LUTHER'S WORLD OF THOUGHT

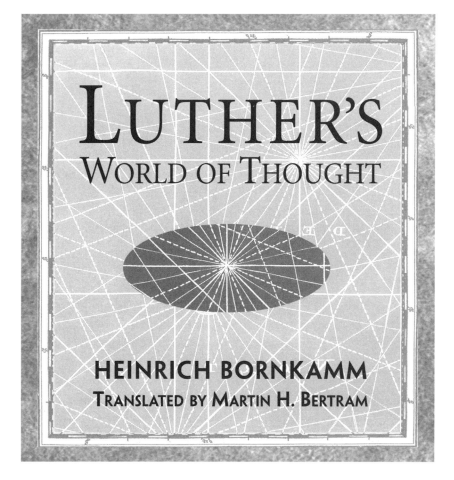

LUTHER'S
WORLD OF THOUGHT

HEINRICH BORNKAMM
TRANSLATED BY MARTIN H. BERTRAM

CONCORDIA PUBLISHING HOUSE · SAINT LOUIS

To Roland H. Bainton

CONTENTS

AUTHOR'S PREFACE

Luther was more than a great theologian. He was a man of wide and varied interests and a thinker whose mind encompassed many fields. Therefore it may be permissible to present his world of thought not in a compact theological system but in a free and easy choice of some of the most significant themes. In this way it may be possible to move some of Luther's less-known ideas into clearer focus and to demonstrate how these bridge the years and are ever alive and relevant.

I am indebted to Concordia Publishing House for making my book accessible to readers in the United States and to Martin H. Bertram for the difficult task of translating it. The quotations are taken from the Weimar Edition of Luther's Works.

Heinrich Bornkamm
Heidelberg, October 1, 1957

TRANSLATOR'S PREFACE

This translation owes its existence to a wish expressed by my son to make several essays of Dr. Heinrich Bornkamm's *Luthers geistige Welt* available in English to his classes at Valparaiso University. Later, Dr. Otto A. Dorn, general manager of Concordia Publishing House, encouraged me to proceed with the entire book. This I was glad to do in the hope that an important contribution to Luther lore would thereby be opened to readers not conversant with the German language.

Martin H. Bertram
June 15, 1957

ABBREVIATIONS

WA   Luther, Martin. *D. Martin Luthers Werke. Kritische Gesamtausgabe. Schriften.* 68 vols. Weimar: Hermann Böhlaus Nachfolger, 1883–1999.

WABr   Luther, Martin. *D. Martin Luthers Werke. Kritische Gesamtausgabe. Briefwechsel.* 18 vols. Weimar: Hermann Böhlaus Nachfolger, 1930–85.

WADB   Luther, Martin. *D. Martin Luthers Werke. Kritische Gesamtausgabe. Die Deutsche Bibel.* 12 vols. in 15. Weimar: Hermann Böhlaus Nachfolger, 1906–61.

WATr   Luther, Martin. *D. Martin Luthers Werke. Kritische Gesamtausgabe. Tischreden.* 6 vols. Weimar: Hermann Böhlaus Nachfolger, 1912–21. Reprinted in 2000.

Martin Luther (1483–1546)

Luther came from a long line of peasants who lived in Möhra on the western slope of the Thuringian Forest. His father, who, as the oldest son, was disqualified as heir to the estate, had turned from the soil to the profitable mining industry in the territory of the counts of Mansfeld. Simplicity, a strict parental discipline tempered by love, and a self-evident piety of the church accompanied Luther through the early years of his life. The contemplativeness and the active charity that he found among the Brethren of the Common Life during his years at the Latin school in Magdeburg and later in the homes of relatives and benefactors in Eisenach showed him the world of medieval religiosity at its best. A serious sense of responsibility to a divine Judge is one of the constantly recurring memories of his youth. His years of philosophical studies at Erfurt (1501–1505) present the picture of a student thirsty for knowledge, cheerful, and given to music making. But there was an undertone of earnestness and melancholy. The conclusion of a long crisis was evidently reached when a bolt of lightning, which struck perilously close on July 2, 1505, wrote the message of the hourly nearness of death into his heart with flaming letters and wrung from him the vow to enter a cloister. To this vow he remained faithful, even in opposition to his father's wish and despite his own doubts and misgivings. On July 17 he rapped for admission at the door of the austere and respected cloister of the Augustinian Order.

With this step, Luther surrendered every vestige of independence. It was by decision of his superiors that this serious-minded and gifted monk became a priest and later a theologian. His entry into the cloister was nothing unusual; for a thousand years the Catholic Church had advised everyone in search of the surest way to God to take this step. Luther subjected body and soul to severe discipline. But the asceticism of the medieval monks and mystics (such as Suso) went far beyond his. Luther's profound earnestness and his deep mental anguish did not stem from excessive fearfulness but from the unyielding consistency with which he practiced the precepts of the church and his monastic order. The church had directed him into monastic life on the supposition that it offered more and purer opportunities than the outside world to share in the sensation of divine love. Luther tried this, only to discover that one's transports of love gave no convincing assurance and certainty. In the confessional, the church and his order demanded, as a prerequisite for divine absolution, a complete and unreserved acknowledgment of every sin committed. Luther complied with this command with heroic honesty. Yet he could not rid himself of doubt regarding the sufficiency of his contrition for the bestowal of divine mercy. In the church's every assurance he found an element of human merit on which this assurance was dependent.

Thus Luther walked the path the church had pointed out to him, but when he came to its end and could never content himself with incomplete solutions, his untiring sense of logic led him to liberty after much travail of soul. Guided by an impassioned zeal to explore Holy Writ, he discovered the primitive Christian Gospel, which had long been covered by the Catholic Church. Many a wise word spoken by Johann von Staupitz, the vicar of his order, clung to his memory and stood him in good stead. Staupitz called the able magister as his successor on the theological faculty of the new University of Wittenberg in 1508 and later, after a short sojourn at Erfurt, back to Wittenberg in 1512. Meanwhile, Luther, still imbued with a strong belief in the saintliness of the Holy City, had journeyed to Rome (1510) on business for his order, but he had returned deeply disturbed and frightened by the decline of spirituality he had noted there.

Luther also followed an independent course as a theologian. Through the late-medieval nominalism of his teachers, he found his way to Augustine; from the systematic formalism of scholasticism he found his way to the Bible. After entering upon the duties of his Wittenberg professorship, Luther never delivered other than biblical-exegetical lectures. The enthusiasm with which he espoused and defended Augustinian theology was soon shared by the rest of the faculty. Through many an internal struggle he progressed and matured from lecture to lecture. Often he had to recapture his conviction concerning salvation by faith alone from the traditional elements of his thinking. His long days of struggling in his convent-tower study and his doubts regarding God's mercy impressed themselves deeply on his memory. By about 1515 he had evolved the essential outlines of his theology. He termed it a "theology of the cross," for only at the cross of Christ do we experience God in a manner that stands the test of reality. God must send us into darkness and into trials and temptations to free us from ourselves and to prepare us for the reception of His grace, which faith, contrary to all expectations, finds solely at the cross. This he had experienced in the course of his own life, and he had become firmly convinced of it. In this way he freed himself from the church's demand to find in her power, in her laws, in her hierarchy, and in her spiritual goods a pledge and guarantee of God's reality on earth. Luther was deeply moved when, in 1516, he again found in the writings of the mystics, especially in Tauler, something about this experiencing of God. But he did not get it from this source, as the later date proves; he merely found some support there. Nor did he ever have anything in common with the real essence of mysticism—the rapturous experience of fusion with God.

Luther felt no other duty incumbent on him than the purification of theology. He kept aloof from the boisterous humanistic demonstrations of these years. The educational reforms of Erasmus he adjudged superficial. In September 1517 he tossed a challenging gauntlet in the form of a series of theses at the feet of scholasticism, the theology of the day. Much to his surprise, there was no success at all. He was all the more astonished when a new series of ninety-five Latin theses, which he had nailed to the door of the Castle Church at Wittenberg (often used for academic announcements) on the eve of All Saints' Day, took their course through Germany in print and reprint at an incredibly fast pace This echo clearly demonstrated that Luther had met the need of the hour. The consciences of many serious-minded laymen and pastors were grievously troubled by the shameless sale of indulgences, which were replenishing the empty coffers of the papal see and of the archbishop of Mainz. The humanists had also pilloried this financial fleecing of Germany. Luther was more incensed by the spiritual fraud and seduction of the Christians who were being misled by a false and hypocritical mode of penitence. His blows were directed not merely at excrescences but at the heart of the matter: the Catholic sacrament of penance, in which the innermost affairs of the heart became an ecclesiastical act and the priest the judge in God's stead. By reviving the original sense of Jesus' words on penance, he broke asunder the most important method of the church's control over the soul. Although the Ninety-five Theses had been composed without any such intent, they nevertheless fomented a revolution of the widest proportions. Luther naively supposed that he was representing the pope's view on indulgence, penitence, and priestly office against the misuses of the preachers of indulgences.

Simultaneous with his lectures at the university, the transcripts of which do not echo any of the public skirmishes, Luther set himself to the task of acquainting the people with the most important content of his theses. This he did in a short, moderately worded German treatise. In a comprehensive Latin work, which he properly submitted to his bishop for approval, he supported his theses. In the spring of 1518 his order honored him by assigning to him the theses for debate at the convention in Heidelberg. The profundity of these Heidelberg theses and the intellectual vigor of his discussion gained Luther a number of enthusiastic young friends, above all, the later Strasbourg reformer Martin Bucer.

But soon lowering clouds appeared on the horizon. At the instigation of the Dominicans, Tetzel's order, a heresy trial was instituted against Luther, and he was cited to Rome. As everyone knew, confinement in a cloister or death awaited him there unless he recanted. However, instead of delivering his professor into the hands of Rome in accord with medieval law, Frederick the Wise demanded, humiliating though this was to the papal see, that Luther be tried on German soil by unbiased judges. To assure himself of the goodwill of the powerful elector at the imminent imperial election, Leo X broke off the trial and delegated Cajetan, legate at the Diet of Augsburg, to pronounce judgment on Luther after a hearing. The cardinal failed to persuade Luther to recant, especially because Luther could in good conscience declare that the doctrine he had attacked—the doctrine regarding the dispensation of indulgences from the treasure of supernumerary merits of Christ and the saints—did not represent the official position of the church. Cajetan confirmed the correctness of Luther's declaration when he asked posthaste for an official pronouncement and promulgation of this doctrine by means of a papal bull.

Thus Luther's opposition to the erroneous opinions of individuals developed into a controversy with the church. Now the formal demand of extradition was presented to the elector. To spare the elector embarrassment and danger, Luther immediately volunteered to leave Germany. As was often done in late-medieval times, he appealed to a future council. Frederick the Wise was in a quandary; it was hard to reach the right decision. When Luther, ready to travel, was bidding his friends farewell, two messengers from the elector appeared. The one urged him to leave; the other ordered him to stay.

At this juncture—decisive so far as Luther's future work was concerned—political events caused an interruption of the trial and brought about a turning point. Emperor Maximilian died in January 1519. Pope Leo X left no stone unturned to thwart the election of his grandson, Charles of Spain, to forestall a strengthening of Spanish power in Italy. But he failed with both of his candidates: Francis I of France and Frederick the Wise. On June 28, 1519, Charles V was elected. The pope's political machinations paralyzed his own energetic efforts against Luther. Consideration for Frederick the Wise forbade persecution of the elector's protégé. This situation was exploited—though without any authorization—by the papal chamberlain, von Miltitz, in an attempt to adjust differences. Luther declared later that this step had been the last possibility for a peaceful settlement. He expressed his readiness to exercise the utmost restraint; the last thing he wanted was a disruption of the church. Not until Professor Eck, from Ingolstadt, attacked him by the circuitous route of a debate between himself and Luther's Wittenberg colleague Karlstadt did Luther feel compelled to come forward anew. With terrifying boldness, he professed his realization, acquired and strengthened meanwhile by historical studies, that the papal system had not been founded by Christ but was merely a historical institution with a legal basis no more than approximately 400 years old, that is, since the codification of canon law. Then the Leipzig Debate confronted Luther with the more far-reaching question regarding an unerring court within the church. As he delved further into the questions that troubled him in Leipzig, the entire Catholic concept of truth, which at the time still found its strongest support in the belief that the councils were infallible, began to crumble. In the end, Holy Writ remained the one and only source of truth to him, and the road to truth was open not to an especially favored class but to every believer. In the face of this "priesthood of all believers," the difference between clergy and congregation ceased to exist for him.

Although both Luther and Eck had been proclaimed victor in the debate by their respective adherents, the former, thanks to his energetic work, undoubtedly remained in control of public opinion in Germany.

The humanists, who were striving to shake Rome's yoke from Germany's neck—or were at least pitting classicism against the fetters of scholasticism—rallied round the banners of this courageous monk. Students flocked to Wittenberg, where Luther had been joined in 1518 by the young celebrity Philipp Melanchthon, who was also eagerly and earnestly espousing the preaching of the pure Gospel, as well as working for a humanistic reform of the university. With his encouragement and with the clarifying insight conveyed by the debate, Luther now cast aside the repressions and inhibitions that still clung to him. He had not rushed ahead rashly but had walked on circumspectly step by step, proceeding from one inescapable conclusion to the other but never receding. Not until now did he become entirely free. Like the rushing of water when there is a breach in a dike, thoughts and images couched in language equal to every subject now stream from his writings. In addition to beautiful, altogether contemplative little writings, he takes up many a gauntlet; finally he attacks. Deeply aggrieved by the accusation that he was destroying moral life, he demonstrated in his "Sermon on Good Works" that deeds of love are the natural fruit growing on the tree of genuine faith. Thus his first theological work of larger design deals with evangelical ethics. Now he also made himself the mouthpiece of popular demands as he called on the "Christian nobility," that is, the princes and magistrates, for active participation in the reformation of the church. All the complaints of national humanism are repeated by him but with an entirely constructive tenor and elevated to the basic struggle against the claim of "canon law's" superiority over secular law. The moral indignation, the well-aimed blows, and the profusion of pertinent ideas on reform contributed to the unprecedented success of this treatise.

Luther again placed public applause, evoked by this tract, at stake when he calmly but unswervingly proceeded from the criticism of abuses to a discussion of the fundamentals of the Catholic Church. In his tract *On the Babylonian Captivity of the Church* he sought to liberate faith from the false bonds of sacramentalism for the simple and obedient acceptance of the divine Word of promise. This learned and forceful work was intended to ameliorate the condition of the church, not to bring about a break with her. That this was Luther's true intent was demonstrated shortly thereafter when he addressed an open and respectful letter to Pope Leo X, in which he submitted the reasons for his fight. Luther could say with a good conscience that matters would not have come to this point if his adversaries, particularly Eck, "who had ventured on an undertaking which he was not man enough to finish, had not provoked him."[1] Luther suspected nothing of this vain Medicean's true character when he naively and frankly suggested by letter to him that he lay down his papal crown and when he, in the same letter, dedicated to him his splendid treatise *On the Liberty of the Christian*. All these writings were reprinted and read to an incredible extent. Their many editions are an exact measure of the esteem in which Luther was held by the people. From 1517 to 1520 his religious writings alone (not counting the large Latin works) appeared in German in more than a quarter million copies, a number hardly conceivable for the printing and book trade of that day—and all this before Luther had adopted the cause of reform in the treatise to the nobility. He was not carried aloft on the wave of national humanism; his fame in the German nation was rooted in his own person.

Luther's complaint that spiritual life in the Roman Church was overgrown with, and crowded out by, politics finds ample proof in his own heresy trial. The interests of papal secular sovereignty irretrievably retarded the execution of this thoroughly spiritual matter. When the trial was resumed and was to be concluded, the elector's attitude and public opinion had long since crystallized. The Reformation had become irresistible. The burning of the papal bull and of canon law (December 10, 1520) was Luther's defiant reply to the threat of excommunication. Thereby he himself excommunicated, as it were, the apostate ecclesiastical rule in the name of Christian truth and the true church. With fear and trepidation, the conviction had grown on him that the Antichrist, in the person of the pope, had seized control of the church.

Both factions now looked to the emperor, who alone could bring about a decision. Frederick the Wise saw to it that Luther was guaranteed safe-conduct when the latter was cited to the Diet of Worms. Because of the persistent machinations of Aleander, the papal nuntius, the ban of the empire followed on the heels of excommunication. This widened the zone of conflict. Through his heroic stand before the diet (April 17–18, 1521), Luther had become the German national hero, and the still more menacing negotiation that followed the diet enhanced his position. Luther's real opponent now entered the arena in the person of Charles V, who adhered faithfully to the tradition of his dynasty and the religious sig-

---

1. "On the Liberty of the Christian," WA 7:8.28.

nificance of his office. Luther's elector saw his hopes shattered. The expedient of concealing Luther at the Wartburg could be but short-lived.

The enforced leisure in this asylum was indefatigably employed. In addition to a number of tracts, Luther now produced his magnificent translation of the New Testament. Linguistically of one mold and reflecting a coherent understanding of the Gospel, it presents, together with the translation of the Old Testament that followed in installments and was completed in 1534, the greatest monument in the history of the German language. In a happy moment this translation made the east-central German dialect ripen on fertile soil into the unifying language of the German-speaking world.

Finally, the confinement at the Wartburg became unbearable for Luther. The restive and ambitious Karlstadt had taken over the leadership of the movement in Wittenberg; fanatical spirits appeared on the scene; old forms of service were being violently pushed aside. In the end the city council had no other choice than to appeal to Luther. And without a moment's hesitation he left the sheltering Wartburg. Before he passed through the territory of his bitter enemy, Duke George of Saxony, he wrote his protector, the elector (who had forbidden him to leave the Wartburg), the most forceful letter of his life (dated March 5, 1522): "He who has the strongest faith is the most powerful protector." Luther's defiant faith and his trust, which no longer asked for protection from the elector but rather offered protection to the latter, already conformed to the external state of affairs, albeit in a manner still hidden from Luther: The weight of the religious movement now exceeded the political power of the elector, who had protected its inception. The magic of Luther's voice soon restored order to turbulent Wittenberg. True to his conviction that faith cannot be coerced, he established the necessary rules and regulations in the city's various parishes and entrusted the further development to the peaceful persuasive power of the preaching of the Gospel.

Years of constructive work followed. Without undue haste, mainly in answer to inquiries and requests, Luther now drafted the basic outlines for a correct congregational organization, for an evangelical purification of the Mass, and for a new educational system. The question may be raised whether Luther fully used the years of the emperor's absence during which the execution of the diet's decisions was held in abeyance. One may ask why he did not strain every effort to establish congregations during those years when the movement faced few obstacles. But the purpose of his message was not the establishment of a new church; he was striving for the restoration of the old one. The thought of forming a new organization was foreign to his mind; his interest lay in growth and betterment. It seemed natural and self-evident to him that any new regulations and laws desired by cities and territories should be inaugurated only by the respective government of city or territory. He availed himself of every opportunity to emphasize the difference between spiritual and secular power. In contrast to the medieval erasure of the line of demarcation between the two and, above all, in opposition to the ascendant domination of the spiritual power, he laid the foundation for a new concept of state during those years. His state derives its charter directly from God; it is a miracle of divine order in a world otherwise doomed to chaos. Therefore Christians owe it full obedience and devotion, unless it demands a denial of faith or manifest wrongdoing.

Because of the clear discernment with which Luther viewed his basic principles, he was not tempted by any offer of alliance with political movements. Thus he turned a cold shoulder to the friendly advances of the empire's knighthood. Conversely, and in conformity with his principles regarding separation of Gospel and politics, he counseled the grandmaster of the Order of German Knights, Albrecht von Brandenburg, to convert his order's territory into a secular duchy—a legitimate political influence of the Reformation that was a great blessing to the German nation. During the Peasants' War (1525), his principle was put to the severest test. Social and religious demands were woven into the program of the revolt; Christian liberty was its sublimest idea. Luther recognized the validity of many of its claims and exhorted princes and nobility to strive for a peaceful settlement. But he strenuously opposed the idea of a rebellion invoked in the name of Christ, even staking his life on the issue. His attempts at conciliation on revolutionary soil placed his life in jeopardy. Finally, he had no choice but to encourage and support the government in its conflict with the wild hordes incited by fanatical instigators such as Müntzer. Just at that time, his elector, whose conscience was deeply troubled by the revolt, closed his eyes in death. Luther then opposed the immoderate rage of the victorious government with the same intrepidity with which he had confronted the mad peasants. But even the tragic consequences of the revolt never made him waver in his conviction that he was in duty bound by Gospel and conscience to fight his battle against those confused minds.

Amid the chaos of the Peasants' War, Luther married, taking a step in which he had been preceded by others whom his opposition to the unnatural and therefore ungodly vows of celibacy had encouraged. Ailing and filled with a foreboding of an early death, he had but scant hope for long domestic happiness. But he did want to fling defiance once more at the devil, who had raged so vehemently in the Peasants' War. At the same time he desired to strengthen doubting consciences with his own example. In Katharina von Bora, who had escaped from the convent because of what he taught and with his help, he found a brave mate and a splendid wife. This step was misconstrued, especially in humanistic circles. But the relationship between humanism and the Reformation was soon to be put to a far more severe test.

Egged on by Luther's adversaries, Erasmus had begun a public discussion with Luther in 1524. Cleverly, he had chosen the point of contact between the interests of classical-humanistic philosophy and Catholic theology: the assertion of the freedom of the will. In his Heidelberg Theses (1518), Luther had termed this "an idea without content." Erasmus was completely different from Luther in his thinking and did not appeal to him. But his philological attainments commanded such great respect that Luther would not have cared much if he could have avoided this controversy. After an unusually long interval, Luther replied to the attack in 1525 with his powerful treatise *On the Bondage of the Will*. Exceedingly incisive in subject matter, it was reserved in form. It is the prelude to the controversy between the reforming Gospel and the spirit of modern rationalism. Luther was not concerned about the philosophical problems of determinism but about the freedom of man before God. As in no other writing, Luther here draws the veil from the depth of his experience of God. In an inscrutable fashion, God's omnipotence is identified with the reality of the world; it bears all that is beautiful and all that is terrible in life, the contending divine and satanic powers between which man is tossed to and fro. But from this mystery, God radiates the liberating light of His revelation in His Son, Jesus. It does not solve all the difficult problems here on earth, but it does offer sufficient support for bearing them with heroic faith instead of dismissing them with rationalistic sham solutions.

With this treatise, opinions and minds came to a parting of the ways. It completed the estrangement of a number of humanists who had previously been offended by many a trenchant word of Luther and by many a stormy scene attendant upon the introduction of the Reformation.

Because Luther was also constrained in 1525 to settle accounts with "the heavenly prophets"—the mystic fanatics such as Karlstadt and Müntzer— this fateful year brought him face-to-face with a number of far-reaching decisions. The struggles of later centuries are delineated against the background of Luther's conflict with Erasmus and his coterie, as also of his rejection of religious individualism and churchless spiritualism.

Circumstances in the cities and territories that had accepted the evangelical faith gradually called for a more closely knit organization. The hope for a reform on a large scale by means of a council or at least a German national convention grew ever fainter. Following the lead of other territories, the Wittenberg reformers petitioned Elector John the Constant to appoint a commission for a visitation and reorganization of the congregations. With unmistakable clarity, Luther stated that thereby they were adhering "to the office of love common to all Christians" and that the elector was obligated to this brotherly service not in his capacity of secular government but in that of a Christian. Thus Luther preserved his principle of separation between secular and spiritual power. It was entirely contrary to the mind of Luther that the princes soon thereafter, and in ever-growing measure, usurped control of the church as a governmental right. Had the evangelical churches been in possession of the organizing talent of a Calvin, they would have received a more independent form. But Luther was always plagued by misgivings regarding his authority for the establishment of a new organization and therefore confined himself to a solution that he regarded as transitional. He considered himself called only for the training of pastors and for the nurture of Christian congregations. As Melanchthon gradually took the education of theologians in hand, Luther created the guideposts for a new Christian community: a new order for the Divine Service—the "German Mass" (1526); the first evangelical hymns; and the catechisms (1529).

During these years, his lectures, his sermons, his work on the translation of the Bible, and his commentaries continued without interruption. In addition, however, his time and attention were claimed more and more by a discussion of Holy Communion with the Swiss reformers. As sharply as Luther had rejected the idea of a constantly renewed unbloody sacrifice in the Mass and the Catholic doctrine of transubstantiation, so little had he wavered in his belief in the real presence of Christ in Holy Communion. To be sure, he had gone through moments of doubt. But the more he felt the temptation of human reason in him and perceived this in others (above all, in the spiritualists Karlstadt and Schwenckfeld and in Zwingli, the disciple of humanism), the more resolutely he adhered to the plain words of Scripture.

Luther's literary discussions with Zwingli also present a chapter in his controversy with the rising rationalism. In these he drew a concept of Christ far transcending the mere treatment of the text, which, arising from the common soil of early-church Christology, by far surpassed that of Zwingli in logical accuracy and religious force. The caustic objection of the opponents that the body of Christ, which had ascended to heaven, could not be present in the elements of Holy Communion did not baffle him in the least. His risen Christ participated actively in the worldwide dominion of God. Luther had merely to give his bold ideas about the immanence of God in all created objects—in tree and leaf, fire and water, and in stone— a Christological turn for a metaphysical explanation of his doctrine of Holy Communion. Thus it happens that his greatest utterances on God's presence in nature, unexcelled by any nature mysticism but entirely unmystical themselves, are to be found in his writings on Holy Communion. As in Luther's great work against Erasmus, there are elements here, neglected by his successors, that not only eclipsed his opponents but also could have led to a proper understanding with the budding modern perception of nature. But Protestant scholastic philosophy again took recourse to the crutches of an Aristotelian *Weltanschauung*. For Luther all this was only the presupposition for what is essential, for the grateful acceptance of one item of the reality of grace, which he found in Holy Communion. And he seized it eagerly because he felt deeply the reality of sin and of satanic power. Particularly in these days his letters give evidence of grave inner conflict. Never, as we know, was his faith a self-evident and uncontested possession.

But even in these days of vehement theological discussions, Luther never closed his eyes to political events in the empire. He was not perturbed by fears (unfounded, as was discovered later) that the evangelical princes had of an offensive alliance of the Catholic estates (*Reichsstände*) but by the ever-growing Turkish menace. In 1529, when the Turks had penetrated to the gates of Vienna, Luther, in two blazing writings, summoned the nation to resistance. His sole concern was the interest of the empire. He rejected a crusade, a war in the name of Christ, as he had in the "Christian" Peasants' War. The prayers and the penitence of the Christians must be the greatest force against the enemy, but a war with weapons may be undertaken only "at the emperor's command, in his name, and under his banner." Even religious difference dare not interfere with answering a call to arms, still less the disuniting selfishness and avarice of the princes. Luther reminded the latter with emphatic earnestness of their obligation to the empire.

But the hoped-for religious conciliation was being most seriously imperiled at that moment. Under the leadership of Ferdinand, brother and representative of Charles V, the Diet of Spires (April 1529) again picked up the sharp weapon forged by the Edict of Worms against the evangelical estates. In a solemn document, the latter fearlessly confessed their faith and avowed their rights ("protestation") and appealed to the emperor and a council. Negotiations for a defensive alliance, which were immediately initiated by the endangered evangelical estates, found a serious obstacle in the theological differences between the Wittenberg and the Strasbourg and Swiss representatives. Although Luther entertained little hope for agreement, he did not withhold his support from an attempt of Landgrave Philipp of Hesse to remove the difficulties. However, these discussions, often erroneously regarded as an open outburst of intra-Protestant discord, developed more favorably than expected. After a rather fruitless exchange of opinions, a compromise was offered by the Lutheran faction. Zwingli, however, declined it because it would still seem too Catholic to his congregations. The Marburg Articles, finally drafted by Luther, declared agreement in fourteen points, disagreement in the fifteenth, and a willingness to bear with one another and to implore God for the proper enlightenment. Marburg might have pointed the way to toleration despite existing differences, but subsequent events opened the wounds anew.

The negotiations for an alliance in Spires received no support from Luther. For years he had disclaimed any legal right to armed resistance against the emperor and had emphasized that hope for success must center solely in the power of God's Word. Therefore among some of the estates grave scruples of conscience made themselves felt about a military alliance, which was urged especially by Philipp of Hesse, the ablest statesman among the Protestant princes. The awkwardness of Protestant politics found its chief cause in this conscientious sense of responsibility, as also in Luther's heroic but unpolitical reliance on God rather than in territorial antagonisms.

Thus all questions regarding the future of the Reformation were still unanswered when Charles V—after a victorious conclusion of peace with France and the pope and after a nine-year absence—returned to his empire in 1530. Friendly undertones in his convocation of the Diet in Augsburg awakened unfounded hopes for a peaceful adjustment of the religious problems at the elector's court, hopes that Luther never shared. At his prince's request, Luther journeyed as far as the Coburg, the southernmost point in the electorate and three days distant from Augsburg. It seemed too venturesome to take the outlawed Luther to the diet. Thus Luther had another Wartburg experience from April to October 1530. Again he occupied himself with the translation of the Bible, with commentaries, and with other writings in astonishing number. Idleness was neither his choice nor his portion. At the Coburg he chafed even more under his forced separation from the arena of important happenings than he had at the Wartburg. His anxiety for the cause of the Gospel, Melanchthon's timidity and attempts to compromise, the frequent absence of news from the diet—all this disquieted him. From a distance he participated by means of comforting and imploring letters. As early as June, the entire diet heard his powerful voice in his "Admonition to the Pastors Assembled at the Diet in Augsburg," perhaps the greatest rendering of accounts on his work to his adversaries. The solitude of the Coburg afforded him the quiet for an extensive retrospective view of his life with its many conflicts. With an overpowering earnestness, he pleaded with the entire church not to ignore the voice of God and not to close her eyes to manifest divine guidance. The look backward filled him with humble pride. To whom was the Catholic Church indebted for having routed the peddlers of indulgences and the indolent monks? And at that, without any hubbub or riot, merely by preaching the pure doctrine. What would have remained of the church if the popular revolt heralded by the grievances submitted at Worms had not been channeled into its proper course by Luther's proclamation of the Gospel? It was absurd to try to brand him as the father of the revolution. After all, whom did Müntzer and the other factious spirits hate more than him? "If I should want to boast, I might even say that we were your protectors and that it was due to us that you have thus far remained to be what you still are." Impetuous pleading and prophetic threatening in the same breath. He felt that the hour of decision had come: "Therefore it is our greatest desire and our humblest plea that you give God honor, know yourselves, repent, and mend your ways. If not, take me and put up with me. If I live, I shall be your pestilence; if I die,

I shall be your death. For God has set me upon you. I must, as Hosea says (13:7), be a bear and a lion unto you. . . . You shall have no respite from my name until you reform or perish."[2] He was happy over the courageous avowal with which the Augsburg Confession was presented on June 25, though he found fault with the concessions made in it. But the subsequent wearisome and dragging negotiations merely confirmed the faint hope he had entertained at the outset. His splendid letters of wrath and comfort purified the atmosphere for the worried friends in Augsburg like an electrical storm. He ridiculed their attempts "to bring the pope and Luther under one hat. The pope will not want to, and Luther declines. Take heed that you have not prodigally squandered your labor." Still he defended the vacillating Melanchthon tenderly against the attacks of others, though he knew full well that he was not able to withstand the mental pressure of these months laden with controversy. Simultaneously, he made it clear to his friends that if they sacrificed any part of the Gospel and hid it in a sack, "then Luther would appear and liberate this eagle gloriously." In the end all that remained for him to do was to urge his friends to break off negotiations and come home. "If war results from it, then let it come. We have pleaded and done enough."

The decisive hour had been wasted. But Luther returned from the Coburg enriched. The difficult translation of the Old Testament prophets was almost completed; a number of writings, some of which had occupied him for a considerable time, were composed, among them the excellent *Sendbrief vom Dolmetschen*, the masterful exposition of his art of translating. Above all, he now clearly perceived the seriousness of the impending decisions. As at all times of conflict, this disposed him to greater happiness. He had hardly arrived home when he took the initiative with his treatise *Warning to His Dear Germans*. As "the prophet of the Germans (for such a proud title I henceforth must assign to myself for the pleasure and delight of my papists and asses)," he once more exhorted to peace. But if the opposition was insistent on war, he let it be known that he did not fear it. He felt no alarm for his person, "for it is well to bear in mind that whosoever kills Dr. Luther in an uprising will find that he [Luther] will not spare many of the clerics. Thus we go to our destination together—they to hell in the name of all the devils, I to heaven in God's name."[3] Nor did he

---

2. WA 30/2:276.339f.

3. WA 30/3:279.19.

fear for his work, for he trusted in the power of prayer and was convinced that God would not let His Gospel perish. But despite all his former intercession for peace, this time, he declared, he would not check an eventual uprising with his voice nor would he forbid his followers to defend themselves. This treatise gives us an idea of the power Luther's pen would have wielded in the Schmalkald Wars if it could still have been enlisted.

The ultimatum delivered at the recess of the Diet in Augsburg and the union formed among the Catholic princes again confronted the Protestants with the question of organizing a league of defense. This they concluded in February 1531 at Schmalkalden. Luther no longer objected because he had been persuaded by juridical opinion that opposition against the emperor, when the latter interfered with the rights of independent governments, was upheld by the laws of the empire. True to his principle of differentiation between spiritual and political matters, Luther left the decision of this question to the jurists, though reluctantly and with the solemn declaration that he himself would never incite the people to resistance. However, the clouds of war again dispersed. Luther's resolute conduct and the Schmalkald League, which also attracted other opponents of the emperor, were impressive. But it was chiefly the new advances of the Turks that forced the emperor and his brother, Ferdinand of Austria (who was especially menaced by them), to seek a peaceful understanding with the Protestants. Luther again urged the Protestants to grasp the proffered hand of peace and not to capitalize on the distress of the foe. In the Bavarian dukes and in the foreign princes he saw unreliable and self-seeking allies. He warned against placing too much reliance in weapons. The conclusion of the Nürnberg Anstand (1532), a preliminary imperial recognition of the Reformation until the convocation of a council, seemed to him like a divine yes to his own conciliatory spirit. He was filled with gratitude to God, "who greets us so graciously. . . . God has mercifully heard our poor prayer."[4] Luther sincerely appreciated the friendly advances of the emperor and again called upon the Protestant estates to come to his aid against the Turks. He himself did his share by praying for the cause of the empire, and he hoped confidently for the victory of the emperor against the rest of the empire's enemies: the French and the pope.

In the more tranquil years that now followed for the Reformation, Luther cheerfully resumed his customary work. In addition to his lectures, he collaborated in the visitation in the electorate of Saxony (1532);

---

4. Correspondence (May—June 29, 1532), WABr 6:310.66, 327.57.

in the reorganization of church life in Wittenberg (1533); and in the reorganization of the theological faculty (1533), which he served as dean to his death, and also of the university, to which Melanchthon had given new statutes in 1536. In these statutes, an alliance between biblical exegesis and classical studies, enduring for centuries, was concluded. Luther's old love for Augustine found expression in a special lecture course. From medieval university life he retained, above all, the disputations in a cleansed form. The professors often had to propose theses for these discussions. Since 1535 we possess a large number of Luther's theses for debates; he himself was a past master in these scholarly verbal skirmishes. The completion of his translation of the Bible (1534) and its revision (begun as early as 1531 in the most careful manner, together with a group of scholars) and a large number of treatises and letters added to his daily work. Now—in contrast to the days of conflict—he often groaned under the burden of work and felt physically unequal to it.

During these years, it seemed that the old adversaries—papists, enthusiasts, and Zwinglians—had, for a time, almost vanished from the field. Only the persecution of the evangelicals at the gates of Wittenberg, in the duchy of George of Saxony, made him sad and angry. Even the Anabaptists occupied him but little, though they were again making their presence felt in central Germany. The mad specter of Münster merely confirmed Luther's belief that the devil was playing a role there. To his great satisfaction, on the other hand, Martin Bucer's efforts to bring about an agreement on the question of the Lord's Supper were beginning to bear fruit. The picture had changed since the Marburg Colloquy. In Augsburg both factions had appeared with different declarations, and the Saxons had assiduously emphasized their points of disagreement with the Swiss. Zwingli's death (1531), the entry of Württemberg into the Lutheran Reformation movement (1534), and other events led at least to an approach between Wittenberg and the South Germans. In the end the compromise rejected at Marburg paved the way for the Wittenberg Concord (1536). Melanchthon induced Luther to give up his old distrust of the inconstant Strasbourg theologians. However, the history of the concord, as well as other happenings of these years, supported Luther's position that resoluteness and firmness of purpose achieve the best results in the end. By such a stand, South Germany was won for Lutheranism; however, the gap between Luther and the Swiss, which the former tried hard to bridge, later was to be widened all the more.

Luther was not faced with momentous political problems again until 1537 when the emperor finally persuaded Pope Paul III to convoke a council in Mantua. Now the question whether there was still a solution for the intricate problems was to find its answer. Luther had already defiantly announced his coming to the papal legate Vergerio, the same Vergerio whom, on the occasion of a visit to Wittenberg in 1535, he had good-naturedly hoaxed and made to quake before the "beast" possessed of the devil. The Protestant princes, too, were inclined to send delegates to a genuinely free and fair papal council. Their expectations were soon shattered by the bull of invitation. But the convocation of a free countercouncil under the auspices of the Schmalkald League, as was now proposed by Elector John Frederick, did not meet with Luther's sanction. As in the past, he was scrupulously avoiding even the semblance of a rupture with the church. But at the request of the elector, he stated the demands that had to be adhered to inflexibly and the concessions that might be made in a spirit of charity (the Schmalkald Articles). The timidity of Melanchthon prevented the acceptance of these articles by the Schmalkald Federal Diet (*Bundestag von Schmalkalden*) in February 1537, but later they were incorporated in the confessional writings of the Lutheran Church. They present Luther's boldest and most spirited confession, his last will and testament to the papacy. In contrast to the feeble, polished language of the Augustana, they are vibrant with life but unwieldy; yet they are inspiring because of the boldness and anger with which they bear testimony. With the best of intentions, Luther included in them a number of articles that might perhaps be subject to debate among scholars; however, he concluded with the statement that he himself could not surrender a single point. Whoever chose to do so would have to settle this with his own conscience. The Schmalkald confederates now issued a strong rejection to the papal and imperial representatives.

For a while it seemed as if the Schmalkald Articles were to become Luther's last will and testament. During the Schmalkald Diet, he suffered such a violent attack of his old ailment that his death seemed imminent. He wanted to die at home. But the ride in a carriage over rough mountain roads accomplished what huge doses of medicine given by the physicians had not been able to do. After terrible attacks of colic, he was rid of the stones. Jubilantly, the messenger cried out before the house of the papal legate: "Lutherus vivit!" Luther recovered slowly, and now he hoped to live at least long enough to deal the papacy one more sound blow.

Luther was correct in his opinion that the Roman Curia was not giving serious thought to a council. The meeting was postponed again and again; finally, it was suspended indefinitely. In these negotiations he had again crossed swords with his old papal adversary. As was his wont after momentous decisions (for example, after the Leipzig Debate and after the Diet of Augsburg), he now delivered a sound afterthrust. Out of comprehensive historical studies grew a disquisition (*Of the Councils and the Church*, 1539) not inferior in incisiveness, depth of thought, and vigor to the writings of earlier years. Bitterly disappointed and, at the same time, filled with patriotic indignation over the treatment accorded the emperor by the pope (as Luther said, he had held out the council to the emperor as a piece of bread to a dog, then hit him on the snout as he was about to snap for it), Luther now buried all hopes of solving the vexing problems by means of a council. But more than this, his study of history destroyed every vestige of traditionalism in him. He became convinced that the unity of the church could not be built on the old councils or on the church fathers, as was attempted then and later. The Word of God alone is the "imperial law" (*Reichsrecht*) of the church or, as he preferred to say, of the people of God, of Christendom. He held that this encompasses three organizations in which every Christian holds membership: the family, the state, and the Christian congregation. All three are directly in like measure responsible to God, every Christian is equally obligated, and they are separated only by the distinctive commission given to each. This great book (*Von den Conciliis und Kirchen*) sums up the outcome of twenty years of conflict: The Reformation is not provisional, awaiting a general reform of the church; it is the Reformation. At the same time this book offers, after various starts, a harmonious doctrine concerning the world and the kingdom of God, rules of Christian conduct, and thus a comprehensive basis of social ethics that conforms to everything Luther ever said on questions of national life, government, vocation, marriage, school, social welfare, and law. How earnest Luther was in his determination to train his people to moral and Christian living was shown not only in his sermons, into which he injected sociological problems ever more frequently, but also in a theological discussion in his own circle, which agitated him as much as any contention with enemies from without. His old pupil Agricola had taught that sinners should be led to repentance not by the imperative of the moral law but solely by the proclamation of the Gospel. Luther knew how greatly man's conscience stands in need of the voice of the Law, and

29

he was horrified to see how here the relationship of Law and Gospel was turned topsy-turvy. Assailed as he was in his struggle, such a presumptuous sense of security made him shudder. In the end both rider and steed would break their necks. For this reason he attacked the antinomians with the severity he would have shown had he been facing enthusiasts (*Schwärmer*) and papists.

What Luther had learned about councils only confirmed his conviction concerning the Roman see—a conviction he had arrived at two decades before this. His great literary settlement of accounts brought to an end what had begun at the time of the Leipzig Debate. One can understand why he held himself aloof from negotiations that aimed at compromise. These had been begun by a number of Erasmian theologians and politicians and finally had been accepted temporarily by the emperor, who again had been hindered by the Turks and the French from taking stern measures against the Protestants. Luther was not hopeful. But in a different and more fateful way, he was again drawn into the political arena. Landgrave Philipp of Hesse, hot-blooded by heredity, intended to abandon his licentious life at the side of an unloved wife by resorting to bigamy. Although forbidden by the law of the realm, this expedient, in view of the Old Testament patriarchs and other precedents (e.g., Count von Gleichen, regarded as historical), did not seem quite so wrong at that time. Philipp's pastor, Bucer, succeeded in rousing Luther's sympathy with the landgrave, who seemed sincerely contrite and who apparently could be reclaimed only in this way. Luther finally declared his willingness to accede to the request if absolutely necessary. But he insisted on the greatest secrecy. In confession, however, he earnestly counseled Philipp to desist. When the story was noised abroad, a second error was born of the first. Luther advised denial of the story so the example would not find any imitators. Both decisions stemmed from his principle that conscience must, in special circumstances, seek its course independently before God, without, or even contrary to, the precepts of the Law. He had been led to this misapplication by his sympathetic weakness toward the landgrave's manifest anguish of soul. This gravest mistake of Luther also took its gravest revenge. The embarrassed landgrave now walked into the emperor's trap and was used by the latter as a tool for the complete checkmating of the Schmalkald League.

However, the Reformation was still advancing irresistibly. Luther had the great satisfaction of finally seeing the Gospel victorious round about

Wittenberg in the lands of his fiercest foes, in the duchy of Saxony (1539), in Brandenburg (1539), and in Cardinal Albrecht's city of Halle (1541). In 1542 he had the pleasure of consecrating an evangelical bishop into office at Naumburg, and thereby, as he hoped, he set an example for correct and proper church government, gradually supplanting the emergency government (*Notregiment*) of a sovereign. The reports of an incipient reformation in the archbishopric of Cologne greatly encouraged him. At the same time he was as blind as the evangelical princes to the far-reaching schemes of Charles V, who was preparing for war against the Protestants. The discord in the Schmalkald League worried him far more. He was shocked above all to see that the antagonism between the Wettin territories, now that the duchy, too, had become evangelical, threatened to develop into a split within Protestant ranks. When the elector and Duke Maurice finally marched against each other, Luther intervened with an open letter in which he addressed them both as boldly as he once did the peasants. But thanks to the mediation of the landgrave, whom Luther supported with all his authority, an armed conflict was avoided.

Even in these years, Luther remained true to his amazing respect for the emperor. When preliminary results of negotiations regarding a compromise at Regensburg (1541) were submitted to him by a delegation, he did his utmost to conciliate opposition. He stood ready to leave a number of important questions open for the time being, provided the emperor permitted the preaching and dissemination of the most basic articles of evangelical faith. But he foresaw correctly that the pope would reject such tolerance. In the same year Luther's national loyalty asserted itself once more when the Turks, after the conquest of Ofen, again stood menacingly at the gates of Germany. He issued a blazing proclamation to his country, summoning all to come to the emperor's aid unhesitatingly and unconditionally, and by prayer and abstention from quarreling, mammon worship, carousing, and blaspheming to ward off the all too well-deserved judgment of God. Shortly before his death, this love of country and resentment against papal interference in national affairs reached its climax. At the Diet of Spires (1544), Charles V had once more deceived the Protestants, against whom the times still forbade an attack, with the promise of a temporary settlement of the religious question by the next diet or a German national council. A papal brief had taken him to task for this severely. Luther, who took the emperor's promise at face value, now dealt the pope his stoutest blow in the treatise *The Papacy of Rome, Founded by the Devil*

(1545). In addition to the old warning against the Antichrist in the papal chair, this unbelievably vehement writing gave expression to German indignation over the popes' claim that they had bestowed empire status on Germany. Pointing to the history of Germany's great emperors, whom he dearly loved, he branded this as a ridiculous falsification of history. What price the empty title of Roman emperor had cost Germany! If the emperors had only always been cognizant of the fact that they owed their dignity and position to their own power, not to papal anointment! To think of Luther with this fervid treatise against the papacy posing as the emperor's second one year before the outbreak of the Schmalkald War! So guileless was he in the world of politics! How steadfastly he still hoped for German unity! There is no more touching picture than this. But during his last years, he beheld with ever-increasing anxiety lowering clouds of misfortune on Germany's horizon. However, he never suspected the emperor's true role in those clouds. His anxiety was caused by his nation's rejection of God's Word, which would compel God "to lay about with fists." As one of the prophets of old, he could then say that only he was staying the arm of God with his prayer but that the blow would fall after his death.

The unheard-of vehemence that has often been criticized in the writings of Luther's declining years springs largely from this concern for the body and soul of his native land. It caused him many a sleepless night. For what he had to say, he pulled out the loudest stops. The closer he felt he was to the grave, the more severe, the more determined, and the coarser he became. Nowhere did he yield an inch. When he supposed that he was detecting new traces of Zwinglian error, he again pronounced judgment but with a severity that destroyed the friendlier relationship established with great difficulty a few years earlier. This testiness and irritability—which his friends now noticed in him and which was womanishly exaggerated, especially by Melanchthon—was undoubtedly also caused by the narrow confines in which his life moved in his last years. He felt the absence of lusty conflict, which had always invigorated him and afforded his wrath release. Now he was wasting his strength on the petty tensions at the university, on the discord among his co-workers, and, above all, on the disorderly ways of the students and citizens of Wittenberg. The unsparing frankness with which he aired his grievances against individual vocations (for example, against avaricious lawyers) provided his adversaries of that and of a later day with cheap objections to his work. The looseness in dress and conduct of his fellow citizens finally repelled him, so in the last year of his life, he startled the Wittenbergians while away on a trip with a notice that he had no desire to return to them. Delegations from the city promised energetic steps against these abuses, and Luther's wrathful outbursts soon ceased.

During his last years, he may also have been depressed by his lack of work on larger theological essays and Bible commentaries, which had once so refreshed him. His daily routine tasks weighed ever more heavily on him: his revision of the Bible, letters, opinions, lectures. Only with great physical strain were his lectures on Genesis completed. Primarily he now addressed himself to subjects suggested by current events and public affairs. At the same time he also returned to matters that had occupied him in earlier years. He again admonished the ministers "to preach against usury" (1540), that is, not against interest in general but against the fast-rising capitalism, the effects of which, especially the unrestricted rates of interest and the helplessness of ruined debtors, he observed with dismay. For this reason he demanded a moderate rate of interest, landed property as security for loans, and, above all, participation of the creditors not only in the gains but also in the losses of their debtors. Whatever God has given us as an insecure possession in life must not be insured at the expense of others. In Luther's eyes this was more than a command of justice; it was a matter of obedience to God. Although his objections have gone unheeded and have been drowned out by the onward march of the capitalist system and thus soon appeared antiquated, nonetheless, he is one of the great monitors on the threshold of the capitalist era.

Luther also resumed his controversy with the Jews. Not only because they again and again brought him face-to-face with the question of usury but essentially—and how could it be otherwise with him?—for reasons of religion. To him, Jesus ushered in a new historical epoch, even for the Jewish people. Therefore Luther's love for the Old Testament, to which he dedicated by far the greatest part of his scholarly efforts, and his rejection of post-New Testament Judaism are two sides of the same thing. In the former he found the coming Redeemer promised and awaited; in the latter he found Him rejected and blasphemed after His appearance. That the Jews regarded themselves as the chosen people and still waited for the Messiah are the "lies" against which he directed his fierce treatise in 1543. If a government does not choose to provoke God's wrath, it must take steps against this open blasphemy. Luther's sense of responsibility explains the sharp measures he advocated for the suppression of the Jews, especially of their divine services. To him the Jewish question was the reversal of the Christ question. Their homelessness and their usurious extortion and impoverishment of nations, which he indignantly indicted, were conclusive proof to Luther of God's punishment and His abandonment of this people for the denial of His revelation, with which He had once favored them. This question agitated him to the last days of his life. Three days before his death, he concluded his final sermon with "a warning against the Jews." If they accepted Christ and desisted from their usury, one should treat them fraternally. However, he had long abandoned all hope of this. If they refused, they should be exiled, for one "can have no patience or fellowship with the blasphemers and profaners of the dear Savior."[5]

This sermon was delivered in Eisleben. A peculiar combination of circumstances brought it about that he returned to the city of his birth to die there. He had been summoned thither to adjust a dispute in the family of the Mansfeld counts. As he saw his death approaching, he was grateful that his last efforts had been devoted to this work of peace. After a short death struggle, he quietly fell asleep on the morning of February 18, 1546. His last word was a firm yes, given in reaffirmation of his faith in his Redeemer and in a reavowal of his work.

Luther once said that God had led him like a blinded horse.[6] A survey of his life bears out the truth of these words. There was little of premeditated planning in it, as there is in the work of a statesman, of a political economist, in a certain sense also in the work of a scholar and even of an artist, if their work is to prosper. Luther had the hand of another draft the pattern of his life and his work, and he merely filled in, feature by feature, as the hour demanded. Because of this, as has already been intimated, one may find organizational flaws in the framework of the Lutheran Church. Yet in the very absence of intention and design lies the secret of his work. His mission and assignment was, after all, not the fulfillment of a definite, single task within the range of the limitless possibilities of the human mind; his mission and commission was the general reformation of the church. This means a reformation and reanimation of the most intimate, most personal decisions and judgments of humankind as had not happened since the days of Christ and has not happened again since Luther. How could Luther have intended and planned this? He was guided by

5. WA 51:196.10.

6. WATr 1, no. 1206; cf. also WATr 1, no. 406; WATr 3, no. 3846.

what God commanded at the time. Only thus could be wrought a revolutionary change that affected the faith of countless numbers on the whole earth and simultaneously, reaching far beyond the religious confines, ushered in (admittedly allied with other forces, though far overshadowing these) a new era of the human spirit. Whatever has been created since then in the field of science and statesmanship, philosophy and law, the arts and literature is unthinkable without Luther's emancipating act. Thus he became Germany's greatest gift to the world.

Only God's guidance and his own passive compliance enabled Luther to bear his mission. To the hundreds of fellow evangelicals exiled from Leipzig because of their faith, he once confessed that in hours of trial he found his greatest comfort in the knowledge "that he had not expelled himself from the papacy."[7] He was often troubled, for he staked far more than his own life on his work. To surrender this would have been easy. How often he complained that he was not deemed worthy of martyrdom for his Lord! But he was involving his nation. Often he was asked—not only by others but also in many a distressful hour by his own conscience— whether he was not, after all, a seducer of his people, one who presumed to contradict one and a half millennia and innumerable teachers of the church. He sallied forth boldly because he was convinced that he had not seized the truth but that the truth had seized him. God's leadership, which he followed passively, always found him consistently the same. If one fixes one's gaze not only, as is so often done, on the young Luther and his early conflict but follows the lines of his life, as we tried to sketch it, from his youth to his old age and death, its inner oneness and uniformity of pattern will be singularly impressive. To be sure, this pattern must be pieced together from a wealth of varying modes of expression born in inexhaustible number from his fervid spirit and his never-failing linguistic power. Luther was not a man of a once-for-all formula nor did he write any textbooks. But this is why he remained the fountain of youth of Protestantism, which has ever found in him its source and strength for regeneration and revival.

If one tries to penetrate to the core of Luther's tremendous power, one discovers that he was a great teacher and educator in the subject of reality. Pressed hard by the reality of God, he unmasked the reality of man without reserve and assigned to man his place in the world of reality. He saw

---

7. "Verantwortung der aufgelegten Aufruhr (1533)," WA 38:119.23.

through the great self-deception on which the Roman Church bases its tradition and its claim to infallibility in the matter of teaching. To him good works were attempts at insurance that do not stand the test of God's penetrating power. For this reason he told man to do his assigned work in the world, not in self-chosen, monkish seclusion. Luther arrived at the vital laws for state and economy not by a study of natural law or of any theories cherished by the church but by sober observation of their real and enduring powers. These natural requirements are understood, without any abstract rules, by the great men, "the miracle men" (*Wunderleute*), and by "the sound heroes" (*gesunde Helden*) whom God sends to a nation from time to time. Luther's concept of empire is different from the romantic medieval dreams of a universal empire, dreams in which even many humanists still indulged. He viewed the empire as the totality of "the German nation." In the political realm he considered a well-articulated public opinion to be the greatest power. This he tried to create and further by means of counsel on education, marriage, hygiene, social welfare, and the administration of justice. Many a point in his program may be termed conservative and patriarchal, but it must be borne in mind that it was not his purpose to set up a program for all time to come. His suggestions sprang from the conviction that reform can grow out of a wise improvement of existing conditions. Thereby he gave those who followed him the latitude to do, within the bounds of conscience, whatever the times enjoin. Decisions dictated by conscience and stern, sober reasoning, indispensable to the world's existence, must also be based on a greater power, namely, on the gentle, clearly heard command of love, which alone can restore to the world here and there some of the beautiful harmony it has lost. The true world of God was divined by Luther also in nature, which is completely pervaded by God. But to recognize it amid all the flaws and defects of the real nature, it is necessary to have learned at the cross of Christ to peer through darkness and gloom into the very heart of God and there to behold the true, hidden reality of God. This is the alpha and omega of Luther's thinking. From this his work has its life.

THE WORLD-HISTORICAL SIGNIFICANCE
OF THE NINETY-FIVE THESES

As late as a few years ago, notices such as this might have been seen tacked to the bulletin board of some German universities: "Theological theses, which the undersigned, with the approval of the dean of the venerable theological faculty, will defend publicly for the attainment of the licentiate [or doctorate] of theology. N. N." Upon appearing on the scene at the appointed time, one witnessed a spectacle suggestive of medieval days. Preceded by the dean, the candidate for the doctorate appeared. He was accompanied by three opponents engaged for the occasion. From a low platform he had to uphold his theses for an hour against the attack launched by the three opponents. Then he betook himself to a higher platform, where, after an address by the dean, he was solemnly pronounced a licentiate or a doctor. All this was a remnant of a definite form of medieval university life. Unfortunately, today all this has vanished; but in those days, it was part and parcel of academic life. It was a method regulated by fixed scientific rules for unearthing the truth. A vast number of theses, as well as the minutes of such learned disputations at medieval universities, are still extant.

No great significance was attached to an invitation to such a debate issued on October 31, 1517, by Luther, professor of theology at Wittenberg, as he tacked his Ninety-five Theses on a church door, which at the time served also as a bulletin board. He introduced his theses with a completely conventional formula closely resembling the modern one: "Prompted by love of the truth and in an attempt to bring the truth to light, the following theses are to be debated in Wittenberg under the chairmanship of the venerable Pater Martin Luther, master of liberal arts and of sacred theology and professor in ordinary at Wittenberg." These are not the only theses ever composed by Luther. Because at that time it was usually the duty of the professor to draw up the theses for the doctoral debates, it stands to reason that he performed this task innumerable times. We still possess hundreds of his trenchant theses. Then why, when there is such a large treasure, do we constantly single out these chance ninety-five? How did it happen that these theses, drawn up for a rather casual debate, made history, whereas scores of others by Luther himself, as well as by others at the universities round about, left scarcely a ripple on the surface of time? A few weeks before this, Luther had published theses against scholastic theology. From these he expected a strong reaction. In them he had made a major attack against the dominant theological system of the day, and almost desperately he waited for the echo. But the echo never came. Here in the Ninety-five Theses he occupied himself with only one question: indulgences. Moreover, he had been induced to do so more by experiences in the confessional than by scholarly considerations. Despite this, the propositions, to his great bewilderment, evoked a tremendous reaction; like a pamphlet, the theses, couched in the Latin of the learned, were soon in great demand.

It is a mistake to try to explain the remarkable effect of the Ninety-five Theses by assuming that they represent a great revolutionary program with which Luther had launched an attack on the entire fortress of the Catholic Church. No, externally there is little indication of a revolutionary program. All the theses revolved around a few ideas: contrition and repentance, punishment of sin and indulgence. They refer to church and papal power only inasmuch as these have a bearing on indulgence and penance. Instead of instigating to revolution all along the line, the theses contain statements that have a peculiar ring to evangelicals of today and demonstrate how cautiously and gradually Luther, yielding only to necessity, separated from the Roman Church. The church's claim still has validity in his eyes: "God forgives no one's sin without at the same time humbling him and subjecting him in everything to His vicar, the priest" (7). He still sees purgatory at the end of life, and for him, the words of the pope—yes, of every bishop and priest—still reach into this realm (25). He is still far removed from deleting indulgence from the Catholic message; indeed, he avers with great zeal: "Whoever speaks against the truth of apostolic indulgence, let him be accursed and damned" (71). For this reason, "bishops and priests are in duty bound to receive the indulgence commissioners with all due reverence" (69). Shall one call this revolution? Consequently, the reason for the wide effect of October 31 must be sought elsewhere. The theses were no slogan or battle cry with which Luther had opened hostilities. But with a single, well-aimed blow, he penetrated the vulnerable spot in the foe's armor and thrust all the way to the heart. But before we can understand this, we must look at the enemy and examine the vulnerable spot in his armor.

One of the most powerful impressions made by the Catholic Church is to be found in the well-thought-out system according to which she guides and embraces the whole life of her adherents. Like columns, seven great sacraments bear the vault of grace that stretches out over the life of the believers. From them spring the fountains of holy powers for the entire course of man's life. In Baptism—according to the teaching of the church—man is not only received into the communion of the church, but also a sacramental grace, working in the realm of the unconscious, is infused into the child; thereby the sin living in it is completely erased. This grace is renewed in confirmation by the episcopal laying on of hands. In the sacrament of marriage, the natural institution of matrimony and of the family receives the consecration of the church. In the sacrament of extreme unction the dying person is once more purged of sin and supplied with imperishable strength. In his ordination the priest is the recipient of a special vocational sacrament. Meanwhile, man can strengthen himself with the Sacrament of the Altar; and in confession, the sacrament of penance, he can assure himself as often as he desires of the remission of his sins.

Of all these Catholic sacraments, only one, confession, is important for everyday life. All the others are received either once or at certain moments in life; they do not affect the questions of daily life or meet the needs of moral conflict. Confession alone is the Catholic's companion on his way through the workaday world. In it he again and again bares his soul as he confesses his sins before the priest; then he goes on his way, fortified by the priest's pronouncement of absolution. Therefore this sacrament occupies a unique position among the Catholic sacraments; it appears almost like a stranger among the sacraments. With the exception of the sacrament of marriage—in which, according to Catholic doctrine, the bridal couple themselves are the dispensers—all the sacraments are consecrations and benedictions of the church, attended by symbolic signs and acts. The sacrament of penance alone consists exclusively of words and calls for an act of the individual, as well as of the church. One notices that in this sacrament, in addition to the other sacred acts that serve for the consecration and the enhancement of life, the basic religious question is heard: What must I do to be saved?

This had also been the question of early Christianity, and the first Christians had replied with Paul: "Believe on the Lord Jesus Christ, and thou shalt be saved, and thy house" (Acts 16:31). To be sure, this reply also implied a stern command. Belief in the Lord Jesus and Baptism obligated the Christian to abstain from sin. Primitive Christianity still asked: Can a redeemed person be a penitent at the same time, that is, can a redeemed person commit sin? For penitence presupposes sin. The early Christians were so powerfully impressed with God's gift of redemption that the thought that man might reward this gift with ingratitude, that is, with sin, was intolerable to them. Consequently, it seemed entirely natural to the early Christians that among them there should no longer be any sin, thus also no penitence for the redeemed. Therefore we read in the Epistle to the Hebrews: "For it is impossible for those who were once enlightened, and have tasted of the heavenly gift, and were made partakers of the Holy Ghost . . . and the powers of the world to come, If they shall fall away, to renew them again unto repentance; seeing they crucify to themselves the Son of God afresh, and put Him to an open shame" (Hebrews 6:4–6). Of course, this idealistic demand could not be reconciled permanently with reality. It was painfully obvious that sin was a power even within Christendom. This realization introduced many attempts to cope with the question of penitence. "The Lord is near; His kingdom is at hand," proclaimed Hermas, a Christian philosopher of the second century. The Lord would grant one more period of grace. Thus also the redeemed were permitted to repent once more of all their sins. But when, after this announcement of Hermas, the Lord did not appear, the predicament returned. Finally, an expedient was found: A distinction was made between venial sins and mortal sins. The former can be expunged by alms and other deeds of charity. For the remission of the latter, a severe process of penance was finally evolved. Whoever committed a mortal sin was excluded from the congregation and could be reinstated only after a complete and frank confession before the entire congregation. Then heavy penalties were imposed on him, such as fasting, castigation, hard labor, or heavy monetary fines. Not until he had performed such acts of penance and, dressed in penitential garb, had participated for a long time in the Divine Service only from the forecourt was the lost one again accepted into the congregation.

In a sector of the church it was keenly felt that in this way penitence had strayed far from Jesus' original purpose. When He initiated His ministry with the words "Repent: for the kingdom of heaven is at hand" (Matthew 4:17), He did not have public confession in the church in mind but each individual's earnest reflection on his daily sins. Of this there was scarcely a vestige left in the church's confession and penitence. Therefore the Greek monks first began to confess their sins to one another. They trained themselves in an ever-closer scrutiny of self; they even searched their thoughts and impulses. According to Greek rule, each brother had to confess every evening in the assembly of the monks not only his sinful deeds but also the impure emotions of the day. Grievous sins were confessed to the abbot. This was a new step in the history of Christian confession—in addition to the public confession, that of individual to individual. The latter was to dominate the future, for it was more profound because it involved also the more refined sinful impulses. Furthermore, it was more secret and avoided the disgrace of a public confession before the entire congregation. Therefore this mode also conquered the monasteries of the Occident. Here it has remained until the present day. But it also took hold of the broad field of the laity. At first the laity flocked to the monks for confession; then the monks were supplanted by the priests. In the course of a thousand years, the old monkish custom of confession grew into a customary religious act of all faithful Catholics.

Confession is composed of three parts: contrition, confession of sin to the priest, and, after receipt of absolution, good works as satisfaction for sin. Neither when doing public penance nor in confession does a man receive complete absolution; he must suffer the penalty for his sin, either here on earth or, for complete purification, in purgatory. The penalty for his sins, as well as the mode of satisfaction (insofar as satisfaction is possible), is determined by the church. The difference between this and the early confessional procedure is this: In the latter the absolution followed the performance of the penitential deeds, whereas in the former it precedes them.

Thus the gigantic system of the Catholic Church extends from heaven to earth and below the earth. It holds the individual so firmly in its grasp that he cannot escape with as much as an impulse. The priest sits in the council of God. God has placed a limit on His own forgiving grace in favor of the church; He has assigned to her an indispensable role in the remission of man's sins. The church holds man firmly in her power because the keys of heaven have been given to her. God has yielded to her the right to impose expiatory deeds on earth and in purgatory for the cancellation of the temporal penalties not remitted in the sacrament. He Himself imposes these temporal penalties through the agency of the Catholic Church.

At this point indulgence establishes contact with the sacrament of penance. Originally indulgence was simply the exchange of certain ecclesiastical penalties for others, for penalties more convenient to the penitent, such as monetary penalties, pilgrimages, prayers, etc. It soon dawned on the church that indulgence offered a valuable means of joining many petty deeds of penance to bigger ones profitable to her, for example, the construction of churches and, since the jubilee indulgences of the "holy years" (observed since 1300), to purposes that served the papal see. This is comparable to converting many small bank accounts into a corporation's share capital. Now as the Catholic Church claims authority not only for the imposition of penalties but also for the exchanging of these penalties, she expands her power immeasurably. At first the exchangeable penalties were content to confine themselves to this world, but soon indulgence also extended its influence to purgatory. Yes, even the dead were affected by this power of the church, provided only that the living met the conditions of indulgence for them. This ecclesiastical power centered in the pope. The theologians adduced reasons in support of the papal prerogative and power to transform incomplete and imperfect human deeds of penance into perfect ones before God, to transform paltry payments of money into adequate penitential deeds. For with the church's arm the pope can draw from the inexhaustible treasure of Christ's and the saints' merits and supply without limit any man's deficiency in penitential deeds.

I refrain from enlarging on the unprecedented abuse and shameless exploitation with which the sale of indulgences was carried on in the late Middle Ages up to the days of Luther. About this there were bitter complaints even in the Middle Ages. Contemporaries of Luther considered it wrong. So do Catholic historians of recent times. Instead of dwelling on the excrescences, it is far more important to expose to view the enormity of the doctrine itself. In accordance with his principle of directing every attack at the center of the fortress and not at any outposts, Luther, in his Ninety-five Theses, assailed, first, the tremendous danger of indulgences to religion rather than the pecuniary fleecing involved. This danger inhered definitely in the mistaking of indulgences for the forgiveness for sin. For later in the Middle Ages, Catholic practice did all it could to let the people know that it is wrong to think that one can buy remission of sins with money.

The Ninety-five Theses jeopardized not only the sale of indulgence but also the entire Catholic system of penance, of which indulgence is only a part. The most important chapter in the religious guidance and education of the Catholic faithful was disputed. The confession is the common proffer of grace by the Catholic Church. For her rule over man it was all-important to make penance a sacrament. In this manner the most intimate thoughts of the individual—his confession to God and the certainty of forgiveness—were placed into the custody of the priest. The extent of the Catholic conception of penance becomes clearest in indulgence. The church lifts one hand to heaven and draws from the treasure of Christ's merits. With the other hand she dispenses mercy on earth and thus wipes out the temporal punishment for sins—punishment imposed by God, not by the church herself! It reaches beyond this world to the dead in purgatory. This was Luther's opponent in the Ninety-five Theses. Here in the system of penance is the source of the power of the Catholic Church over mankind. This is the heart and—if hit—the mortally vulnerable spot in her influence.

In the first four of his theses, Luther directed his attack sharply and tellingly at this point. "Our Lord and Master Jesus Christ, in saying: Repent ye! intended that the whole life of believers should be penitence" (1).

> This word cannot be understood of sacramental penance, that is, of the confession and satisfaction which are performed under the ministry of priests. (2)

> It does not, however, refer solely to inward penitence; nay, such inward penitence is naught unless it outwardly produces various mortifications of the flesh. (3)

> The penalty thus continues as long as the hatred of self, that is, true inward penitence, continues, namely, until our entrance into the kingdom of heaven. (4)

These four statements introduce a world-historical revolution. They rend the tie between the Catholic sacrament of penance and Christ's words on penitence. They deprive the sacrament of penance of any binding power, for it would be ridiculous for a Christian to pursue a mode of penance that does not conform to Christ's demand. Luther reflects Jesus' meaning when he speaks of the daily drowning of the old Adam and the daily renewal and rising of the new man. Simultaneously, he points out most clearly the real offense of the Catholic doctrine of penance. If penance is made a sacrament, it is torn asunder into many separate acts; the acts of confession become somewhat intermittent. Corresponding to this, God always issues His grace piecemeal, as it were. It must be granted anew from one confession to the next; for according to Catholic belief, the priest not only proclaims forgiveness, but he also remits sin in God's stead. Furthermore, God does not grant complete forgiveness in the rite of absolution. No, the temporal penalties remain in force. For Luther, however, real penance is something complete and final. It is determinative for man daily and hourly; it is at the same time a penetrating searching of the heart and a proper conduct of life. When God grants man His forgiveness, He does not detract from it by means of ecclesiastical penalties or purgatory.

This is the simple basic thought underlying Luther's criticism of the penitential system. His attack on indulgence is equally simple. What is the aim and purpose of indulgence? Relief from the temporal penalties for sin imposed by the church in the sacrament of penance, commutation into more convenient and less burdensome penalties. For Luther this represented a position far removed from true repentance. His opposition was expressed most simply and profoundly in the fortieth thesis: "True contrition seeks and loves punishment, while the leniency of indulgence remits it and causes men to hate it." This brings the entire religious antithesis to the fore. The Catholic sacrament of penance and indulgence bear man in mind and are intent on making things easy for him. Indulgence is supported by natural human love of self. Man wants to stand before God as righteous as possible—also because of purgatory, hell, and judgment—but at the same time he wants this to be as convenient as possible. Assurance of protection against God and deliverance from as much penalty as possible are the two aims of indulgence. Luther's conception of penitence bears God in mind and demands that man submit completely to His will and service. True penitence, for Luther, implies a ready willingness to suffer for sins and an earnest attempt to make amends, albeit full amends can really never be made. The Catholic purchaser of indulgence has regard only for himself; the Lutheran penitent has regard only for God, without giving thought to the burdens he may bear in His service. This is a heroic position about which not much can be said. For Luther it was the natural disposition of true repentance. At the same time he knew how rarely this is found among men. This thought he expressed in one of his theses: "Rare as is a true penitent, so rare is one who truly gains indulgence, that is to say, very rare" (31).

Thereby Luther cut the ground from under the feet of the Catholic conception in the most salient area. In accordance with the true sense of Christ's message, he converts penitence—which in the sacrament of confession consists of separate penitential steps—into a daily and complete confession. He delivers man from his self-love, which, through indulgences, would like to attain forgiveness with as little trouble as possible, to the loftier naturalness of true penitence, which no longer seeks its own comfort but gladly bears whatever is imposed. It is easy to foresee what changes in the church's doctrine and practice were to result from this simple but radical return to biblical truth. With remarkable accuracy of aim, Luther hit the extraordinarily dangerous point of indulgence; he struck at the baseness of the old Adam, who fain would escape with as light a penalty as possible. This is the antithesis of a true penitential attitude. Luther contended against indulgence because he took repentance seriously, more seriously than did the Catholic Church. Furthermore, the fundamental danger of indulgence had grown in the practice of the late-medieval church into a destructive force because, for the sake of making money, the difference between indulgence (dispensation from penitential penalties) and remission of sin (release from guilt) was erased and practically done away with. The church sinned hideously against the Christian conscience by countenancing the idea of the purchase of remission of sin. Thereby indulgence supplanted the Gospel. In sharp and pungent theses, Luther brought the contrast into bold relief: "The true treasure of the church is the holy Gospel of the glory and grace of God. Naturally, however, this treasure is most hateful because it causes the first to be the last. Naturally, however, the treasure of indulgence is most acceptable because it causes the last to be first" (62–64).

Luther moves in on indulgence from yet another side. He recognizes it as a selfish work by means of which man seeks his own ease. For this reason any measure demanding true unselfishness is preferable. In a series of pointed theses (41–50), Luther impresses upon his readers that a work of indulgence is far inferior to any work of love. He even assumes that the pope is convinced that the sale of indulgences is in no way comparable to a deed of mercy. It is always better to give alms to the poor or to save your money for any proper household item than to squander it on indulgence. Yes, Luther even believes that if the pope knew about the indulgence traffic, he most certainly would rather set fire to St. Peter's Church than let his flock be fleeced for its construction. With wonderful simplicity, Luther states the principle that guides him in his criticism of indulgence: "For love increases by a work of love, and man becomes better. Through indulgences, however, he does not become better but only freer from punishment" (44). This thesis is like a portal through which we catch a glimpse of the approaching Reformation. Any act of love performed in the routine of daily life takes rank above all services prescribed by the church and rendered for the attainment of salvation. Luther rated all ordinary and unselfish deeds of love higher than the religious acts performed for the sake of one's own salvation.

As we saw earlier, it was not Luther's plan to abolish indulgence completely. What was his objective? With the eye of a historian of genius, he beheld the original function of indulgence: nothing but the remission of the church's penalties. Naturally, the church, like every teacher in school, has the right to prescribe penalties. At the time Luther is still convinced that his action reflects the pope's own viewpoint. He believes that the pope does not or cannot grant a dispensation from any penalties other than those he himself has imposed (5, 84). To be sure, he does feel that this necessitates a change in the wording of the most current formula of indulgence: "Therefore the pope, when he speaks of a plenary remission of all penalties, does not mean simply of all but only of those imposed by him" (20).

From the history of penance we have learned to appreciate the significance of this. The hand of the church reaches into heaven; Luther slaps it down. No longer is there any talk of the church remitting God-imposed penalties, only ecclesiastical, no others. Furthermore, there is no longer a piecemeal mercy of God that leaves some penalties to be atoned for to the advantage of the church. The priest is again banished from the council of God. God's mercy is no longer incomplete and imperfect; it is perfect and complete. In the same manner Luther slaps back the Catholic Church's other hand, which is stretched out toward purgatory and presumes to bind and unbind the dead. Although Luther still believes in a purgatory, he disclaims any relationship between the penalties of purgatory and the church penalties. Therefore he writes with stinging irony: "Those tares about changing the church penalty into the penalty of purgatory surely seem to have been sown while the bishops were asleep" (11). The dead are definitely beyond the power of the church and stand before the judgment seat of God, at whose side no pope and no priest is to be found. Thus the church is repelled and driven back to the original view on indulgence: temporal remission of temporal penalties.

Luther saw through the game the church was playing when she changed the temporal prerogatives into eternal prerogatives and church penalties into God's penalties. In this way she achieved a power over the faithful from which they could not extricate themselves. Luther's penetrating eye also detected that the late-medieval indulgence policy no longer concerned itself with man but with money. But the Gospel's whole interest revolves around man. Once more, therefore, he drives home with satirical scorn the difference between the Gospel and indulgence: "The treasures of the Gospel are nets wherewith of old they fished for men of means. The treasures of indulgence are nets wherewith they now fish for the means of men. The indulgences which the preachers loudly proclaim to be the greatest graces are seen to be truly such as regard the promotion of gain" (65–67). Now another trait manifested itself in Luther's strategy: It pointed to the future. In his fight for the Gospel, for purity and truth of Christian doctrine, he simultaneously made himself the mouthpiece of the people's offended sense of justice. If the pope can, as he claims, deliver souls from purgatory, why does he not do this for love rather than for money? Why, then, does he not do it a hundred times daily rather than just once for every believer? Why keep on issuing new indulgences if they are to have the same effect the old ones had? If souls are delivered from purgatory through indulgences, why, then, are those moneys expended for requiems for souls now delivered not refunded? Why does the pope not invest his own money in the construction of St. Peter's Church instead of mulcting his poor faithful? (81–89). Luther's purpose in voicing these pointed questions of the laity was not to ridicule the church but to issue an earnest warning: "Repressing these scruples and arguments of the laity by force alone and not solving them by giving reasons for so doing is to expose the church and the pope to the ridicule of their enemies and to make Christian men unhappy" (90).

When Luther destroyed the scheme of indulgence, he simultaneously struck a blow at the heart of Catholic piety. He contradicted the preachers of indulgence who ascribed to the pope the right to deliver souls from purgatory (21). "The pope acts most rightly in granting remission to souls, not by the power of the keys (which is of no avail in this case), but by way of intercession" (26). It must not be overlooked that "the intercession of the church depends on the will of God alone" (28). Above all, the pope possesses no personal power of forgiveness. He can only confirm that God wants to pardon the penitent (6). The pope merely has the authority for "a declaration of divine remission" (38). The eternal merits earned by Christ for humanity do not require the assistance of the pope as a treasurer who apportions and parcels them out to man; they are constantly creating, "independently of the pope, grace to the inner man and the cross, death, and hell to the outer man" (58). In place of the piecemeal distribution of grace held in the church's safekeeping, Luther now proclaims the comforting message of the Gospel: "Every Christian who feels true compunction over his sins has plenary remission of pain and guilt, even without a letter of indulgence" (36).

The Ninety-five Theses are more than a mere document born of a certain historical moment, they are a mighty prelude to the proclamation of evangelical truth, in which the leitmotif of the coming message is already being sounded. We shall select just four of the basic thoughts.

1. God demands the whole man; He cannot be put off with a few occasional penitential acts. In conformity with Jesus' words, penitence is again the internal repentance, which dare not desert man for a moment and therefore must show itself in moral conduct and discipline. Luther's basic rule—"True contrition seeks and loves punishment" (40)—wants to show the Christian the attitude that gladly suffers, would like to make amends, and uncomplainingly prefers the difficult path of penitence and suffering to the easier one of indulgence.

2. Any and every deed of love transcends all that man may do for himself, no matter how pious the motive, for all that man does for himself necessarily implies a claim before God and the wish to make an impression, as it were, on Him. But before God, the last shall be first, and before Him those are justified who serve their neighbor unselfishly and with sanctified naturalness.

3. The church is not an institution of salvation in the sense that she possesses absolute power over the keys to the gates of eternity. She is no religious insurance company in which works of indulgence or penitential deeds can purchase a policy. But she is the communion of believers, all of whom stand before God naked, poor, and insecure

but who, nevertheless, can give one another the greatest protection, namely, the intercession of genuine love. However, this church, as the communion of saints, never forgets that "the intercession of the church depends on the will of God alone" (28).

4. With his Ninety-five Theses, Luther removed the priest and gave Christendom the pastor (*Pfarrer*). The priest who binds and unbinds sin as if he sat in the councils of God and as if God had entrusted to him the administration of a portion of His grace was banished from the church. In his criticism of pope and priest, Luther gave us a picture of the true pastor as he envisaged him: as the preacher of the Word who offers up intercessory prayer for his congregation and comforts the conscience with Jesus' assurance that God Himself forgives sins.

Luther concluded his theses with two pairs of antitheses: "Away with all those prophets who say to the people of Christ: 'Peace! Peace!' though there is no peace!" (92). This was Luther's final judgment of Roman Catholicism: that it proclaims peace where there is no peace, for the Catholic Church attempts to soothe man and put his conscience at ease with canonical works of penance, which are inadequate. Luther demanded that man must rely solely on God's words of forgiveness. On the other hand, "Blessed be all those prophets who say to the people of Christ: 'The cross! The cross!' and there is no cross" (93). This is to say that only he who takes up his cross and is sincerely repentant finds his cross of conscience removed and is now filled with true comfort.

These theses still address themselves to us today. We are ready to make peace with God and, thoughtlessly and oblivious to our guilt, to go on our way without asking whether God is able to make peace with us in our present condition. How often we speak without hesitation of the Divine in us, almost as if He were like us! Even we Christians listen to the Gospel without living according to it, and we act as if God were so good-natured that He overlooks all our faults. For everything we do we lay claim in so frivolous a manner to God's blessing, as if He did not have stern and humiliating things to say to us about all that we do and are. Therefore Luther's warning "Away with the false prophets who say: 'Peace! Peace!' when there is no peace!" is applicable also today where the Gospel and faith are preached without earnestness and without reverence for His divine majesty. The last two theses of Luther have validity for every Christian: "Christians should be exhorted to strive to follow Christ, their Head, through punishments, death, and hell, and thus to be confident of entering heaven through many tribulations rather than in the security of peace" (94–95).

Is this event of October 31, 1517, identified as it is with the intimate questions of conscience regarding penitence and indulgence, really world history? How can world-historical significance be attributed to it? Yes, it was world history in the most real and literal sense of the word. The two greatest revolutionary changes of human history (viewed politically, culturally, and intellectually) emerged from two events that at first were altogether inconspicuous. When Jesus said, "Repent ye, for the kingdom of heaven is at hand!" the first of these two turning points was ushered in. Luther initiated the second with the first of his Ninety-five Theses: "Our Lord Jesus Christ, in saying: Repent ye! intended that the whole life of believers should be penitence." No ruler, statesman, general, philosopher, or minister of culture has influenced the course of history as much as these two Christian proclamations. Not only the inner life of Christians but also the political and cultural structure of the West have been more profoundly changed by these proclamations than by any other historical happening. Everyone, whether Christian or non-Christian, will find this corroborated by history.

Are we living in a third era of world history today, an era characterized and determined by the words "Do not repent, for modern man has no need of repentance"? The effects of such a period would be just as far-reaching for all human life as the great revolutions wrought by Christ's message of repentance and by the renewal of that message through Luther's Reformation. It remains an incontrovertible historical truth that religious faith spells the life of nations and that unbelief spells their doom. Therefore the Ninety-five Theses—with which Luther wanted to awaken his church to sincere repentance, to a stricter discipline, and to a fearless faith—are of world-historical importance.

THE HIDDEN AND THE REVEALED GOD

Christianity has no name for God; in this respect it differs from other religions. The latter address the divinity with a specific name; it is immaterial whether the cult is polytheistic or, as in Islam, monotheistic. We Christians apply the same word *god* with which we address our heavenly Father in prayer also to the various pagan divinities. We call Zeus the supreme god of the Greeks or Allah the god of Islam. The Greeks, on the other hand, could not speak of a Zeus of the Persians nor could the Arabs speak of an Allah of the Christians, for these are proper names. Although these may often be traced to concepts expressive of divine attributes, they have nevertheless become names that cannot be transferred. We have no name for God but only a concept for Him. For us name and concept coincide. God is the nameless one, whereas we men and all creatures were provided with names, as the story of creation so beautifully relates.

The significance of this unique position of Christianity in the family of religions is easily felt when one places a modern scholarly Old Testament translation, which retains the Hebrew name Jahwe, beside Luther's translation: "Jahwe ist mein Hirte, mir wird nichts mangeln." Or "Preise, meine Seele, Jahwe, und vergiss nich alle seine Taten" (Psalm 103:1–2). The difference is felt immediately: Jahwe is a strange God of no concern to us. On the other hand, in Luther's words the psalm becomes our own song of praise. Whatever I can call by name is known to me, thus it is delimitable and determinable. It is no longer full of deep mystery, of weirdness, or of a mysterious, boundless love. For this reason it seems unworthy of God to assign a name to Him. Even those among us who wanted to lead us Germans back to the religion of our Germanic forebears were not inclined to address their god as Odin or Thor. Christianity has given us a deeper, a more spiritual concept of God, which has become the natural and self-evident possession of everybody in our nation, Christians and non-Christians alike.

But now many confront us with the question: Must we not advance much further with the spiritualization and refinement of God? You Christians, they declare, stop halfway. You have comprehended the nameless God, but what about the personal God in whom you believe? You conceive of God as being far too much like a human being. A God who created and preserves the world, who watches over my every step and guides me, a God with whom I speak in prayer as with a good friend or a father, who is angry with me because of my sins, who loves me, who in the person of Jesus sent His Son and ambassador into the world and revealed Himself in Him—all this is completely unthinkable. You divest God of His peculiar mystery, of His greatness, and of His incomparableness by investing Him with so many intimately personal qualities and acts. Those are the objections we all know. For this reason man resorts to the adoption of abstract terms such as Providence, Fate, Higher Power, Divinity to avoid the personal element that surrounds the word *God* for us. Obviously, such expressions are gaining ground in modern colloquial speech. Behind these designations can be heard the intimation of a god who is not only nameless but also impersonal, faceless, and formless. To many this seems to be the only logical manner of reproducing and delineating the divine mystery in our language.

But let us counter with the question: Where do you, who reject a personal, demanding will and a revelation, find the divinity? Where does man encounter it? In life itself, in the altogether unfathomable depth and in the infinite breadth of life's happenings, in the operation of nature, in the primal force of historical life. All this is replete with the divinity; it surrounds us like the air we breathe. It meets us in the current of nascent growth, in the winds of the future. You discover nothing of this God, they say, if you gaze entranced at the one book, the Bible, and at the one figure, Christ. You Christians know nothing of this true, expansive, incomprehensible, near, and distant God.

Do we really know nothing of Him? Must we surrender life, nature, the historical world to retain the God of commandment and of grace, the God who addresses us personally in Christ? Much depends on this question for a proper understanding between us and the de-Christianized people of our nation. Let us first consult Luther for an answer. The reply of an individual Christian or theologian may not be of great consequence, but the answer that can be derived from the origin and the basis of our evangelical faith is important. We are also prompted to confer with Luther because this mighty thinker and man of God has surprises in store of which too few evangelical Christians are aware.

Surely we all know that Luther had a great fondness for animals and flowers and a fine knowledge of the realm of nature. Many are acquainted with the charming complaint of the birds that Luther addressed to his servant, who was addicted to bird catching. It is generally known how he could marvel at the wonders of nature. "If you should examine a kernel of grain on the field minutely, you would die of wonder."[1] And we remember how Luther embellished his speech with rich imagery taken from nature. But Luther makes a far richer contribution to our question than open eyes for nature and a plenitude of metaphors. He himself thought this question through thoroughly and could answer it boldly. Yes, God Himself is the tempestuous life in His creation; He dwells in all and penetrates all. The insight reflected in Goethe's words "Ihm ziemt's, die Welt im Innern zu bewegen, Natur in sich, sich in Natur zu hegen" comes to mind when we hear Luther say:

> God is a supernatural, inscrutable Being who resides simultaneously and entirely in every kernel of grain and still is in all and above all and outside all creatures.[2]

> God sends forth no magistrates or angels when He creates, fashions, or preserves something, but all this is the peculiar work of His divine power. But if He is to create and preserve it, He must necessarily be present and create and preserve His creation both in its innermost and outmost particles, around it and about it, through and through, below and above, in front and behind, so that nothing can be present or within all creatures but God Himself with His power.[3]

> His divine being can be entirely in all creatures and in each individually, deeper, more intimately, more present than the creature itself, and yet again be encompassed nowhere and by none, so that He, to be sure,

---

1. "Sermon von dem Sakrament (1526)," WA 19:496.11; cf. pp. 157ff.

2. "Vom Abendmahl Christi (1528)," WA 26:339.34.

3. "Dass diese Worte Christi . . . (1527)," WA 23:132.32.

encompasses all things and is in all things, but without having any creature in Him and without being encompassed by any.[4]

No poet and no nature mystic has ever discoursed more boldly and more fervidly on the immanence of God in His creation as its living breath, its real life. If we recall how many people have become confused in recent centuries in their Christian faith over this subject of God and nature, one must deplore deeply that this profound and life-giving viewpoint of Luther was consigned to oblivion in the church for so long. If these liberating ideas of Luther had remained alive, then the naive picture of an earth-removed and humanlike Master Builder, Organizer, and Preserver of the world would long have disappeared from evangelical pronouncements. It was really unnecessary for mankind to torment itself in the seventeenth or in the nineteenth century with an image of God that had already temporarily bewildered the faith of young Augustine in the fourth century.

No less bold and magnificent is Luther's conception of the God who is operative in history and confronts man in history.[5] The power with which he portrays the Lord who holds the reins of history finds a parallel only in that of the Old Testament prophets. While Isaiah calls powerful Egypt a fly and Assyria a bee that God can summon with a mere hiss for the destruction of Israel (Isaiah 7:18), Luther depicts God as a sharpshooter who has one nation shot down by another when its measure of iniquity is filled:

> Do you see the guns loaded? . . . He shot the Jews with the Romans, the Romans with the Goths and the Wends, the Chaldeans with the Persians, the Greeks with the Turks.[6]

> Indeed, He permits cities and rulers to begin to rise a little; but before they are aware of it, He topples them over, and, as a rule, the greater the kingdoms, the sooner they fall. And even though they prevail for a while, to God this is barely a beginning; and not one has ever reached the goal to which it aspired. . . . And all their splendor is nothing but a game of God, who permitted them to rise a little and then always knocked them over, one after the other.[7]

---

4. "Dass diese Worte Christi . . . (1527)," WA 23:136.31.

5. Cf. pp. 169ff.

6. "Psalm 118 (1529–1530)," WA 31/1:126.13.

7. "Psalm 127 (1524)," WA 15:370.20.

God is able "to scatter cities as a peasant strews kernels of grain; yes, He can overthrow kingdoms."[8]

These pictures of Luther of the sovereign power of God that holds sway in history according to its own inscrutable will affect us with primal force amid the vast revolutionary changes we have been experiencing for decades. We behold empires fall and nations die; for decades we have heard the panting of warring nations. Therefore this language of Luther is more intelligible to us than it was in uneventful and more peaceful times. However, we must have our eyes opened for a still bolder glance cast by Luther into the depths of historical happenings. There man meets the masked God Himself. History is not only God's playground or arena, where all takes its course in accordance with His will, but in all its varied phases and forms He Himself is hidden as behind a mask.

> He Himself acts through us, and we are only His mask behind which He conceals Himself and performs all in all, as is well known to us Christians.[9]

> It may surely be said that the course of the world and especially the life of His saints is God's disguise in which He hides Himself and reigns and busies Himself so wonderfully in the world.[10]

Viewed superficially, it always appears as though the stronger prevails and obtains the victory. This view, as Luther says, gave rise to the saying: God helps the strongest. But in reality, another fought here and made the strong one mighty that he might be victorious. "God defeated the others through the prince who won the war."[11] These words contain an earnest admonition to the victor not to ascribe victory to his own might but to God, who chose him to be His mask. Otherwise God might withdraw His hand from him and cast him aside as an empty mask.

Luther's pictures of nature and of history show similar lines. God's reign in the most minute details of nature and of history cannot be described more forcefully, fully, and logically. The masked God meets us at every turn. Stone and tree are His mask as much as people and nations. He permeates everything with His glowing breath; He is the pulsating life in all that lives. Whoever has steeped himself in this portrayal of God knows

---

8. "Zechariah (1527)," WA 23:519.34ff.

9. "Vorrede zu Lichtenbergers Weissagung (1527)," WA 23:8.36.

10. "Psalm 127 (1524)," WA 15:373.7.

11. "Magnificat (1521)," WA 7:585.33.

that the Christian faith, too, can find expression for this conviction that the mystics and many modern non-Christians claim for themselves. The Christian belief in God is by no means poorer than theirs; it is much richer. It must, however, become conscious of its riches. It may be sure that it need not waive its claim to God's presence in a single fraction or fragment of life. Whatever may be said of God's thorough penetration of nature and of history is also part and parcel of the Christian faith. It may make liberal use of all that has ever been said by poet and philosopher, not as of borrowed goods but as of its own possessions. The Christian is aware, however, that here he is standing only on the threshold of the question concerning God and that the panorama of real mysteries is unfolded beyond this.

The real question concerning God begins at the point at which they stop who claim to find Him in life itself. Whatever we can behold with our eyes in nature and in history is only the mask of God, only earthly phenomena. In nature we witness blossoming and withering, growth and decay; in history we see victor and vanquished, bane and blessing, rise and fall. But who hides behind all these masks? We sense the working of God in all life; we know that He is the cause and the pulse of the world. But who is this God?

Or may one not pose this query? Whoever thinks thus and would like to suppress this question knows not what he is doing. For that is tantamount to waiving all claim to the entire question concerning God. Then the word *God* may just as well be supplanted with another word. Then both question and answer become meaningless. Then the question concerning good and evil, right and wrong, also becomes senseless. Then everything collapses in deep doubt and inescapable nihilism. But in reality no one who as much as searches for a purpose and aim for his own life can ignore the question: Who is this God? Where do I meet Him that I may catch at least a glimpse of Him? What are His designs with this world that He leads over such strangely tortuous paths? What is the purpose of all the weal and the woe He metes out to me? We may despair of obtaining an answer to our queries, yet we cannot desist from asking. This is what makes us human beings; the animals cannot ask concerning God.

Who is the God who encompasses us? Tree and rock are mute; nature utters no intelligible speech. Do flowers bloom merely to wither, or do they wither to produce new seed? Whose power is final, life's or death's? Is nature a realm of ineffable peace and tranquillity that we sense and seek when we flee to her from the bruised and battered world of man? Or is nature also subject to the never-ending conflict, subject to the law of dog eat dog? Are the forest trees also embroiled in a rivalry for a place in the sun?

History is no less mysterious and confusing. What is the meaning of the unceasing alternation between ascent and descent, rise and decline? Does all this have a purpose and a goal? What about justice in a world in which the strong always conquer and disregard all laws? Is it not perhaps, after all, a game in which God alone participates arbitrarily by loading His musket, aiming at the nations, and gloating as they topple? Is not this God a hard-hearted, coldly planning, or perhaps plan-less fate? We often get this impression when probing into the meaning of occurrences in our own life as in that of nations. How many have shouted their accusations against this unknown and unknowable Master of the universe and against this absurd and incongruous course of life!

It would be appalling if our knowledge of God were confined to the realization that He is the power of life in everything that lives. For everything, the sublime and the beautiful as well as the vile and the ugly, owes its existence to this power. God's omnipotence preserves the good and the evil; by the mere bestowal of life it permits the one to grow better and purer, the other to become always more vile. Both good and evil propagate themselves without end in this world. Even the ungodly owe their existence to God's power. Why does He not withhold life from them? Why does He not put an end to suffering, war, and death, which could not endure without His omnipotent hand? Why does He not force all men on the right path if they themselves are unable to find it? Why does He permit them to stray hopelessly in gloom and despair? Questions and riddles without end!

Small wonder that Luther declared that this God, who dwells in everything that lives and whom he beheld there as clearly as ever poet and philosopher did, is a hidden God, a God to whom no path of our philosophical contemplation leads us. If we assume that we can comprehend Him in a discordant and contradictory life, in which He is indeed hidden, then our reflections must carry us into insoluble contradictions. Luther knew that to faith there is no alternative but imprecation and blasphemy. He was well aware that the human mind can snap because of this question and be driven into insanity. All profound thinkers who skirted the rim of this precipice have either known or experienced this (Goethe, Hölderlin, Nietzsche).

Only one, God Himself, can lead the way out of this maze of questions. This Luther knew positively. It is futile for reason to remonstrate and rebel. But does this mean that we should lay our hands in our laps and patiently await enlightenment? By no means. We must learn to put the question concerning God correctly. This is imperative. Then the comprehension of the answer will be easier. The fact that our attempt to apprehend God in nature and in history as the totality of life leads us into a blind alley need not be fruitless. If this quest carried us adrift, then the mistake did not occur at the end but at the beginning. We must retrace our steps and seek a correct starting point. Did we actually look for God when we sought Him in the aggregate of life? Or were we not groping rather for a concept of the ultimate unity of the world? To find the coherent elements of the world is the never-ending task of the philosopher, but this is not the core of the question concerning God. To trace the living world to its ultimate cause and to deduce a philosophical system from this, and to believe in God, are two radically different matters. The former stems from our strong urge and thirst for knowledge and cognition. But the result of this philosophical investigation still has no bearing on my attitude and my conduct of life. One may have the most varying views on this primary unity in all life; one may speak about God or about a primal power, the universe, fate, primal substance, primal spirit—all this is immaterial to, and without any effect on, our heart, our conscience, and our conduct in daily life. On the other hand, everything in life does depend on the question whether I truly believe in God. A genuine faith in God must transform me into another man. The real question concerning God is not only a question asked by us but also one addressed to us. The one is a question of cognition; the other, a question of life. The two can become one only if I know both. Here true faith in God is greater than any power of human thinking. In faith an answer to the question about the ultimate cause and origin of the world is also included; but the philosophical concept of origin contains no answer for my conduct of life, no duties and obligations, no help, and no comfort. Therefore we must learn to formulate the question concerning God correctly.

Luther often put and answered this question in a wonderfully informal, human, and undogmatic manner, particularly in his well-known explanation of the First Commandment (Large Catechism). "What does it mean to have a God, or what is God?" Answer: "God is that to which I must look for all that is good and to whom I must flee in every need."[12] This simple sentence, from which one could evolve Luther's whole theology and his view of the essence of all religions, is far different from most concepts of God. We would perhaps answer this question thus: God is the world cause or life absolute; the unfathomable power that supports and directs life and the world; or the demanding will that I hear in my conscience. We find nothing of this in Luther's statement: "That to which I must look for all that is good and to which I must flee in every need." Luther was well aware that man places his trust in various things in life. The one believes that, after all, money rules the world and conducts himself accordingly. Whether or not he possesses in addition a dim and hazy perception of God is of little practical importance. The other probably relies, in the end, on the gifts of body or mind with which he is endowed and glories in his own powers, which will see him through every difficulty. Others find what they consider complete security in the position and reputation they have acquired. Many trust in their luck, in their good blood, in the high respect in which their family is held, in their education; many gain strength and confidence in life from the fact that they are citizens of their country. If we sincerely searched our hearts and candidly confessed the real source of our confidence and trust, what amazingly heterogeneous things would come to light! How rarely will a person be able to say: I place my reliance solely on God! "To whatever your heart cleaves and on whatever it relies, that is really your god." Thus idols are not confined to heathendom. God and idol lie in such close proximity in our hearts that they are often hardly distinguishable. They are identifiable, however, by the true mainstay in our life.

Accordingly, having God means: "To possess something on which the heart places all its reliance."[13] This is the answer given by the same Luther who knew how to depict God's activity in creation so fervently and thrillingly. How does this harmonize? We realize that it transcends the bounds of our imagination. No concept, no image, no metaphor of our fantasy is adequate for an undivided and coherent view of God. Yet the two views concerning God belong together. It is inconsequential whether I can make many profound statements about God. It is of the greatest importance, however, for me to know that He is my God, that He is at my side, a God on whom I can depend implicitly at all times. Whoever has failed to

---

12. WA 30/1:133.

13. WA 30/1:134.

understand this difference can never have an inkling about a true belief in God, for to believe in God does not mean to believe that there is a God but to believe that He is my God. This is the simple difference between semblance and truth. Even pious pagans, for example, our Germanic ancestors, perceived this. They were fully convinced of the power of their gods and commended themselves to their protection by prayer and by sacrifice. There is no religion in this world in which man does not seek protection and security from his god, no matter how much he fears this god.

On the other hand, the current belief in God today—the assumption of a supreme being, a supreme fate—is no real belief in God, not even a pagan one. Even the belief in God of many Christians is often little more than a traditional, anemic conviction that somehow there must be a supreme being, a God. But in daily life they prefer to be guided by more practical considerations than by His commandments and to rely on things more tangible than His incalculable help. This is a mere caricature of a genuine belief. Because one, as they say, cannot have any definite knowledge of the existence of a higher power, they declare: I believe. To them belief is a type of knowledge with less probability. A tragic confusion! No, to believe in God means "to rely on Him for all good things and to flee to Him in every need."

Then we shall also understand that these apparently disparate images of God merge and harmonize in Luther's view of Christian faith: the God who lives all-powerfully in history and nature and the God on whom I may and must rely with all my heart, for whoever has confidence in this God will look upon nature and upon the fluctuations of history as a single mighty testimony to the power of the God in whom he may trust. Strength and comfort will spring even from the terrors of inscrutable divine acts for the faith that has learned to worship the hidden wisdom of the Father both in joy and in sorrow.

But perhaps we have already advanced too far for some and have said too much because we had originally set out only in quest of the correct question concerning God. Does the answer, in the final analysis, not rest with God alone, when He elects to grant an individual in a miraculous way, unseen by others and independent of others, the assurance of His encompassing presence? This, of course, cannot be gainsaid. When this conviction has thus been vouchsafed, all further discussion is superfluous. When God's clear light shines into our hearts, we need not elaborate further. However, God does not come to us before He has prepared our hearts and made them receptive for Him. This implies, among many other things, that He corrects our thinking and sets our questioning to rights.

If we have learned from Luther that everything hinges on pulling together the two widely separated ends of our question concerning God so they touch and this illuminating spark flashes across: The almighty God of heaven and earth is my God; He is favorably disposed toward me; I can rely on Him for every good thing and flee to Him in every need—then we are ready to draw the final conclusion. The people who assume that God reveals Himself in nature and history are mistaken. He is present there, but He is concealed. We behold His mask there but not His countenance. We are aware of His might, but we do not learn His will. We feel His breath, but we do not look into His heart. Who is hidden behind this mask? Luther said fittingly: "Therefore we are skilled to distinguish between God and His mask. The world is not able to do this."[14] Whoever supposes that he can grasp God in nature or in history with his hands, as it were, confuses God with His masks and does not differentiate between these. He gropes and reaches out into the dark. Here there is no room for reliance and confidence. I can rely only on him whose heart is known to me.

Perhaps it is now dawning on us that the true God far transcends the surging power in all life and existence, namely, that He is also a heart, a commanding and loving will, something personal, a thou who speaks to me and with whom I can converse. Power and person together in a unity not penetrable by our thoughts form the mystery of the true God. Whoever disregards the one or the other surrenders the entire God. Those who think the Christian God too personal must be apprised of this. If they suppose that it is sufficient to designate Him as an omnipotent, all-causative life, they fail to perceive that they are still not speaking about God at all but only about the profound unity of the world. On the other hand, we must also inform many Christians that they are making a similar mistake when they relinquish the stormy, creative power of life to the pantheists and virtually obstruct the path to the Christian faith for many by their naive, humanlike conception of God. They, too, forfeit not only half of God but the whole God. There is such a thing as a familiarity that deprives God of His majesty. Wherever He is stripped of this, He is just as little as He is to those who think they can get along with the masks of His majesty and without His heart.

---

14. "Lecture on Galatians (1531)," WA 40/1:174.3.

In Luther's faith the personality of God is incomparable and something free from all naive resemblance to humankind. When Luther speaks of the heavenly Father, the totality of life permeated by God always rings in his words. But just because God is concealed and not revealed in this life, faith is constrained, by reason of God's intangible presence, to seek Him as a person, as a fatherly heart on which it relies for every good and where it seeks refuge in every need.

To seek—even the last step of which our reflection is capable will not carry us beyond this. After we have revised the incorrect question concerning God, the question about the ultimate cause, and have grasped the true question about God, the question regarding Him who is my God, then we have completed the preparation. We can do no more than put the question; someone else will have to give the answer.

He has already given it. The only thing a God-seeking person must still understand is this: that he need take not a single step further but that he has already arrived at the goal. He must merely open his eyes and turn to the source from which clarity and the presence of God have been promised him. To be sure, the question must remain correct and unimpaired. We must not ask for a concept of God equipped with all that appears to us necessary for, and suited to, God; we must not ask for proofs. There are none. We must not ask for a compelling categorical imperative, but we must ask only whether our heart can rely on this God, the God whom Jesus proclaimed and portrayed thus:

"No one but the only God is good."

"For your heavenly Father knoweth that ye have need of all these things."

"They sow not, neither do they reap, nor gather into barns; yet your heavenly Father feedeth them."

"But when he was yet a great way off, his father saw him, and had compassion, and ran, and fell on his neck, and kissed him."

"I say unto you, that likewise joy shall be in heaven over one sinner that repenteth, more than over ninety and nine just persons."

"God is a Spirit: and they that worship Him must worship Him in spirit and in truth."

Is this a God, the God on whom we can depend even in the darkest hours? Let him who questions Jesus' right and authority to proclaim the grace of

God investigate whether Jesus really knows the human heart and whether we can elude Him who said:

> "Be ye therefore perfect, even as your Father, which is in heaven, is perfect."

> "Whosoever looketh on a woman to lust after her hath committed adultery with her already in his heart."

> "Ye cannot serve God and mammon."

> "In the world ye shall have tribulation . . ."

Does Jesus know our heart? Can we evade Him? Or does He speak the truth? When we finally gaze into the face of Jesus, the lonely suppliant on the mount, the Son of Man who had come not to be served but to serve, who unmasks the Pharisees and hypocrites intrepidly and judges them irrefutably, who calls the little children unto Himself, who comforts the adulteress, who heals wounds and remits sin wherever He goes, who weeps over His people—when we hear the Man of Sorrows of Gethsemane and of Golgotha saying: "Not My will, but Thine . . ." "Father, forgive them for they know not what they do!" did Luther then say too much when he called Him the mirror of the fatherly heart? No logical and clear proofs can be adduced for this certainty. But Jesus can bring an open and sincere heart under His spell and convince it of His truth more effectively with gentle force than with a thousand reasons. His only guarantee and pledge is His life itself, even to His dying on the cross. There He descended as a brother into all the woe and forsakenness man can experience, and by His death He bore witness to the truth that God is nigh amid pain and anguish of heart and can be found where our human mind is least inclined to seek Him. Where our blurred eyes behold nothing but darkness and tragedy in Jesus' life, there the eyes of faith see an immeasurable light bursting upon the world. God is concealed from the blind, but to the seeing He is revealed. Because then Christians know for what purpose they must bear their own cross, just as they know Him who helps them bear it.

But if someone should ask, "Why must this be none other than Jesus, this unphilosophical mind, this Jew from Palestine, that remote corner of the globe?" we have no reply to offer. Whoever asks such questions has not yet comprehended the essence of God. He still treats Him as a sort of president of the world with whose politics he is at variance and for whom he will not again cast his vote in the next election. This is not the way to deal with God. Whoever presumes to be able to prescribe to God how He should reveal Himself destroys the one thing in himself that he can do to meet God, namely, to behold where God's hand is to be seen and to hear where His Word is to be heard.

To express the presence and the revelation of God in Christ, Luther was especially fond of calling Jesus "the Word of God." That is a metaphor taken from the beginning of the Gospel according to St. John. That, too, we must seek to understand anew. And the more firmly we fix our gaze on Christ and the more candidly and freely we search for His footprints in the Bible, the better will we understand this Book.

Luther was so fond of calling Christ "the Word of God" because there is no more exact agency for self-communication than words. They reveal one's spirit, one's mind. Each of our words betrays us, intentionally or unintentionally, for they emanate from our innermost being. Even if we use words to conceal our thoughts, they reveal part of our character, namely, the ability to be untruthful. Word and character are inseparable; we even think in words. Our words are merely our character exposed to view. Luther wanted to express this most intimate communion between the heart of God and the spirit of Jesus Christ when he adopted the term "Word of God." At the same time he used the singular might of the unpretentious word as a metaphor for the wonderful might of Christ. A word is the weakest thing in the world, a mere breath of air, yet it is the mightiest. Words can affect the whole human race, decide the fate of nations, introduce new eras. Similarly unprepossessing, insignificant, and seemingly defeated, Jesus stands among the rulers of the world, yet what power has issued from Him, visibly and invisibly! As words not only reflect the mind but also contain it as their real substance, so Jesus' words and His whole person are not only a doctrine concerning God; God's grace is not merely proclaimed in them, but it is also imparted by them. In Him God is near us, clearly and definitely. He demands a decision, just as every word spoken by man demands a yes or a no. We must accept it or reject it, take it at its face value or call it into question. Thus Christ is not only the bearer of a message, He is also the personified question of God, the question that asks us whether we want to put our trust in Him and accept Him as our God. At the same time He is the personified pledge of God, the pledge that assures us that we may rely on Him for every good and flee to Him in every need.

To be sure, this requires courage. Death, sin, need, and pain are a Christian's lot as well as that of any other person. Therefore even for the believing soul the profound mystery of God always arises anew from the depths. The enigma of the incomprehensible power of God that holds the life of nature and of history in its hand and keeps it in stormy motion again and again forces the question to our lips: Is the God who demands our trust and pledges His help, which we often fail to see amid our sorrow and tribulation, not just a dream, a great self-delusion of man? Luther applied the old military term *Anfechtung* to this distress of the heart. For these are not merely questions or weary doubts and misgivings, they are attacks of an enemy skilled in fighting (*Fechten*). For our comfort Luther informed us that in this respect we are only sharing the experiences of Christ, who emptied this cup to the dregs, and that in this way God purifies and refines our faith and our trust in Him. "I did not learn my theology at one time, but I had to meditate deeper and deeper. Then my *Anfechtungen* carried me thither. For this cannot be acquired without experience."[15] This teaches us—especially young people—to exercise patience when the question concerning God staggers us and can silence our saucy accusations and hasty renunciation. Because Luther had experienced the blessing of doubts and *Anfechtung*, he called them "God's embraces."[16] Faith must transform the terrifying aspects of these painful embraces of the hidden God into the gracious countenance of the revealed God.[17]

Christian faith encompasses and overcomes the immense tension between the glowing life of God in all phenomena of nature and of history and the kindly disposed God, whose heart we may behold mirrored in Christ. The more thoroughly we understand that the question concerning God involves a dual view and not a shift from one point of view to another, the easier will it be to bear the intellectual contradictions that reason continues to present. For the more penetrating eye of faith these contradictions dissolve by themselves. For faith asks for no definite formula concerning God; it knows that it can reach into mystery and darkness and there find a hand that will hold and guide it. In the end all brooding and all reflections on God are reduced to the simple truth expressed by Conrad Ferdinand Meyer: "Was Gott ist, wird in Ewigkeit kein Mensch ergründen, Doch will er treu sich allezeit mit uns verbünden."

---

15. WATr 1, no. 352.

16. "Psalm 45 (1532)," WA 40/2:582.5.

17. "Lecture on Genesis (1535–1545)," WA 43:460: "If you believe in the revealed God and accept His Word, then He will also gradually reveal the hidden God to you."

FAITH

The evangelical Lutheran churches that are found everywhere in the world are the only large Christian denominations named for a man. The others call themselves Catholic, Orthodox, Reformed, etc. Does this not mean that we are in danger of falling into a kind of human hero worship instead of tying ourselves solely to the great truths of the Gospel? If we understand our relationship to Luther aright, we are aware that we are not binding ourselves to any man. After all, Luther was not the founder of a religion; he was a servant of the Lord, nothing more. The real Luther himself forestalls any attempt to worship him and his person.

Yet we enjoy an immense advantage over other church bodies inasmuch as we can steep ourselves again and again in a study of the man Luther. He is not only a heroic figure in German history; he is that, too, and one of the greatest. He is not the author of absolutely authoritative textbooks. We are not bound and obligated to his opinion as infallible dogma. Luther himself always expressly accorded his followers every freedom from his person—to be sure, only a freedom to, and never away from, the Gospel. He is no Christ for us, no saint, but he is an exemplary Christian. He, as no one else, is our exemplar of life, of faith, of prayer— in earth-bound humanity, it is true, but nurtured and strengthened from the fountain of divine power. For this reason his soul conflicts, his struggles, and his faith are not to be relegated to the past; they are living and present today. If we bear this in mind, we are rendering ourselves an indispensable service. For temptations and trials teach—according to Luther's beautiful translation of Isaiah 28:19—to take note not only of the Word but also of the ideal and pattern. Therefore we direct our attention to the significance of Luther's faith as a force in his life and in his

67

thoughts—not only to the thought content of his faith, mentioned so often in this book—as we try to reduce this faith to four simple formulas.

I

Luther's faith is an unconditional faith. In his quest for God and man's relationship to God, he knows no if and no but, no halting on a course once chosen. His whole life is one great proof of this.

To be sure, our conventional notions, retained from childhood days, of Luther's development, especially of his trials and conflicts in the monastery, often make it harder rather than easier for us to understand this. There is hardly anyone among us whom Luther's heartrending anguish of soul did not impress as unusual, yes, as strange and terrifying. Is it not abnormal for a young, healthy, and highly gifted man to torture himself to the quick with the question concerning God, not only to mortify and crush himself but also to break down again and again in despair before the holy God? Was this not exaggerated? After all, what sin did this monk who watched over himself so conscientiously have to atone for? A good son, a diligent pupil and student, who, as we know from many reliable sources, had won the love and affection of friends and fellow men— was it not nonsensical for him to regard himself as lost before God because of his sins? If he had had at least some great fault to atone for, like many another who for this reason was driven to monastic expiation! Even if there had been only the passions of youth, the kind young Augustine had to overcome! But there was nothing of this. Whenever Luther came to confession, he had so few downright and evident sins to confess that his mfather confessors chided him and told him not to torment himself with such trivial offenses. Why, then, this terrible struggling? We shall never rid ourselves of the impression of what is unnecessary, yes, of what is unnatural, almost morbid, if we fail to realize that Luther did not seek and devise this toilsome monastic life for himself but that he merely followed the course to which the church had directed him. For more than a thousand years she had counseled all who were serious about God and a truly holy life to take the monastic vows and by constant self-discipline and penance to live in a far more intimate communion with God than was possible outside the cloister walls. The Catholic Church pursues that policy to this day. Hundreds of thousands had gone the same way before Luther and had tormented and mortified themselves no less—often worse—than he. The only difference between them and Luther was that he walked the way consistently to its end.

The question with which we commonly epitomize Luther's conflicts in the cloister—"How do I gain a gracious God?"—was not, as it often seems to us, Luther's own peculiar question. This question was put to him; he was confronted with it. It was the question of the church before his time; it was the question of all Christendom. It was peculiar to Luther only insofar as he stood his ground and stayed with the question down to its ultimate deductions and consequences; it was his own only inasmuch as he took seriously the answer given to him by his church. In all that his church had to say by way of command and consolation he took her at her word. This is the secret of his conflicts of soul in the cloister. When the church told him, "You must search yourself daily before God and penetrate to the innermost recesses of your thoughts and emotions," he complied, and in doing so he discovered that we human beings never achieve perfect truthfulness before God but that we are all too prone quickly to draw a veil over many hidden thoughts. When the church's official decree informed him, "You must acknowledge and enumerate all your sins in confession," he tried it, and in doing so he realized that we never reach the end and never really unveil all our sins completely before God. What, then, did confession avail him if the remission of sins proclaimed in confession was predicated on the impossible confession of every sin without exception? When his monastic superiors told him, "In the monastery you have found a higher route to God, for here you can elevate your whole inner being to God much oftener and more effectively in moments of unalloyed love," then he tried this too. He did have profound experiences during which he felt himself carried closer to God. But a pure love for God? Such a thing is not found in the human heart. What value can be attached even to the loftiest outbursts of love if my whole life is not a single dedication to God and devotion to my neighbor? Who will make such a statement about himself? If the advantages and the merits of the monastic order hinged on such special deeds of pure love for God, then this was a cruel deception.

Luther invented neither the question concerning a gracious God nor the answer to it. To enter the cloister and attempt the forms of monastic saintliness was nothing extraordinary for a Catholic Christian. Only one thing was extraordinary in Luther's case: that he took everything literally and seriously, both the question and the answers, that he followed the course to its end. It was not in him to stop halfway or to forego a solution and answer. Just because he did not yield and evade the issue, he overcame and exhausted all the answers given by the Catholic Church and monasticism in reply to the question concerning a gracious God. He arrived at the correct answer by no different method. After his discovery of the ineffectiveness and futility of ecclesiastical doctrine, he now took God Himself at His word and dared believe that God accepts the believer with all his sins as His child in accordance with His promise in Christ. God makes good His promise without any if and but. That became Luther's liberating conviction after he had burrowed to the bottom of all the ifs and buts of Catholic doctrine.

Anyone surveying the path Luther trod will no longer regard this man's conflicts of soul in the cloister as curious exaggerations but as an expression of an unerring and logical judgment. Luther progressed step by step. Never a step too fast; rather, one has the impression that it was too slow. Not until ten years after his controversy on the sale of indulgences did he proceed with the establishment of new congregations. Luther always let necessity dictate the way; he never rushed on wildly and rashly. But then he followed his course irresistibly and irrevocably.

A biographer of Luther could easily demonstrate how this man's whole life reflects an unswerving firmness in every situation and a consistent pursuit of every chosen course to its end. He never resorted to the expediency of following more convenient and comfortable byways. When his friends offered him safe asylum on Franz von Sickingen's Ebernburg toward the end of his journey to Worms, considered by many a certain road to death, he declined; he walked the road to its end and thus became the hero of Germany. When his elector hid him behind the protecting walls of the Wartburg, he remained only as long as he could reconcile this with his conscience. Then, contrary to the strict prohibition of his protector, he returned to Wittenberg. Thus he became the reformer of Wittenberg. When the peasants issued their social demands, most of which were approved by Luther, as deductions from the Gospel and in this way tried to make the cause of Christ a political affair, he opposed them unyieldingly and thus prevented the Reformation from becoming a political revolution. When he felt seriously ill and thought that his end was at hand, he still took a step for the sake of the conscience of others. But he promised himself little from this. He married and thus became the founder of the evangelical parsonage. When the dangers menacing the new Reformation impelled some of the Protestant princes to conclude a defensive alliance against the emperor, he intervened several times, persuaded that armed resistance against the sovereign of the empire was inadmissible, and in this way he kept the evangelical movement from becoming the basis for an oppositional league of princes. Whatever he regarded as God's will and order, he executed with unflinching steadfastness. This was the fruit of his faith, which was not hedged in by conditions and tactical considerations. Half-measures were alien to him because he knew that they did not pass muster before God.

II

Luther's faith was a belief in reality, a belief that accepted life's reality at its face value and did not lend itself to any illusions.

The first and most decisive feature of this faith was the fact that for him God was a reality. Luther's whole life can be understood only if one knows what this means. We humans, even we Christians, are, for the most part, far removed from recognizing God as the essential, yes, as fundamentally the only reality. The earthly, visible things usually appear much more real to us. To earn a livelihood for ourselves and our families, to hold our own in our professions, to advance, to acquire money and a good position, to write a few scholarly books that promote learning, to give our children a good education, to fulfill our duties faithfully toward our country, etc.— these seem to be the real questions and problems of our life. Compared to these, God and our association with Him must play second fiddle. Of course, we concede that God is important too, but He must content Himself with our superfluous time and strength. Luther said the opposite. He granted that all my tasks in life are certainly important too, but most important and most real is God; all else is secondary. To talk with God was just as real to him as a conversation with a friend. The thought never came to Luther that it was unnecessary to tell God about our worries and cares because He Himself, in view of His omniscience, knew everything. Naturally, He knows all, says Luther, but I have a right to talk to Him about it, to tell Him what I have to say, and to listen to what He has to say to me. For one dare not forget that prayer has two component parts: talking and listening. How can we expect God to listen to us if we do not listen to Him? As a rule, we think of prayer only when we are in trouble up to our ears. And when those prayers fail of fulfillment, we turn away from God, embittered and disappointed, and say: "God has not heard us." Probably we did not ask ourselves a single time whether we heard God. Luther says: "If we want our prayers to be heard, we must first hear God's Word; otherwise He will not hear us either, no matter if we weep and shout till we burst!"[1] One time when Melanchthon was seriously sick, Luther implored God not to deprive him of his friend because he could not dispense with the services Melanchthon rendered by preaching the Gospel. He talked with God as ardently and intimately as with a bosom friend to whom he could confide the whole truth. It sounded almost irreverent, yet his words flowed from the deepest reverence, which had taught him to converse with God as children do with their father and which had learned, both in fulfillment and in denial, to say: "The name of the Lord be praised!" Thus Luther spoke with God, often for hours, even—and especially—in the days devoted to his most arduous tasks and his most difficult decisions. We must not imagine that thoughts and wishes sprang from his heart continuously during these long hours of praying, then new thoughts and ideas would soon have failed him too. No, he spoke with God and listened to Him as he read the Bible, meditated on the text, or recited the catechism for the purpose of putting his daily life in order. But in all this he took for granted that God was not a beautiful thought or the unknown master architect of the universe or an object for sublime reflections in quiet moments but that He was absolute reality. Compared with this real God, all else was trivial to him: emperor and diet, pope and university, friend or foe. His whole life long he set his compass unerringly on the course toward this one reality. To him all other things man is wont to regard as so important were clouds he traversed on the way to his goal.

But Luther took everything else in the realm of reality just as seriously. Because God was so inescapably real to him, he knew that he was in duty bound unrelentingly to examine the reality in which we ourselves stand before the eyes of God. Because he was aware of being constantly in the presence of God, he was not tempted to draw a veil over the heart's dark abysses. God, of course, cannot be deceived by such a subterfuge. And that is all that matters. Without this deep conviction of Luther regarding the real, living God, his crushing judgment on man, who is forged to the chains of sin, cannot be understood. Luther was anything but a pessimist. That boundless, exuberant joyousness that breaks forth from him despite all sadness has nothing in common with the rather sour humor of a

---

1. "Zechariah Lectures (1525–1526)," WA 13:615.10.

melancholy person. But he uncovered sin in man so unmercifully as no one else since New Testament days only because God demands unrestricted recognition of reality from us. Here unsparing honesty is the best policy; it is the most merciful because man can be helped only in this way. This is the only course that points to freedom. A sick person cannot be helped by the physician as long as he imagines that he is well and requires no cure. With a penetrating eye, Luther recognized this spasmodic claiming to be well before God as humanity's most dangerous sickness, the conviction that one is not so bad after all as its vilest sin. When Luther spoke of humankind's hopeless abandonment to sin, he was far from envisaging mankind as a band of criminals. No, but the worst thing was the fact that we human beings feel insulted when we are called sinners and that we appear to be far too respectable in our own sight to require repentance. Privately we are too prone to measure ourselves according to how far we surpass others, whom we regard as our inferiors, not by the distance that separates us from our God and His commandments. So long as we do this, we will not understand a single word about God. For what He says about us men always has a double message: "Ye shall be holy: for I the LORD your God am holy!" and "For there is no difference: for all have sinned, and come short of the glory of God!" This is reality. If we recognize God as reality, then we also see our own reality. The two are indissolubly connected. That we have lost our contact with the real, living God so alarmingly is undoubtedly caused by the fact that we have lost sight of our true selves and, in place of our human reality, behold a man of straw clothed in our wishes and illusions. To recognize God also means to recognize our sins. To see one's sins also means to behold the holiness of God. Whoever speaks about God and does not know that in His sight he is a guilty person has not felt a trace of God's reality. It is impossible to have the one half without the other. God's majesty and our sin—the two together constitute the entire reality. Luther's faith was a real faith because it comprised both halves.

Luther views the reality of the world just as soberly and honestly. As with his own nature, so man has also at all times indulged in curious and fantastic views with regard to the world; with numberless theories he has concealed this or that segment of reality or spread a beautiful, delusive semblance over the whole. Because Luther was so deeply imbued with the reality of God, he was not hampered by wishes and dreams. Therefore he could see the world as it actually is. This is true especially in a twofold respect.

In the first place, if our German nation has learned that the world is a realm full of endless misery—particularly where it has been fashioned by man—it owes Luther a debt of gratitude for such insight. Yes, gratitude. For no matter how unpopular this realization may be, the fact remains that he who pronounces this truth is deserving of gratitude. He rids us of the illusions with which we like to befog our world. When great catastrophes and times of trial come, we are rudely tossed out of our beautiful dream-world and are unable to find our way in this world of reality. Now what has become of the beautiful dreams about the maturity of the nations, about the progress of humanity to an ever higher moral level, about the good fortune that comes to the masses as a result of the blessings of science and civilization? Suffering, conflict, and tribulation are part of the reality of the world. They are our daily bread. But not exclusively, thank God! The world offers much joy and happiness. But injustice and affliction are inseparable companions of the sin-laden history of mankind.

Death, too, is a part of reality. Luther discoursed on death as naturally as he did on life. It never occurred to him to pass over this piece of reality in silence or to sidestep it. Life derives its seriousness from death. Death makes everything inescapable, and for this reason it is a special messenger of God. The fact that everything earthly is mortal constitutes the reality of the world.

But Luther's faith also encompasses an entirely different aspect of reality; it sees not only sorrow, conflict, and death but also the power of divine dominion in a world forfeit to death. Just because injustice triumphs so often in the world, law is a divine miracle in the world. Because humankind, if left to itself, would transform the world into a desert, the state is a divine institution, a wondrous agency in this chaotic world.[2] Luther's remarkable insight into reality becomes manifest especially in his views on political science.

In contrast to the illusory theories so often advanced in the history of political science—that the state was founded on a natural urge of fellowship and association among men or that it represents a free contractual agreement between a nation and its ruler and that this will someday develop into a glorious paradise of justice and social adjustment—Luther

2. Cf. pp. 207ff.

declared simply: The state must exist because the world is full of sin. In the absence of law and government, nothing would endure. Not that the state itself is sinful, but men are sinful, self-evidently those, too, who administer the state. But the state itself is a miraculous institution established by God's directing and preserving hand. For this reason Luther held that public office was second only in importance to service in the church.

Luther sees still another miracle in the reality of the world: God's pulsing activity in nature.[3] Occasionally it seems as if it were the privilege of those outside the church to bear witness of God's life in nature. Then how astonished we are when we turn to Luther's works and find the power and the passion, surpassed by no nature mystic, with which he described God's hand in nature! For Luther, God has His being in every tree and leaf, in fire, in water, in stone. To be sure, many people of his day misunderstood this and were shocked by it. It was so difficult to reconcile this with the conventional picture of God, whom one thought of so naively as a great and august man and whom one separated widely from the works of His creation. But Luther also thought this out to its conclusion and was not afraid to use a surprising expression, an expression that at first seemed strange. Luther reflected on and illustrated God's vibrant indwelling in nature with matchless reasoning power. God Himself is the ultimate basis for the reality of nature. He lives, moves, and has His being in the world. He, who for Luther is reality absolute, encompasses all.

But what rents and rifts are to be found in this world! It is God's world, borne and ruled by Him, yet it is a world full of sin, sorrow, death, war, chaos, the tide of which God Himself must stem by means of the state. What sort of God is this who tolerates such contradictions? Is this view of reality not a great disappointment? A self-deception? No matter how often we call, no reply comes from the beyond. To be sure, the reality of this God is not visible. Often everything seems to refute the assertion that God is at work; perhaps it is the devil, fate, chance. This is exactly what made Luther's faith real; he did not make the world his own ideal nor did he see only what fits into the human picture of God. Later, the Age of Enlightenment saw only what is meaningful, progressive, and harmonious in the world. But Luther leaves these questions open and views reality as it is. This is possible only because his faith has, in addition, a third characteristic.

---

3. Cf. pp. 153f.

III

Luther's faith is a daring faith; it looks to Christ. His open eyes for reality with all its profundities and tensions had made it apparent to him that God is not visible, not demonstrable, not calculable, but that belief in Him calls for a venture, a leap into the dark.

Faith is a venture to recognize this vile world as God's creation despite its depravity, a venture to believe in merciful, forgiving love despite our enslavement in sin, a venture to comfort ourselves with the hope of life eternal despite death and the grief of parting, which we must experience again and again. Luther once described this daring leap of faith beautifully:

> If God chose to show us life in death, and showed our soul place and space, way and manner, where and how it is to appear, whither it is to go and remain, then death would not be bitter; it would be like a leap over a shallow stream on the banks of which one sees and feels firm ground. But He does not reveal any of this to us, and we are compelled to jump from the safe shore of this life over into the abyss where we feel nothing, see nothing, and have no footing or support, but entirely at God's suggestion and with His support.[4]

According to Luther, only one thing sustains us in this leap from life's safe shore into the abyss: Over this abyss God has erected the sign of the cross. Even the cross is no proof that we shall spring into the arms of God. Even on the cross we behold nothing of God's victory. If one views the cross with eyes other than those of faith, one could say that a cruelly deluded fanatic expired there. Even the leap toward the cross remains a blind venture. But Luther ventured it, and he knew that whoever has the courage to do so achieves assurance and conviction that can no longer be driven away by any darkness. Luther's faith was a conviction that, though assailed again and again, was always regained; it was not a heroically borne uncertainty as some have declared. "This is the nature of faith that it boldly takes the grace of God for granted, forms an opinion of confidence toward Him, and feels assured that God will regard him favorably and not forsake him. . . . Faith does not require information, knowledge, or certainty, but free submission and joyful venturing upon God's unfelt, untried, and unrecognized goodness."[5] This means that the certainty of faith is not

---

4. "Jonah Exegesis (1526)," WA 19:217.15.

5. "Sermon (1522)," WA 10/3:239.13.

based on human experiences and on visible tokens of God's rule in the world. These may be deceptive. But this certainty rests on faith's knowledge of another aspect of God's reality in the world: His hidden presence in Jesus Christ. To be sure, this runs counter to all outward appearance and to all reason. Reason cannot grasp the mystery:

> Who, clothed in garb of flesh and blood,
> Dost take a manger for Thy throne,
> While worlds on worlds are Thine alone.

It cannot comprehend the cross of Christ. But this cross becomes faith's pledge of the merciful love of God, which does not abandon man even when he rejects it. Consequently, for faith the cross becomes the focal point of history. Here time and eternity meet. How insignificant all transitory events in history appear beside this, no matter how important and imposing they may loom in their day!

He who lives in this faith can venture all for it. When necessary, Luther gladly staked his life for it. The finest proof of this is contained in the letter that Luther wrote to his elector on March 5, 1522, when, against the latter's will, he returned to Wittenberg from the security of the Wartburg. At the same time this letter is one of the most magnificent monuments of the German language. This journey took Luther through the territory of his great enemy, Duke George of Saxony. He assured his elector that this prospect failed to evoke the slightest fear in him. He would even have gone to Worms, no matter "if I had known that as many devils were lying in wait for me as there are tiles on the roofs, I nevertheless would joyfully have jumped into the midst of them." But Duke George is much less than a single devil, and Luther has no thought of evading him. He is resolved to ride in "even if it rained nothing but Duke Georges for nine days and each one raged nine times as much as this one. He regards my Lord Christ a man woven of straw." "I am coming to Wittenberg with much higher protection than that of the elector." Luther considered himself more able to protect the elector than the latter was able to protect him, for "he who believes most will protect most here. Since I feel that Your Ducal Grace is still weak in the faith, I can by no means regard Your Ducal Grace as the man to protect or save me." Luther did not want the elector to incur any harm or danger because of him, "for Christ has not taught me to be a Christian at the expense of someone else." In conclusion he repeats: "If Your Ducal Grace believed, you would behold God's glory; but since you do not yet believe, you have not yet seen anything. God be loved and praised forever. Amen." Accordingly, Christ, Christ, Christ is the beginning, the middle, and the end of Luther's venture in faith.

But Luther hazarded more than his life. He also hazarded his nation. The most perplexing question confronting him all the days of his life was: "Can your viewpoint be correct compared to that of the whole Catholic Church and that of countless theologians and believers for more than a thousand years? Are you yourself not the corrupter? Are you not seducing your nation?" But he had to venture to go alone and to lead his people in implicit reliance on the divine truth that had come to him and on his Lord Jesus. Thus he hazarded not only himself but also the soul of his nation. He knew, however, that in God's keeping it was safer than in any human tradition, no matter how ancient.

IV

Faith is life that proceeds from the strength of Christ. He who finds redemption from sin and peace with God at the cross receives from Christ new and genuine strength for life in this world. For Christ is not only the teacher of a new theology, but "Christ is a living, active, fruitful Being who does not rest but works unceasingly wherever He is." Therefore the words apply: "Wherever the works of Christ are absent, there Christ, too, is absent." Christ's miracles are not His only works; these no one can imitate. But "Christ has done other works too, such as patience, love, meekness, and the like, which everyone should do. Do them, and today, too, Christ will still be recognized by His works."[6]

Thus faith flowers in good works. Luther was far from divorcing these two or from declaring good works to be unnecessary, as Catholic writers have often charged. For this reason he wrote his "Sermon on Good Works" (1520) as a first evangelical system of ethics, as a guide for the performance of Christian works.[7] He assigned both works and faith to their proper place, which is determined by the fact that Christ must be the center of a Christian's life. A Christian's faith is directed solely toward Him, and a Christian's good works spring only from Him. Therefore, as Luther said, a Christian's whole life consists of "faith and love or receiving and doing good works. . . . Faith receives Christ's good works; love performs good works for the neighbors." But Luther took vehement exception to the

---

6. "Adventspostille (Matthew 11:2ff.; 1522)," WA 10/1.2:153.20ff.

7. Cf. pp. 148f.

fallacy that man can accomplish anything before God with his good works and thereby assure himself of salvation. Before God the *sola fide*, the "by faith alone," is valid to the exclusion of everything else. "The only work God demands of us is faith in Christ; this is sufficient for Him. Therewith we give honor to Him as to Him who is gracious, merciful, wise, good, and truthful." He who performs good works for the purpose of winning or increasing God's mercy or to achieve any merit whatsoever before God is on a road that is terribly wrong. God's mercy can be obtained only by faith. But the recipient of such love and mercy must pass it on to others. From it there springs ever anew a great transformation in the Christian's life.

> After this has taken place, do not be minded otherwise than: Do unto your neighbor as Christ has done unto you, and let all your works, together with your whole life, be directed toward your neighbor. Search out the poor, the sick, and all sorts of needy persons. Help them to the limit of your ability with body, property, and honor. Let this be your daily habit. Then those who are in need of your help will benefit from you.[8]

Both faith and works are therefore equally necessary in a Christian's life but both in their correct relationship: Faith must be directed toward God, good works toward one's neighbor. Only when the two are joined does a Christian live his life in the spirit of Christ. The assumption that only faith and not love is demanded of a Christian would be as great a fallacy as every kind of works-righteousness. Yes, strictly speaking, this would not even be faith. "Those, too, who like to hear and who understand this doctrine of true faith but do not begin to serve their neighbor, just as if they wanted to be saved by a faith devoid of works, do not perceive that their faith is no faith, no more than an image reflected in the mirror is a face but only the reflection of it." To bolster this view, Luther approvingly cited St. James (1:22ff.), whom he otherwise found wanting in some respects.[9]

True faith gauges itself by the example of Christ. Because Christ is "a living, active, fruitful Being," it must follow that

> faith is a living, active, mighty thing, so that it is impossible for it not to do good continuously. Nor does it ask whether there are any good works to be performed; but before one can ask, faith has already performed them and is always in them. . . . Faith is a living, resolute confidence in God's mercy;

---

8. "Adventspostille (1522)," WA 10/1.11:167.10ff., 168.18ff.

9. "Adventspostille (1522)," WA 10/1.1:169.34ff.

faith is so strong and confident that it would die a thousand times because of it. And such confidence in, and recognition of, God's mercy makes one happy, intrepid, and eager toward God and all creatures. This the Holy Ghost works by faith. Therefore man becomes willing and eager to do good to everyone spontaneously, to serve everyone, to suffer all manner of things for the love of, and in praise of, God, who has shown man such mercy. Accordingly, it is just as impossible to separate works from faith as it is to sever burning and glowing from fire.[10]

These four basic traits of Luther's faith constitute an internal unity: His unconditional faith, which trod to its end every path on which he knew God was leading him, did not draw its breath from a security based on human reason or tradition but from his venture directed toward Christ. This venture was anchored solely in the reality of God vouchsafed him in faith, which by love becomes a reality in the life of man.

10. "Prefatory Remarks to Letter to the Romans (1522)," WADB 7:10.9ff.

THE SACRAMENTS[1]

Luther's view of the sacraments is often covered by formulas woven by theology for centuries and obscuring our insight into its ultimate objectives and internal associations. That is all the more regrettable because the question at issue is not one of minor importance that might be yielded to a few captious theologians for the amplification of their system. It projects itself into the church life of every individual. It was important enough to split the great Protestant denominations on the words "This is My body," which Luther inscribed with chalk before him at the Marburg Colloquy. The question confronts us daily in our intercourse with the Catholic Church, which regards Christ present day after day in transubstantiation in that exalted moment when the bright Mass bell resounds and the priest elevates the monstrance and the chalice. This church treats all great religious and civic questions at her festive world congresses under the badge of the eucharistic Christ, the Christ who appears in the Sacrament of the Altar. All this constantly suggests and urges the question regarding our evangelical conception of the sacraments. As we recall Luther's doctrine, we are self-evidently aware that this can be only the indispensable preliminary but that it can never conveniently supplant the task assigned anew to every epoch of the church: to strive for an interpretation of the sacraments.

I

Luther's viewpoint on the sacraments can be understood only if one lifts

---

1. A few passages of this essay have been omitted by the translator with the author's kind permission.

it out of the isolated position into which it has too often been forced and places it in the totality of his theology. Only in this way will its most profound dynamic forces and motives become visible, and especially only in this way is the inner unity of his vast world of ideas revealed. This is all-important for a proper understanding of Luther. His theology is by no means designed for textbooks; but amid a wealth of expressions, it possesses a hidden force of logical thought that impresses anyone pondering it almost like a phenomenon of nature. The constituent parts of his theology lucidly and logically crystallize into a whole, affording a view of the basic structure also in its derived doctrines. To note this correspondence between the parts and the whole is not only imperative for any student of Luther, it is also a most fascinating task.

It is clear that in Luther's teaching the sacraments are not a unit in themselves, not an isolated section of his theology. Consequently, they should not be taken from their context and viewed by themselves. We are repeatedly startled by statements of Luther that almost let the sacraments appear dispensable and secondary. So long as man has the words, that is, so long as he believes the message to be proclaimed in the sacraments, it may be that he can dispense with the signs, with the sacraments themselves. Salvation is possible without the sacraments but not without the Testament, that is, the Gospel.[2] To the end of his days, Luther conceded that some people may not need the sacraments. To be sure, he did not include himself in this number, and he thought of such people without envy, rather with a secret shudder. For in this precarious life in which man has to contend hard for his soul's salvation, it is foolhardy to forego such powerful assurances of grace as Baptism and Holy Communion. But this does not alter the fact that Luther conceived of faith even without the sacraments. He who refused the Swiss the hand of brotherhood because of a difference of opinion on the doctrine of Holy Communion is protected from the suspicion that he slighted the sacraments. Why, then, those statements that declare the sacraments unnecessary for him who possesses complete trust and implicit faith in God's Word? Because the sacraments in themselves mean nothing to Luther; they give no occasion to experience something not contained in the Word of God. The Gospel is found only in the Word of God. "The Word, and only the Word, is the means of God's grace."[3] Therefore the sacraments are nothing other than a separate

---

2. "Sermon on the New Testament (1520)," WA 6:363.7.

3. "Commentary on Galatians (1519)," WA 2:509.14.

instance of the proclamation of the Gospel. They are not an occasion for an immediate mystical meeting with God in supramundane bliss, but in them the one Gospel voice brings me again and again the message that the immeasurable and unfathomable, revered and awesome Lord of the universe is my God in Christ. The sacraments are only another form of the Word of God. This basic thought is the key to Luther's teaching concerning the sacraments. It alone wards off any misunderstanding that a perception of the mystery in the sacraments had induced Luther to indulge in strange theological speculations or in an untested reproduction of traditional but really long outworn doctrines. This basic thought also contains the decisive principle for a proper judgment of all attempts at liturgical reform. In addition, they give one a correct evangelical view of the sacraments.

If the sacraments ultimately transmit nothing more than the words of the Gospel do, if they offer no experiences other than those found elsewhere in the gift of the church, what, then, is their significance? What is Luther's meaning of the sacraments? Again he has a surprise in store for us. Luther applies the term "sacrament" not only to the rites that the term conventionally designated, but his use of the term is wider by far. With the same authority with which he designates the sacraments as the Word, he reverses the order and calls the Word "sacrament." The stories of the Gospel, he wrote, are "sacraments, that is, holy signs through which God effects in the believers what those stories indicate." He even goes beyond this. The passion of Christ contains a sacrament; it works forgiveness of sin for us. Yes, Christ Himself is a sacrament, namely, whenever He is more to us than a tutor whose conduct we follow, when He is to us the revelation of God Himself.[4]

Behind this peculiar and many-sided use of the term, the identical idea is hidden everywhere. A sacrament is a God-given token that is to point to Him. The words are signs, for in these concise and limited human words God pronounces His eternal truth. The passion is a token, for in it Christ becomes the redeemer of mankind. Christ is the perfect and consummate sign from God and to God, for God deposited His entire revelation into Christ's wretched human life. Thus a sacrament is, as Luther declared in his unforgettable "Sermon on Preparation for Dying" (1519),

---

4. Cf. Heinrich Bornkamm, *Das Wort Gottes bei Luther*, Schriftenreihe der Luthergesellschaft 7 (München: Christian Kaiser, 1933), 18ff.

a visible sign of the divine mind, to which one must cling with firm faith as to the good staff with which the patriarch Jacob walked through the Jordan, or a lantern by which one must be guided and on which one must diligently fix one's eyes on the dark path of death, sin, and hell. . . . Nothing else will avail in the anguish of death; for with that sign all are saved who are saved. It directs you to Christ and His image and enables you to say in the face of death, sin, and hell: God has given me His promise, and in His Sacraments He has offered me a sure sign of His mercy that Christ's life has overcome my death in His death, that His obedience expunged my sin in His suffering, that His love has destroyed my hell in His forsakenness. The sign, the assurance of my salvation, will not lie to me or deceive me. God has said this; God cannot lie.[5]

To Luther the sacraments were tall guideposts along life's highway. In token of this he adhered to the custom of elevating the bread and the wine in the Divine Service at Wittenberg long after the abolition of the Mass.

Luther did not use the word *sign* (*Zeichen*) in the sense in which we speak of symbols. The symbol is not necessarily related to its object. The snake is a symbol of deceit, but this does not imply any internal connection between the snake and deceit. The symbol is merely a figure of speech, a figurative indication of what is meant. This is not what Luther had in mind when he used the word *sign*. Otherwise he could not say, for example, that the words of Christ are sacraments by means of which He effects our salvation. Otherwise he could not in the same breath designate the sacraments as "signs" and as "words," that is, acts of God in which something real happens. Mere signs, signs in the sense of symbols, as Luther observes correctly, always refer to an absent object. The sign he had in mind is an effective one. Whatever it represents actually happens. Baptism and Holy Communion do not only speak of forgiveness of sin, they also contain and effect it. They are, therefore, the image of an object that is present yet invisible. They not only picture a distant reality, they contain it.[6] That applies to whatever Luther called a sacrament. The words of Christ are only "signs," only a reference to the unfathomable truths of God announced therein—yet they contain the entire divine truth, and he

---

5. WA 2:692.37ff.

6. "Dass diese Worte Christi . . . (1527)," WA 23:213.15, 235.33. Ernst Sommerlath, *Der Sinn des Abendmahls nach Luthers Gedanken über das Abendmahl, 1527–29* (Leipzig: Doerffling & Francke, 1930), 112ff.

who believes them is saved. Christ, too, is truly only a "sign," a homely figure succumbing in life—yet the eternal God became incarnate in it. This is also true with regard to the sacraments of the church. There are no less innocuous signs than the sprinkling with water or the consumption of bread and wine—yet he who believes the words of the sacraments receives what they promise: forgiveness of sins.

If we envisage the sacrament in this comprehensive sense as a real, an effective, and a conclusive sign from God, we touch upon the most profound question in Luther's theology and in all theology: the question concerning the knowledge of God. For the signs—the Word, Christ, the sacraments—are the God-given means of knowing God; they are places where He reveals Himself and where He is present. But let us remember that they remain signs in the sense just discussed. Luther knew well that God's eternal truth is deeper than the Bible, that He is greater than the simple personal life of Jesus. But what knowledge would we have of God without this sign of the Bible, without the sign Jesus Christ? According to Luther, God cannot be recognized at all other than in signs. To be known by us, God avails Himself of these signs, enters them, and is in them the real, divine truth for us as we, with our human limitations, can comprehend Him. We never have God without these masks and veils. Luther is fully convinced that there is no way to a more immediate knowledge of God, no supposedly more intellectual knowledge of God, which might view Him without such veils and covers and enter into a more intimate association with Him and a purer contemplation of Him. The Spirit, he once said, cannot dwell among us other "than in physical things, as the Word, water, Christ's body, and in the saints on earth."[7] Thereby Luther parted company with any attempts to know God through lofty flights of abstraction or through meditative submersion in, and intoxication by, mystical experience. He had tasted all this, yet he retained nothing but a horror of these experiments in assurance because they always left him in doubt whether he was experiencing God or himself. No, the Spirit of God meets us in an inexpressibly simple and earthly manner in the plain and clear words of Christ; in His person; in the consecrated Christians, the saints on earth; and finally even in the sacraments. God speaks—and how would He be understood otherwise?—in human fashion to man, with words of sharp and abasing command and with words of comforting and uplifting promise. He comes to us

---

7. "Dass diese Worte Christi . . . (1527)," WA 23:193.31.

amid our earthly existence, amid the problems and tasks of our daily life, and puts us, as it were, in communication with Christ. With great forethought Luther placed the reality and the concreteness of God's revelation in line with our whole earthly environment. As really as father, mother, master, servant, or neighbor stand before us and as truly as we must love and aid them, just so really and intelligibly God stands before us and speaks to us through Christ and His Word. In other words, God does meet us, not outside but within the history of our human experience. He does not wait for man to soar into His incorporeal realm beyond the reality of man's own life, but He reveals Himself to man amid his reality so simply and clearly that no one can find an excuse before Him.

This view of Luther regarding the revelation of God is relatively easy to understand if one thinks of the person and the work of Christ. That these are "body" (*Leib*) of the divine Spirit, as Luther is wont to say, is a simple thought. But what does Luther mean when he also numbers the sacraments—the water and the body and blood of Christ in Holy Communion—among the physical veils and covers of the divine Spirit? Self-evidently he is not thinking of any special, magical presence of God in the water or in the bread and wine. For Luther the sacraments were only another and special instance of the Word; they have no other content than the Scriptures do. They are signs of the divine presence in the same sense as are the other means of revelation.

This lays bare the deepest root of Luther's doctrine of the sacraments, a root reaching down into the primal question of theology. If one does not want to regard his doctrine as an isolated speculation, one must trace its origin from these basic questions. Only in this way is its internal unity unfolded. It will also facilitate our deliberations on the sacraments and will obviate a number of misunderstandings at the beginning if we bear firmly in mind two basic ideas of the general context: (1) The sacraments are only a distinct type of the Word; they have the same content. (2) The sacraments are God-given signs in which God Himself is present and active.

These two thoughts contain the principle that Luther applied to test the reality and the validity of a sacrament as he used the term. In his treatise *On the Babylonian Captivity of the Church,* he recognized only two of the seven Catholic sacraments as genuine and evangelical: Baptism and Holy Communion. He could not justify his rejection of the other five by asserting, let us say, that they were not based on, or found in, Scripture and for this reason were not acceptable to the church. This applied only to confirmation and to ordination but not to marriage, for example. A sacrament must be recognizable by its content and by its outward form. It must have the same content that the Gospel has: the message of forgiveness. Without Christ's clear words of promise, there is no sacrament, for example, in extreme unction, which cannot cite a single word of Christ in its behalf but looks to James 5:14f. Nor does extreme unction have anything to do with forgiveness of sin (in James, as elsewhere, forgiveness is promised only as the answer to earnest prayer); nor is it even "extreme" unction in the Epistle of James. It is strange that a sacrament for the dying has developed from the ancient custom in the early church to anoint the sick and to pray for their recovery (prompted by the words of James: "The prayer of faith shall save the sick, and the Lord shall raise him up"). The sacraments of confirmation and ordination have a similarly strange origin.

Furthermore, a sacrament requires a formal, distinctive mark, a symbolic act, an "external sign." In the sacrament of penance, which Luther could easily have retained as a sacrament in the evangelical sense of confession and absolution, the outward sign or symbol is wanting. Luther was still wavering in his treatise *On the Babylonian Captivity*, but in the end he discarded this third sacrament because it lacked the formal mark or sign. The sacrament of marriage lacks everything—both the promise of forgiveness and the external sacramental sign. Thus applying the test of Christ's promise and the presence of the outward sign, Luther eliminated all but Baptism and Holy Communion. All the others are fine ecclesiastical customs that, if evangelically purified, could be observed in the church of the Reformation as well as in the Catholic Church, but they are not sacraments.

This critical sifting of the Catholic sacraments was not the outcome of caviling and quibbling about inconsequential detail; it was completely logical. It clearly defines the uniformity of Luther's idea of a sacrament. The sacraments are external signs of one and the same thing: the message of the Gospel. In the close compass of Luther's definition there is no room for the injection of any physical, magical, or subconscious element but only for that which fits into the area of promise—faith, the area around which Luther's whole theology revolves. To be sure, the sacraments are outward signs, but they are signs of a spiritual act. Symbolically they proclaim a clear message and demand a clear and sure faith. "For a Sacrament is an affair of faith in which nothing but the Word of God shall happen and be done through His Word."[8]

---

8. "Von Anbeten des Sakraments (1523)," WA 11:448.29.

II

In our study of the general meaning of sacrament and sacraments in Luther's view of the two evangelical sacraments, we discover that his doctrine of Baptism requires but a relatively brief discussion, for it presents far fewer difficulties than the doctrine of Holy Communion. It is his theology in miniature; it is an astonishingly rich prelude in which all the great motifs of his faith are already sounded. The classical words of the Small Catechism acquaint us with the basic lines of the Sacrament of Baptism. Christ is its author, the author of its command and of its promise: "Go ye therefore, and teach all nations, baptizing them" (Matthew 28:19) and "He that believeth and is baptized shall be saved" (Mark 16:16). Its sign is the water "comprehended in God's command and connected with God's Word." Its meaning is twofold, as is indicated by its effective sign. "It works forgiveness of sins, delivers from death and the devil, and gives eternal salvation to all who believe this." At the same time it is a symbol; it signifies "that the old Adam in us should, by daily contrition and repentance, be drowned." All this not by virtue of the act of Baptism by water but by reason of the Word, which is in and with the water, and by faith. All the essential characteristics of a sacrament recur here.

In his sermons, in his popular expository works, in his "Sermon on Baptism" (1519), in his *Booklet on Baptism* (*Taufbüchlein*), and in his Large Catechism, Luther enlarged on the theme and meaning of Baptism so clearly and with such a picturesque wealth of expressions that it would be easy to evolve his whole theology from this small chapter. Baptism reveals his picture of God, who is seen by man only in masks, in human words, human form, human actions; of the God who waits for man with His words of mercy and anticipates the first thoughts a man can have. Baptism is Luther's picture of Christ, who Himself became a sacrament for mankind in His death and into whose death we are buried by Baptism that by His power we might "walk in newness of life." Baptism looks ahead into man's earthly life. Here life's battles are already fought over the baptized child. Luther reminded parents and sponsors in his *Taufbüchlein* that it is not child's play to cope with the devil and drive him away from the child and that it is no light matter to incur the enmity of such a mighty, lifelong foe for the child in Baptism.[9] In this conflict man has no other weapon

---

9. *Die Bekenntnisschriften der evangelisch-lutherischen Kirche* (Göttingen: Vandenhoeck & Ruprecht, 1952), 536.8ff.

than a word—the word of Baptism with which God pledged man His fidelity for the first time, a pledge that He observes inviolably. Oh, that we would keep our pledge! Therefore a reminder of Baptism, God's first word spoken over man, affords such comfort in *Anfechtung* and in the battle of life. The first effect of Baptism, the forgiveness of sin, is the basis for its second: the effective mortification of the sinful flesh throughout life. Baptism, as it were, accompanies man through life and, as Luther wonderfully expressed it in his "Sermon on Baptism" (1519), renders "all afflictions, and especially death, useful and helpful" for its work, so these have to assist it in mortifying sin in man. Baptism leaves man no peace in life; rather, it converts, as Luther said in the same sermon, "this life's tranquility, ease, and complacency as an obstacle to its [Baptism's] work into sheer poison for him." For with comfortable enjoyment, "love for this life, horror at the thought of eternal life, fear of death, and flight from the extermination of sin" increase.[10] Thus in the moment in which God calls man by name for the first time and the latter thereby (for that is the significance of assigning man a name) becomes a person before God and in His communion, the word about death (which he is to experience daily spiritually and someday also physically) already sounds in his ears. Baptism joins the beginning and the end of life and opens the gates to life eternal.

This is only a small fraction of the rich blessings Luther evolves again and again from Baptism. His view of the church reveals the same things. For when Luther regards the church as the communion of saints, that is, an alliance of Christians with a responsibility toward one another, then the responsibility of parents, sponsors, and the congregation for the baptized children appears as one of its chief articles. In his *Booklet on Baptism* he writes: "I fear that people so often go astray after Baptism because they have been treated so coldly and carelessly and because they have been prayed for in Baptism altogether without earnestness."[11] According to Luther, only the believer can belong to the true church; mere outward membership means nothing. For this reason no pressure should be exerted to receive the sacraments. This also applies to Baptism wherever a free and independent decision is possible.[12]

---

10. "Sermon on Baptism (1519)," WA 2:734.14ff.

11. *Bekenntnisschriften*, 536.20.

12. Karl Holl, *Gesammelte Aufsätze zur Kirchengeschichte* (Tübingen: Mohr, 1932), 1:344.

Luther's assumption of faith in infants is the part of his teaching about Baptism most difficult to understand. First, it presupposes that Luther adhered to infant Baptism rather than the adult Baptism of the so-called Anabaptists. Luther defended it not only because of Jesus' words "Suffer the little children to come unto Me" but also for two objective reasons that sprang from the core of his theology. First, there is no clearer sign of God's gift of grace than infant Baptism, which is entirely free from any cooperation on our part. Second, it is extremely dangerous to wait until one feels strong enough in faith to ask for Baptism, for one is "not sure of one's faith."[13] Thereby man would rely on himself and on his heart as a condition of divine pardon, not on unconditional grace itself.

Therefore it is an error to make the administration of Baptism contingent on the presence of faith. However, faith is necessary indeed to make the Sacrament effective. And this faith man cannot give to himself. We must hope, pray, and believe that God will bestow it on children as well as on adults. Luther was distressed when he observed that the pious Bohemian Brethren, the descendants of a branch of the Hussites and ancestors of the founders of Herrnhut, had their children baptized on their future faith, not on the faith they had at the time. It was better not to baptize children at all than to baptize them without faith. But it is certain that God, because of the faith and in answer to the prayers of the church, grants children that measure of faith that is indispensable for the proper reception of the Sacrament.[14] This conviction of Luther was based not on an antiquated child psychology but on the boundless miracle-working power of God. To him the miracle that works faith in a sinful adult was not secondary to the miracle of God's bestowal of faith on infants.

Here it is important to clarify the motive from which this part of Luther's doctrine of Baptism stemmed. He deduced it from his basic thought that a sacrament is a token of the promise that must be believed. But this basic idea is independent of this pointed deduction. Even without it, the evangelical doctrine of Baptism can remain Lutheran in the best sense. Intimations of this are found in Luther himself, for example, in his Large Catechism. Although he was firmly convinced of infant faith in Baptism, this Sacrament would nonetheless be meaningful even in the absence of such faith. For it is not human receptiveness that makes Baptism a

---

13. "Von der Wiedertaufe (1528)," WA 26:154.32.

14. "Von Anbeten des Sakraments (1523)," WA 11:452.25ff. Cf. also "Fastenpostille (1525)," WA 17/2:79ff.

sacrament but God's command and promise. "We bring the child to Baptism with the conviction and hope that it will believe, and we pray that God may grant it faith; but we do not baptize it in view of this, but solely by reason of God's command." Luther consoles anyone who harbored doubt regarding his receipt of faith in Baptism with the words: "If you did not believe then, then believe now, and say: The Baptism was proper and correct. Unfortunately, however, I did not receive it properly." The grace conferred in Baptism is preserved for man; God remains true to His pledge.[15]

III

The real problems posed by what Luther teaches concerning the sacraments are found in connection with Holy Communion. Naturally, our understanding will be aided if we again keep in mind Luther's general basic concept: sacrament and Word are identical in substance; the sacrament is a sign in which God is effective; it emanates from God, and it points to God.

Especially in Holy Communion Luther emphasizes that the words of promise, the Words of Institution, are more important than the Sacrament. "The words are of far greater consequence than the Sacrament itself, and the Christian must become accustomed to pay far greater heed to these words than to the Sacraments."[16] The people in the Catholic Church who were taught to adore the Sacrament but not to understand the words must be directed from the Sacrament to the words.[17] For this reason Luther thought it particularly absurd in the Catholic Mass that the Canon Missae with the Words of Institution is spoken softly.

To be sure, in Holy Communion the words cannot be separated from the Sacrament as easily as in Baptism. For the Words of Institution, which contain the promise of the Sacrament, refer at the same time to the elements of Holy Communion. "This [the bread] is My body; this [the wine] is My blood, which is shed for you for the remission of sins." Belief in these words also implies a special contemplation of the elements. In Baptism the relationship is altogether different. Baptism's words of promise—"He that believeth and is baptized shall be saved"—say nothing about the water and

---

15. *Bekenntnisschriften*, 702.

16. "Von Anbeten des Sakraments (1523)," WA 11:432.25.

17. "Von Anbeten des Sakraments (1523)," WA 11:433.3.

do not demand belief in a special miracle in the water. Here the words and the outward sign are easily differentiated, and the danger of ascribing religious significance to the water as such is slight. In Holy Communion both are linked together by the Words of Institution, and the danger of confusing the two is tremendous. That poses the real exegetical difficulty in connection with the doctrine of Holy Communion. To me this also seems to be the reason for the sad experiences the doctrine of Holy Communion has passed through in the history of Christianity. For in Christendom there has not been a gnostic, mystic, theosophical, naturalistic, or magic-primitive current that did not find in Holy Communion fertile soil for the culture of its speculations. Countless theological delusions, adducing the Words of Institution, sprang from the belief that God was objectively and tangibly present in Holy Communion in a manner otherwise unknown to the Christian faith. Here Luther's doctrine of the sacrament as a sign—not as an empty sign but as an index of a latently present reality—discloses its real significance and its real difficulties.

We must abstain from developing, as we did with Baptism, the full riches of Luther's theology pertaining to Holy Communion from the simple, basic ideas in the Small Catechism. All that we found there regarding Baptism can also be said about Holy Communion. The illustrations used with reference to Baptism must suffice. But we must add that the symbolism bearing on Holy Communion is found chiefly in Luther's early writings, for example, in his "Sermon on Holy Communion" (1519). Here he speaks with special beauty about the fact that in the Lord's Supper we are integrated as members into the body of Christ and that we receive a token of this in the Sacrament as citizens are granted a charter for their city. Holy Communion is a sacrament of love in which we experience Christ's goodness and in which, at the same time, we may exchange our sorrows and our love with the congregation. Luther allegorized the bread, composed of many kernels, as "the one cake, one bread, one body, one drink" to which Christ and the congregation are united. This communion with Christ is the highest comfort in all trouble. Its most precious gift to us is the forgiveness of sin, the exchange of Christ's righteousness for our sinfulness.[18]

Gradually the central significance of Holy Communion gains ever-growing prominence in Luther's writings. The other symbolism recedes more and more. Luther concentrates on expounding and clarifying the

---

18. "Sermon von dem hochwürdigen Sakrament (1519)," WA 2:743ff.

essential promise and its pertinent sign: the real presence of Christ in the elements of Holy Communion. Self-evidently he never harbored any doubts with regard to the real presence. However, since 1523–1524 he was confronted by a steadily increasing number of opponents of this view— Karlstadt, the Anabaptists and the Spiritualists, Zwingli, the Swiss, and the Strasbourgers. This constrained him to deepen and develop this part of the doctrine, which, up to this time, he had considered self-evident. His later writings, especially those of 1527–1528, are still almost filled with his wrestling and struggling for the meaning of the Words of Institution and of the bodily presence of Christ. It was more than an external battle; for him it was an internal struggle as well. As late as 1524 Luther confessed how strongly he had been enticed and how he was then still tempted by the thought of a symbolic interpretation of the Words of Institution. "Unfortunately I am all too greatly inclined to this; so much do I feel my old Adam." "But I am a captive; I cannot extricate myself. The text is too powerful and cannot be eradicated from the mind with words."[19]

If we recall Luther's meaning of sign and revelation, it will become clear that his belief in the Words of Institution was more than a slavish literalism. According to him, God's revelation must be most tangible and concrete, whether this be in the sign, in the elements, or in the words of Holy Writ. He was firmly convinced of the correctness of his interpretation; yes, he could not understand how anyone could expound the words "This is My body" differently. With unparalleled acumen and powerful dialectic superiority, he defended his explanation against his opponents. He fought with comprehensive grammatical and exegetical armor yet in complete candor. He raised objections to his own viewpoint. Did Jesus Himself partake of the Last Supper?[20] Does Jesus not speak with "a new word," in a parable, as the Bible does innumerable times?[21] But he knew how to refute his own objections. Nor could stronger opponents have convinced him; he was resolved to remain unalterably obedient to the words of the text. In long years of growth he himself had overcome the allegorical Bible interpretation of the old and the medieval church in favor of a simple exposition on the basis of the meaning of the words. This is his great accomplishment in the history of exegesis. He was all the more averse

---

19. "To the Christians in Strassburg (1524)," WA 15:394.12ff.

20. Holl, *Gesammelte Aufsätze,* 1:575.

21. "Vom Abendmahl Christi (1528)," WA 26:277ff.

to renouncing the simple wording of the text because reason made this so desirable. If he permitted reason to sit in judgment on God's Word here, no end was in sight. As it happens, divine things run counter to reason. Here it is imperative to repeat God's Word in all simplicity, "as a child repeats the Creed or the Lord's Prayer after its father. For here it is necessary to walk blindfolded in darkness and simply to adhere to and follow the words."[22]

Luther, who often treated biblical words with startling freedom, would not have held so unflinchingly to the literal sense of the Words of Institution if his holiest and most precious possession, the Sacrament, the token of forgiveness, had not been at stake. His opposition to Zwingli and the Spiritualists reached much deeper than the difference in the interpretation of the Words of Institution. Zwingli had deprived Holy Communion of its real meaning. Because he had discarded the doctrine of the real presence—which he, too, had once espoused—it was to him no longer an act of divine revelation in which God wishes to grasp man with His grace but merely a pleasing, symbolic celebration of the congregation. It was no longer a sign in which the presence of God is concealed but merely a historical commemoration, a memorial meal, a meal of rejoicing akin to a patriotic celebration, a feast of confession, and a renewal of moral obligations. It was no longer a gift of grace but a human institution. Zwingli converted Luther's sign into a symbol, an arbitrary, symbolic act. This was, in the final analysis, tantamount to saying that God required no sign for His recognition. Instinctively Luther sensed in Zwingli a philosophical religion that believed in a general, immediate meeting of the spirit with God, and therefore he embraced all the more defiantly the God-proffered means of God's presence: the Word, the Sacrament, and the bodily presence of Christ in the Sacrament. Zwingli tried to visualize Christ in Holy Communion; Luther believed that He was actually present. Zwingli pictured Him from his memory; Luther believed that he felt Him, yes, tasted Him in the gift of the Last Supper. For if the presence of God were dependent on the strength of my remembrance and the earnestness of my meditation, then I would ever again revert to myself and rely on myself.

> If I, in conformity with Karlstadt's doctrine, exercised my recollection and my recognition of Christ with such fervor and earnestness as to sweat blood and be consumed over it, all would be for nothing and lost; for this

---

22. "Vom Abendmahl Christi (1528)," WA 26:440.2.

would amount to nothing but works and commandment and would present no gifts and no words of God which offer me Christ's body and His blood.[23]

Christ's presence is, therefore, also independent of my faith. Luther thought his doctrine through logically and to its final consequences: Unbelievers, too, receive Christ's body and blood but, as Paul says, to their damnation. That is an exact parallel to the doctrine of Baptism, especially infant Baptism. God's presence is not contingent on the faith of man. But it brings blessing only to the believer; to the unbeliever it remains closed and thus passes sentence on him.

To accentuate his opposition to Zwingli and the Spiritualists, Luther couched his belief in the reality of Christ's presence in Holy Communion in the most challenging and defiant terms. Christ's body is actually eaten with the mouth and ground with the teeth. For Luther this was neither an unfortunate deduction from rigid biblical literalism nor a peculiar remnant of a broad, animistic religion of magic. Here his view on the presence and the revelation of God in signs had to find verification. The question affected his greatest treasure: the forgiveness of sins. He believed that here God was as palpably close to him as his own sins were. Luther yearned for a reality of grace no less real than his sins. His doctrine of Holy Communion is an expression of his faith in this reality of God amid the world's reality and the reality of man's *Anfechtungen*; it is the ultimate deduction of his belief in the reality of forgiveness.

One must not infer from this that Luther regarded the elements in Holy Communion as a divine substance on earth. He parted company definitely with the Catholic doctrine, which believes that Christ is bodily present for all time in the consecrated wafer and for this reason displays the host for adoration even outside the Mass or carries it about in the church's festive processions. For Luther, Christ is present only in the action, in the proclamation. The elements are only the perceptible sign of the mysterious presence of Christ, with which He is close to man as He addresses him, the believer to his salvation, the unbeliever to his damnation. In Luther's mind the physical presence is never to be equated to the substance; it is always an act, a creative deed of God in an effective sign.[24]

---

23. "Wider die himmlischen Propheten (1525)," WA 18:203.3.

24. Cf. Erwin Metzke, *Sakrament und Metaphysik*, Lebendige Wissenschaft 9 (Stuttgart: Kreuz-Verlag, 1948).

The objections of the adversaries to Luther's doctrine of Holy Communion were exceedingly naive so far as they did not pertain to the Words of Institution. Unanimously they remonstrated that Christ could by no means be present in Holy Communion because since His ascension He was seated on the right hand of His Father. Luther found this objection laughable. He ridiculed the Christ of Zwingli, who sat in heaven like a bird in a cage. But Zwingli's objection afforded Luther an opportunity to develop the final metaphysical background of his doctrine. These expositions number among his most profound theologically and particularly philosophically. Philosophically, Luther far outstripped Zwingli and the Spiritualists. He exposed their belief that Jesus was outside space—namely, in heaven—as a naive contradiction. For, after all, they regarded this supposedly extraspatial heaven as a space or a place in which they localized the exalted Christ. The expression that Christ sits on the right hand of God has an entirely different meaning for Luther: It signifies Christ's participation in God's omnipresence and in His omnipotent rule over the universe. For Luther, God exists literally as a vibrant and vigorous force in every creature, also in inanimate creatures, in fire, in water, in a leaf, in a stone. Luther rejects the childishly anthropomorphizing picture of the Creator, who, after creating the world, now sits enthroned in heaven far away from it; he rejects the God of naive preachers, the God who so tormented Jakob Böhme, for example. Mysticism never expressed the idea of God's immanence in the world more forcefully than Luther did. And Christ partakes of that God in this world; for Christ, after all, is nothing other than that side of God that is turned toward man. This means the whole Christ, both His divine and His human nature. For if God really became flesh, then He became flesh entirely; then the divine and the human nature can no longer be separated. Thus Christ is omnipresent with God. However, He, like God, can be found only where He has promised that He will be found: in Word and Sacrament. There He has given a sign of Himself, and to this sign He has bound Himself, so to speak. Therefore man should not grope for God elsewhere; if he does, he will go hopelessly astray. "Wherever the Word is, there follow and feel your way."[25]

Consequently, the elements of Holy Communion in which Christ is present are not a piece of divine substance fallen from heaven. On the contrary, the fact that God is immanent in a thing is nothing unusual; it is

---

25. "Sermon von dem Sakrament (1526)," WA 19:492.23.

self-evident. He dwells in all things, though hidden and unrecognizable. Here the unusual and novel feature is His selection of one thing as a sign in which He is present with His gift of grace. In this sign the explanatory words, without which we would know nothing about God, are added to His presence.

Luther's doctrine of the bodily presence of Christ also bears out the one central and basic idea of his view of the Sacrament: that God confirms His words of grace in the visible sign of the Sacrament and actually and really bestows forgiveness. The bread of the Sacrament is broken and dispensed to hungry faith only in the Word. Only if Holy Communion is recognized as an indication of the presence of God, not as a symbol, will it remain a Sacrament in the Lutheran and evangelical sense. Only then will the words of Luther's Small Catechism remain true: "He that believes these words has what they say and express, namely, the forgiveness of sins."

LIVING AND DYING

In the late Middle Ages a type of essay flourished that is virtually nonexistent today despite our abundance of books. At that time these writings—called *Ars moriendi* ("The Art of Dying")—were considered of such importance that they were published for all cultural levels: in Latin for the learned, in German for the uneducated. For those who could not read there were publications containing powerfully expressive woodcuts and no text at all. The peculiar concept, the art of dying, that they created has become extinct today, together with these writings. We still know something about the art of living, and we dub him an "artist of life" (*Lebenskünstler*) who is able to derive the greatest satisfaction from life, who can appreciate to the full the charms and allurements that life offers to the senses or to the mind, or who is able to find within himself a haven of peace when fate glowers. But we no longer speak of the art of dying; we would, in fact, be embarrassed and at a loss as to what to say if we were pressed for a definition of that term. Yet its meaning is not so foreign to us. In fact, today our nation is more familiar with it than it has been for centuries since the Thirty Years' War.

The breath of death, unceasingly and palpably wafted toward us from the carnage of the battlefields, and the hallowing sacrificial death of those who gave their lives for their nation or for justice and truth have again aroused in all of us a realization that dying is something that requires a skill. At the same time we have become convinced that the art of dying and the true art of living are closely allied and that actually the one cannot be mentioned to the exclusion of the other.

But when we Christians ask for an opportunity to say a word about this subject, we immediately encounter one of the most serious objections raised against us. It is generally admitted that Christians know how to die. The songs and the music of the church, the dying of famous Christians, and the confident heroism in death of countless unnamed Christians about whom pastors, sisters, and physicians report speak too impressive and convincing a language. But a knowledge of the art of dying is conceded us mainly because it appears easier to question our knowledge of how to live. It is said dying is much easier for Christians than for others because their life is in reality a constant dying and because even here their eyes are fixed on another, better life. We shall not try to defend ourselves against this objection nor are we able to do so; the facts are too obvious. Yes, we will go beyond this and even place a weapon in the hands of the world by quoting Luther, who said that we "view this temporal life only through a painted glass, blinkingly, as it were; but we view yonder eternal life with clear, open eyes."[1] These words, as well as the objections that the Christian faith must expect today, as at all times, make one fact irrefutably clear: that one cannot speak either about living or about dying alone but must discuss them together, otherwise everything will be muddled and distorted in advance. Now, though we must go far afield in our deliberations on this subject, we shall choose our path so it will again lead us past the words of Luther.

First, Luther's Christian does not lead a life apart from that of other people. He is well aware that we human beings do not exist as detached individuals but that we can have our being only within the confines of family, neighborhood, and nation. Only in living together in these groups do we become what we are. For this reason the Christian gladly integrates himself into them. All the riches of life, its goods, and its tasks are open to him as they are to all others. We leave it to the sectarians and un-Lutheran pietists to draw their barbwire barriers around a genuine and vigorous joy of living. We are different from the Roman Church, which forbids marriage to its servants, the priests and the monks. No other boundaries have been drawn for the evangelical Christian than those that exist for every serious-minded and clean human being.

But what, in the final analysis, is the basis of this life that is common to us all? What makes it worth living? This question leads us beyond the natural continuity of a life inherited from our parents, preserved by daily bread, and passed on by us to the next generation. The animals, too, share

---

1. "Sermon on Titus 2:13 (1531)," WA 34/2:110.26.

in this phase of life. The question is: What makes life worthwhile for us as human beings? I believe there are two fountains that nourish life for all of us in a higher and not only in a physical sense and the waters of which fructify all parts, all tasks, and all forms of community life. One of these is love.

Man cannot live without love. We are not restricting this to conjugal love, that is, love between the sexes. Every human relationship—that between parents and children, friendship, between ruler and nation, between superiors and subordinates, between teacher and pupil, the relationship in the community of believers, vocational or professional relationships—all these, if they are genuine, are sustained by an element of love, perhaps only a deeply hidden ingredient of love. Where this is lacking, everything is sham. Wherever nothing but lovelessness and unkindness grimace at us, we feel a cold hand reaching for our throats, and we find it impossible to tarry there. Perhaps we can still put on a mask and play a stage role, but our actions and our words are no longer the same. It is impossible for us to live truly without being the recipients or the donors of some token of love. We may expend our love on human beings or on animals, even on plants, books, or pictures—man can live only by his devotion to someone or to something. Thus love may be as imperfect, as peculiar, as timid as it will; but in it there dwells a vestige of the divine image. And the church has never ceased to discourse on this, though she knows how this image has been mutilated and desecrated by us. Even the simplest person can understand that real living requires more than a satisfaction of physical desires and needs, and that love given and received really imparts the possibility for true and genuine living. If man does not understand this, then he ranks far below the noble animals, which sense this law of life.

The other secret fountain of our life is honor. Without honor man cannot live either. Again we do not mean to say that man cannot live without a special honor, such as professional honor, perhaps an officer's honor, an official's honor, student honor, etc. All these are merely derivatives, in part distorted copies and cheap imitations of the original state of honor that we need for our lives. No one can live without being taken seriously as man, without being appreciated by other members of the community, without being respected in his class. In all the human relationships enumerated before—such as that between parents and children, friends, comrades, etc.—there must be found, in addition to a bit of love, an unexpressed ingredient of honor that lets the other be what he is and respects him for what he is, that acknowledges and appreciates him both in his person and in his vocation: the farmer, the laborer, the academician, etc. The honor that we pay one another holds the entire framework of community life together. Exactly what we said of love also holds true with regard to honor: We cannot live and breathe in a circle of human beings in which we are held to be without honor. He who has really become honorless has been deprived of one of the elements requisite for living. He who has been maliciously defrauded of his honor has been robbed of the very air necessary for life—at least in this circle. We are far from claiming that every slander and defamation means a forfeiture of our honor. It may happen that my nation passes a sentence of dishonor on me for the espousal of a good cause. In that case I could still keep my honor. Even a lonely and despised person may derive honor from the very thing for which he is despised. The honor that comes from fulfillment of a solemn duty sustains us all, no matter how lonely we are and how poor in honor because of others. However, without honor we cannot live a free life; then we merely eke out a forced existence. Honor lost through or without our fault was often the initial step toward a complete catastrophe in life. Schiller's *Criminal through Lost Honor* illustrates this.

However, both love and honor—our most precious possessions and the true fountains of all genuine life—are at the same time the hard rocks that make us fall and the causes of our wrongdoing. For both are not only goods that we own but also demands made on us by our fellow man. Love, when turned toward us, says: "Thou shalt love thy neighbor as thyself!" Luther explains this:

> You cannot excuse yourself by pleading ignorance as to what and how much you owe your neighbor. . . . The word has been deeply inscribed in your heart, with letters so large that you can grasp them with your hands. . . . "As thyself" you shall love, not less than yourself. . . . This lesson will be the index of the state of your Christianity. There you can find whom you love and whom you do not love, how far you have progressed, and where you are wanting. For if there is even only a single person to whom you are not kindly disposed, you count for nothing, even though you could perform miracles. This rule teaches you without a schoolmaster to differentiate between mere works and good works.[2]

---

2. "Commentary on Galatians (1519)," WA 2:578.11ff., 579.32ff.

If this is the law of love, if we all live on love, if my neighbor's life is dependent on my love—who can then still actually have the effrontery to deny that he sins daily?

The demand of honor, without which none of us can live, reads: "In honour preferring one another" (Romans 12:10). Let us listen to Luther:

> Pride also confers honor, but it lets the other person take precedence in bestowing it; humility, however, always precedes the other person. Pride waits for the other person to take the first step, but humility would not even want to be second in showing honor. It knows that it alone may precede. What a wonderful thing to yield honor to the other person! ... We must show honor to one another even though the other person pays us no honor either before or afterwards.[3]

This is the Christian contribution to honor. It would not be bad for a community or a nation to adopt this law of life: It is better to give honor than to receive it. Such a bond of mutual respect and deference would be stronger than all others; yes, it would be the only protection against the disruptive forces that always menace the stability of a nation in the form of class antagonisms and class interests. The Christian church, too, knows something about honor and has a message for it. She has never forbidden to challenge infamous defamation resolutely with the weapon of truth. But the church has a more convincing approach to the defamer than a cold verdict, namely, a profound and superior compassion with him who is possessed by a spirit of untruth, by his ego. Luther asks: "What pure joy may they whose conscience can find no peace experience, even though all their wishes are fulfilled?"[4] Only with the spirit born of such an attitude can the hidden fires smoldering in a nation be extinguished, the fires that will never be reached by our human attempts to work through laws and education. Again we say that if the law of honor plays such a powerful role in human life, if we cannot live without honor, if my neighbor has a fair claim to my esteem—esteem anticipating his—who may then deny his shortcomings?

As Lutheran Christians we live in this life, the greatest possessions of which also make the highest demands on us. We live in no special sphere outside this life. It is common to us all. The topic of guilt has by no means

---

3. Romans 12:10, in "Lectures on Romans (1515–1516)," WA 56:462.23ff. Cf. Johannes Ficker, ed., *Luthers Vorlesung über den Römerbrief, 1515/1516,* Anfänge reformatorischer Bibelauslegung 1 (Leipzig: Dieterich, 1908), 2:285.17ff.
4. "Tessaradecas (1520)," WA 6:114.39.

been exhausted. But it is the guilt we all have by sinning daily against life and the profound commandments governing it. This we all sense to a greater or lesser degree. Every person who is sincere and not superficial knows something about his guilt. We cannot be made to believe that our nation has been brought so low that the conscience of great numbers can no longer be aroused and alarmed sincerely and profoundly. The life of every one of us has flaws and cracks, the jarring of which we can all hear in every sound if we listen honestly. All that we think, do, and are bears the hallmark of the incomplete and imperfect. Even the objects of all our affection—our marriage, our labors, the service to our country—are tainted with guilt. All this is anything but a pessimistic or melancholy philosophy of life. On the contrary, no other than Luther emphasized again and again that this world harbors far more of the good and the beautiful than of the evil. If we fail to perceive this, then we are ungrateful and do not have our eyes open.[5] The accusation of guilt is directed against us, not against the order of the world. In this situation we can help along in only one way: with radical honesty.

It is true that as a rule we resort to a totally different, very ingenious self-aid. In the face of the actuality of our guilt, we flee into a land of fantasy, into the land of good intentions. Good intentions are our most important intellectual victuals. Without them not a single person who does not regard himself as a stupid animal and does not sense at least a trace of the chasm between his willing and his doing could bear life. Desperately man looks for a way out of his extremity. If his past causes him anxiety and pain, he believes that it will be better for him in the future. It is immaterial if delusion adds its voice to say that restitution can be made for past wrongs (in reality, this is impossible); it is all-important for man to believe for at least one happy moment that he can reform. For one happy moment—for here we come to the parting of the ways. The one clings to this hope, for, after all, this hope is at his beck and call. He can still believe in it; it has not yet been refuted by experience. With this escape that man opens for himself, he counterbalances his entire past guilt. The Lutheran Christian, however, disillusioned by life's experiences and overcome by the truth of the divine Word, must concur with Luther: "In our life we are not sure of our good intentions even for a moment."[6]

---

5. "Tessaradecas (1520)," WA 6:121.1ff.

6. "Tessaradecas (1520)," WA 6:110.7.

This is not tantamount to an admission of all lack of moral progress in our life, of no visible victory over weaknesses. The Lutheran faith is not that blind. Yet we are not sure of our next step on life's journey because our old uncharitableness, presumption, or avarice may descend on us the very next moment with tenfold force. What do the few steps mean that we may take here and there toward the unattainably lofty goal of the commandment: "Thou shalt love thy neighbor as thyself"? It is strange that the more we occupy ourselves with God's commandment, the harder its onset; the more ardently we try to fulfill it, the more it reveals its profundity and its earnestness. Thus we become ever more conscious of our guilt. With every step forward, we discover more clearly that thereby we do not escape our guilt by as much as an inch.

Above all our resolutions and good intentions—and this pricks the bubble of our deceptive hopes—we find inscribed the same words that were said about the agricultural plans of the rich farmer who wanted to raze his barns and construct larger ones in which to stow his bountiful crop: "Thou fool, this night thy soul shall be required of thee" (Luke 12:20). The moment will come when it is too late even for good resolutions, when our life is reduced to the past and no future remains for the balancing of past accounts. This moment is not a distant future that can be computed; it threatens tomorrow and the day after tomorrow. My guilt and my derelictions cannot be evaded because this may be my last day. Life derives its seriousness from death. Conversely, however, death derives its seriousness from life. The two are inextricably intertwined.

Sincerely and soberly we must admit that our faith has undergone a change today and is no longer that of former generations. It is not the threat of hell and physical punishment that makes death an object of terror to us; rather, it is the abrupt termination of our unbalanced accounts of life that will be scrutinized and audited by the eyes of another. Then, together with all the rubble and wreckage of our life (which we can no longer conceal, gloss over, or supplement), we must pass through the gloomy portals of death and face God. All the sins committed by us, sins originally committed against men, are offenses against God. For here the simple equation that dominates Luther's entire theology applies: "Service to one's neighbor is service to God."[7] Consequently, whatever we have withheld from our neighbor, we have withheld from God. It is a terrible thought to have to face this revelation.

---

7. "Ob man vor dem Sterben fliehen möge (1527)," WA 23:358.16.

Amid this trouble, this dread of death (which is not a sign of cowardice but of truthfulness and of strength), the joyful, consoling promise of the Gospel, which Luther conveys to us again, intervenes: "Natural life is a part of life eternal; but it terminates with death, because it does not acknowledge and honor Him who gave it. This sin cuts it off. Therefore it must die eternally. On the other hand, those who believe and acknowledge Him through whom they live will never die; but their natural life extends into life eternal. Therefore it will never taste death."[8] To believe and acknowledge Him through whom we have life—this is Luther's simple summary of all reflections on living and on dying. Luther was so impressed by this that he often declared that even our experiences in life permit us to perceive something of the God through whom we live. "For when we contemplate our past life, does it not surprise us that we have thought, done, wished, or said something which we could not at all foresee? How differently would we have conducted our life if it had depended on our free will!"[9] Of himself he confessed that he walked through life like a blinded horse, not according to free will and resolve. None of us can claim that he has lived his life course according to his own pattern and according to his own designs. Every one of us experiences a bit of being girded and led whither we would not go (John 21:18). No one has predetermined and fashioned his life alone.

But to believe and acknowledge Him through whom we have life has a deeper meaning. It means to believe and to trust Him in life and especially in death—Him who extends His hand to us when we flounder about helplessly, who "offers Himself as Helper when no man can help." It means the reversal, so to speak, of things in our life, for it is not we who resolve to perform good works and systematically to reform in accordance with good resolutions, but we ourselves are the good work that God Himself has planned. We must let this come to pass in us even where it runs counter to our wishes, our insight, our pride, our doubts. With confidence inspired by the words "He which hath begun a good work in you will perform it until the day of Jesus Christ" (Philippians 1:6), our faith can make its way through death, past the exposure of our imperfect and fragmentary life, into life eternal in which God has promised us completeness and perfection. Reversal of the landmarks of our life means to acknowledge uncon-

---

8. "Kirchenpostille (1522)," WA 10/1.1:200.3ff.

9. "Tessaradecas (1520)," WA 6:125.14. Cf. also "Tessaradecas (1520)," WA 6:110.37ff.

ditionally and unqualifiedly that we enter the portals of death poor, naked, and entirely dependent on God's forgiving mercy. Luther expressed this wonderfully in his most beautiful treatise on dying, *Von der Bereitung zum Sterben* (1519): "God gives you nothing because of your worthiness. Nor does He build His Word and Sacrament on your worthiness, but out of sheer mercy He builds you unworthy one on His Word and sign. . . . Faith makes one worthy; doubt makes one unworthy."[10]

"Faith makes one worthy." This alone stands the test in the all-revealing, merciful/unmerciful light of death. And this light radiates back into our life. By means of this light, the life of the Christian becomes radically different from that of the non-Christian. We expressed only half of the truth when we said before that the life of the Lutheran Christian does not distinguish itself from that of others. In its content, in the areas it embraces, it is not different; it is just as boundlessly rich and great as the life of all other people. The Christian neither detracts from nor adds to life's outer confines. However, because his is a life of faith, everything in his innermost nature must become different. For the Christian must live his life fully aware that its every detail is open to the view of God and that his life is designed for eternal perfection and completeness. He recognizes God's presence in everything, and he knows that all guilt is judged and canceled by God's mercy. His life becomes clear and meaningful solely in the light of its eternal destiny. Because he knows how destructive and unbridled our innermost nature is, he appreciates the miracle of the divine institutions of state, church, and marriage, which God has established in an evil and devil-infested world. He serves them with a joy that divines perfection beyond them. To him marriage is a token of the mercy that from the beginning took cognizance of man's need: "It is not good that the man should be alone" (Genesis 2:18). In his vocation the Christian hears God's summons, which exempts him from the manifold other tasks and demands surrounding him. He is not bound to do this or that to which inclination or a sense of duty may try to impel him. His duty is clearly prescribed in his calling, thus he is excused by God from the thousand and one tasks that life may place at his door. With good conscience, he may decline the challenge of urgent service if the latter conflicts with the duties of his vocation. He devotes himself wholeheartedly to the service to God and state assigned to him by God. This will never involve any moral con-

---

10. "Von der Bereitung zum Sterben (1519)," WA 2:694.7ff., 694.2f.

flicts, for he believes firmly that he is rendering the state his best service, even when he finds it necessary, for the Gospel's sake, to obey God rather than man and though that service may involve the role of martyrdom. In all this the Lutheran Christian is liberated from slavish legalism and is emboldened to courageous action by the instinctive assurance of love. Finally, he knows that by faith he has been delivered from the accusations of tasks unfulfilled, accusations that follow him from life into death. Confidently he commits these to Him who can balance the books of his life.

The fact will ever go unchallenged that faith must produce its masterpiece for the hour of death, when our whole life is compressed into one overpowering present, assails us, and turns us out into impenetrable darkness. Luther knew well how hard it is to die confidently and how difficult fearless and honest premeditation on death is.

> We have all been ordered to die, and no one will be able to die for another. But each one will be obliged to contend against death in his own person. We may be able to shout into one another's ears, but each one will have to be fit for himself at the time of death. I shall not be with you, nor you with me. For this reason everyone will have to know well the chief articles that pertain to a Christian; he must be equipped.[11]

Luther always classed loneliness among the grave *Anfechtungen* that will confront us in the hour of death. Therefore Luther and Lutheranism ardently practiced the "shouting in the ears," the supporting and helpful custom of praying with a dying person and leading him in prayer, quite in contrast to us. A false shyness has made us cruel toward those who are sorely assailed on their dying beds. In their gravest hour we desert them, or, what is often still worse, we deceive them with regard to the gravity of their condition. At that we never know whether they do not see through our deception. Who of us has the courage to repeat the words of Karl Holl: "I should not like to be cheated out of death" ("Ich möchte um den Tod nicht betrogen sein")? Therefore Luther, in his *Sterbebüchlein*, left no stone unturned in his effort to show that man is not deserted in his dying hour. "No Christian should doubt at his end that he is not alone when dying, but he should be confident that very many eyes are looking at him." The eyes of God and of Christ, the eyes of the angels, the eyes of the deceased and the living Christians. Now in this moment, everything that the church of all times and all places (or, as Luther liked to put it, the communion of saints) has of love, intercession, and supporting power is

---

11. "Invocavit Sermon (1522)," WA 10/3:1.7ff.

present for him, the lonely individual. "A Christian should envisage this and should have no doubt regarding it. This emboldens him to die."[12]

The fact that the entire burden of our life again threatens to bear down upon us in the hour of death gives loneliness its sting. The dissonance of our life, our imperfections, our unworthiness, the question of election, which has tortured so many—all this again looms huge before us. For this reason it is too late to try to come to terms with death at life's end. "We should think about death while we are alive, and we should summon him while he is still far away and is not pressing us. But when we are dying, when he is present of himself and with power all too great, this is dangerous and to no avail. Then one must want to erase his picture and not be willing to see it."[13] It is the real art of faith, difficult to acquire, and its indescribable privilege is to brush lightly aside all the oppressing questions that sharpen the sting of death and to place all our worries into the hands of God alone. All worrisome questions find their answer in Luther's wonderfully comforting words: "You must let God be God; He knows more about you than you yourself."[14]

But all of this would have been feeble words for Luther if every word of faith and about faith were not a reference to, and a testimony of, Him who conquered death, sin, and the devil for us. In Christ alone this faith, which must stand the test of the severest trials, finds its goal and its strength.

> It is a high art and a lesson which no saint has been able to master or fathom unless he has been in despair, in the anguish of death, or in extreme danger. For there one sees that faith overcomes sin, death, devil, and hell. These are no ordinary enemies; they make you sweat, crush your bones, and make heaven and earth too confining for you. At such a time there is no one who could help you but this Person alone, who says: It must be I who dare not lose you. This is the Father's will.[15]

The onslaught of these powers that make one sweat and that crush bones has been borne to the utmost by Christ. In contrast to the Catholic Church, Luther described again and again how Christ was not only smit-

---

12. "Von der Bereitung zum Sterben (1519)," WA 2:695.16ff.

13. "Von der Bereitung zum Sterben (1519)," WA 2:687.11.

14. "Von Anbeten des Sakraments (1523)," WA 11:452.25ff. Cf. also "Fastenpostille (1525)," WA 17/2.79ff.

15. "Wochenpredigten on John 6–8 (1530–1532)," WA 33:110.14ff.

ten and tortured physically but that His soul, too, tasted to the dregs all the anguish and loneliness of man. His bloody sweat was a symptom of a real and natural dread of death, a dread that Luther courageously admitted again and again. It was a terrible reality that God had forsaken Him. Nothing of the depths of man's fear and despair of election was spared Him nor did He suffer this only partially or apparently. Only in this way did He overcome death on the cross, not by protesting and fighting against it but by silent submission and by calmly surveying the images of death, sin, and hell—the sources of sorrow and anguish for Him and for us. "He paid heed to the cherished wish of His Father so completely that He forgot His death, His sin, His hell that were unleashed against Him and prayed for them, for their death, sin, and hell."[16] God has taken Him, the victor, unto Himself and has promised Him to us for our constant companionship, so even the loneliest person is never alone in death but has Christ at his side. Long before we could extend our hand to Him, He reached forth, rescued us from the gulf that separated us from God and that Luther called eternal death, and gained for us a home with God.

Now death, if we view it properly, begins to reveal its deep comfort. It is not our death because we have a home with the Father, but it is the death of our sin, the end of our imperfections. Our incompleteness shall come to an end; death refines us into the purity and perfection of a divine work. Where, then, are death's terrors? For us there remains not a thing to endure but a

> little death, yes, a sweet death, since a Christian dies after the flesh, that is, passes from unbelief to belief, from the remnants of sin to eternal righteousness, from all misery, sadness, and affliction to all the eternal joys. For all the life, all the goods, all the joys and pleasures of this world cannot make a person so happy as the ability to die with a good conscience, in the certain belief in, and comfort of, life eternal.[17]

In view of this we human beings should boldly dare and defy death. In all of Luther's writings on death, no other words recur so often as the words "to venture joyously" (*fröhlich wagen*). "Faith which relies on such a promise and ventures joyously must be present. What sort of savior or god would he be who could not or would not save us from death, sin, and hell? What the true God promises and carries out must be something big."[18] If

---

16. "Von der Bereitung zum Sterben (1519)," WA 2:692.14.

17. "Sommerpostille (1536)," WA 22:101.10ff.

18. "Von der Bereitung zum Sterben (1519)," WA 2:693.31.

He has promised us life eternal, we can dismiss all our worries and mis-givings about how there can be eternal life for us. It is unfortunate that Christians and non-Christians place such obstacles in one another's way where life and death are involved: the non-Christians by trying to fix the limitations of God's might with their impertinent and irreverent ideas and prohibitions, we Christians by presuming to know more with our immoderate imagination than we are able to know and thereby, as Jesus said to the Pharisees, closing heaven to many others (Matthew 23:13). Let us be content to speak metaphorically about this as Luther did so incom-parably: "We should not use the terms 'buried and decayed,' but speak in real heavenly German about being sown [gesäet]. . . . This is the language of God; therefore we, too, should learn to speak like this."[19]

The terrors of death become transformed into nothing but good things, dying into sheer living. Therefore Luther and the true Lutheran Church are in agreement when they speak of death as the workshop of life, the object of our longing and our love. The music of the Lutheran Church has sung the message in a manner transcending all understanding: "Death has become my sleep" ("Der Tod ist mein Schlaf worden"). These words have more meaning than the ancient pictures portraying death as a slum-ber or as a portal to life. Luther's words are more than pictures that dis-pense fleeting comfort in the pleasing guise of a metaphor. For the slum-ber into which our death takes us has become reality in Christ and is, in fact, already reality in our own life through our faith in Him. "Natural life is a part of life eternal and a beginning . . . and extends into life eternal."[20] Of course, not our sin-laden, self-seeking, natural existence but the deeply hidden divine image, on which the promise of fulfillment is beaming, though we, by our own strength, cannot rid it of the hard layers with which it is encrusted. Of this, too, we have a natural presentiment or, more accurately, a presentiment made natural to us by our nation's long Christian history. Hans Carossa spoke the beautiful words: "While the lowliest animal may regard itself as a finished and perfect product, we humans feel our whole life long that we are but a preliminary sketch" ("Während sich das niedrigste Tier als abgeschlossen und vollkommen empfinden darf, fühlen wir Menschen das ganze Leben lang, dasz wir nur

19. "Sermon (4th Advent, 1532)," WA 36:644.3.

20. "Kirchenpostille (1522)," WA 10/1.1:200.3ff.

ein Entwurf sind").[21] The Christian faith, however, may safely go a few steps beyond this presentiment. We are not a sketch for an ideal perfecting of our nature, a perfecting that we can derive, so to speak, from the concept that we are human beings; however, hidden and utterly impossible of awakening by us, the image of God, which has become reality in Christ Jesus, slumbers in us. Solely through contact with Him, through a rebirth, can it come to life in us. Even then it is not simply our property; it is not in our control. It is not as if, let us say, we have a new motor installed in our machine of life by the Holy Spirit and could now demand definite things from this motor and depend on it. This new life born of the Spirit, our real life, is still our own; at the same time, it is strange to us. Perhaps we can only divine (and no more) the import of the apostle's words: "Your life is hid with Christ in God" (Colossians 3:3). Or paraphrasing this: The Christian faith points beyond this foreboding to which Carossa testified, in the words of Luther: "Just try to find yourself in Christ, and not in yourself; then you will find yourself eternally in Him."[22]

I trust that we are now protected from being misunderstood when we say that our common existence here appears unreal compared to this hidden and real life. This is by no means equivalent to saying that the Lutheran Christian does not really live this earthly life. No, he is at hand when needed, unreservedly and ready to stake his all. Sorrow is real to him, as are death, hunger, duty, and joy; everything is as real and pulsating with life to him as to any other person. He has not a smaller but a larger share in life. For this reason we are not at all disposed always to take the defensive diffidently and timidly, but we take the offensive against the world because it is still ignorant of the riches of our life. As the recipients of unmerited gifts, we cannot do otherwise than laud our Father's goodness so as to open the hearts of others. However, our riches consist in the fact that what is palpable and visible does not constitute the whole of life but that our real life is hidden and will be revealed to us yonder, according to the promise we have.

Perhaps we now understand a little better that the entire art of living and the entire art of dying converge in the words of Luther with which we began our discussion: "that we view this temporal life only through a painted glass and, as it were, blinkingly, but yonder eternal life with clear, open eyes."

---

21. Hans Carossa, *Eine Kindheit* (Leipzig: Insel-verlag, 1922), 57.
22. "Sermon von der Bereitung zum Sterben (1519)," WA 2:690.24.

What Is the Church?

> Thank God, a child seven years old knows what the church is, namely, the holy believers and the lambs that hear their Shepherd's voice. For the children pray thus: "I believe in a holy Christian church." This holiness does not consist in surplices, tonsures, long clerical gowns, and other ceremonies of theirs, fabricated by them without the warrant of Holy Writ, but in God's Word and in true faith.

Thus Luther wrote in a well-known passage of the only document composed by him expressly as a confessional writing of his church, the Schmalkald Articles (III, 12). It cannot be denied that theological research has always viewed this 7-year-old child with some envy or perhaps with a bit of doubt. At all events, church and theology have not known and remembered Luther's definition of the church as clearly as that child. There has been much guessing about this matter. And the history of the Protestant concept of the church is an interesting story of strata of other intellectual movements superimposed on the problem of the church. At the time of the old patriarchal state, the church was regarded as one object of the sovereign's paternal solicitude; his sphere also extended to the salvation of the souls of his subjects. In the rising absolutism the church appeared as part of the absolute power of the state. Because this power derived its strength for civic morality from the church, it also had to concern itself with the morals of its subjects. During the Enlightenment, the church was a free society of the believers for the purpose of a common cult and a common religious worship. In the eyes of romanticism the church was the expression of holy emotional forces slumbering in man in varying degrees, thus automatically resulting in a natural gradation and in an organic communion between leaders and followers in the church, as between artists and lovers of the arts. In the liberal nineteenth century the idea of the Enlightenment continued; the church was a religious club, a free society of like-minded people that may claim complete freedom and independent existence in the unsectarian state. In the early days of National Socialism, voices were raised that presumed to conclude from the essence of the totalitarian state that the church was a state institution with the mission to glorify its national festivals and celebrations and to enhance important events in the life of the individual, such as birth, marriage, and death.

As we visualize only these few stages through which the concept of the church has passed, we look somewhat shamefacedly at the childlike simplicity of Luther's definition of the church in the Schmalkald Articles. On the one hand, his words reject holy objects and institutions, which, according to Catholic opinion, belong to the essence of the church; on the other hand, they point to the constituent parts of the church's true holiness, namely, the Word of God and true faith. Thus Luther himself hands us the key to all the hidden chambers of his theology, including his concept of the church.

When we attempt to understand any part of Luther's theology, it is always advisable to proceed from its core: his view of the Word of God, of revelation. The premises of all theology are: God has addressed Himself to us; He has spoken to us and still speaks to us. Luther included our spiritual relationship to God in a wonderful manner in this metaphor of the "Word." A word is the immediate expression of the mind. I reveal or conceal myself by means of my words. Intentionally or unintentionally, I always betray part of my nature in my words. Therefore Luther could find no more fitting expression for Christ than that taken from the beginning of the Gospel of St. John: the Word. For Christ is as closely identified with God as words are with the mind. He is part of the inmost essence and heart of God, just as our words are part of us. As our words reveal heart and mind, so Christ reveals the heart and mind of the Father. Just as there can be no differences between words and mind, so there can be no differences between Christ and the Father. Luther thus spiritualized and deepened in a fine manner any too naturalistic conceptions of the divine origin and character of Christ.

The Word begets faith. Faith is our response to God's Word. Luther regards faith as entirely spiritual. It is not a special and innate quality of the soul. Nor is faith a natural endowment; therefore man cannot excuse himself by saying that he is not gifted spiritually or religiously. No, faith is something that must be presented to us; it is man's breakthrough to liberty before God. Nor is faith a quality of the soul that, as Catholic doctrine alleges, is infused into us in a mysterious, supernatural manner in the Sacrament. No, faith is a clear spiritual act; it is our grateful amen to God's friendly promise. For Luther, Christianity represented a simple relationship: on the one hand, God's promise; on the other, man's faith. This is his understanding of the essence of Christianity. Therefore he rejected whatever is foreign to this simple relationship. Some of the Catholic sacraments have nothing to do with God's forgiveness and promise; therefore Luther could not give them room in the Christian religion. The sacraments accepted by him—Baptism and the Lord's Supper—are not, as some suppose, something independent of and additional to the Word; they are visible signs of their spiritual content, the promise and the confirmation of God's words of grace. They are the "visible Word," as Luther is wont to say with Augustine.

Thus Luther also understood the church. It is born of God's Word, created by God's Word. "The whole life and nature of the church exists in the Word of God."[1] The believers who hear and preserve the Word of God are the church. These two are indissolubly united: "God's Word cannot be without God's people [*Volk*]; on the other hand, God's people cannot be without God's Word."[2]

This quotation acquaints us with Luther's most beautiful name for the church: God's nation or people (*Gottes Volk*). In a figurative sense we can put into the word *Volk* all the thoughts and emotions it usually stirs up in our hearts: the harmony of hearts found only among countrymen, felt most vividly when confronted by foreigners; a common type and a common history; a genuine spirit of brotherliness; mutual attraction; an understanding often not expressed in words; a willingness to sacrifice for one another; a common pride; and a common love for something bigger and greater than we are. But before we try to clarify this further for ourselves, we must note in what respect Luther's view differs from earlier concepts of the church. "God's people" (*Gottes Volk*) is an old term; its history is that of the Christian concept of the church through the centuries.

1. "Ad librum Ambrosii Catharini responsio (1521)," WA 7:721.12.
2. "Von den Konziliis und Kirchen (1539)," WA 50:629.34.

The idea of the *Gottesvolk* is one of the beautiful concepts that the Christian church took from the Old Testament and later repeatedly adapted to the needs of its respective epochs. For four reasons the children of Israel regarded themselves as the chosen nation, the people of God. First, God had miraculously espoused their cause and had delivered them again and again from the hands of their enemies, above all, from slavery in Egypt. Therefore the prophets speak to the people again and again "in the name of the Lord God, who led you out of Egypt." Second, the children of Israel were in possession of the Law; this had been entrusted solely to them. Third, they had the proper Divine Service, for they worshiped the one true God in the temple in Jerusalem in contrast to pagan polytheism, which persistently sought entry into Israel. Fourth, the Israelites had a token of the covenant concluded, as they thought, exclusively with them, namely, circumcision.

Then came the Christians. They, especially St. Paul, recognized that this claim of the Jewish people had been meaningless, even sinful. Faith in the Lord Jesus is the sole criterion for membership in the people of God. The New Testament applied the term "God's people" to Christendom. Those whom God had gathered from Jews and Gentiles made up the people of God. The Christians repeatedly predicated this claim on the beautiful words of Hosea: "I will say to them which were not My people, Thou art My people; and they shall say, Thou art my God" (Hosea 2:23; cf. Romans 9:25; 1 Peter 2:10). The warnings of the prophets up to the days of Jesus were now fulfilled: God had assembled His people whence He willed; He had raised up children unto Abraham from the stones (Matthew 3:9). Therefore the Christians called themselves the people of God not because of any external signs—they had neither a temple nor circumcision—but for two reasons. First, their era, too, was marked by great events in sacred history: the advent, the death, and the resurrection of Christ. But this sacred history was entirely different from that of the Old Testament. The Old Testament events were indubitably certain; they were apparent to all. The Egyptians had found out to their grief that the God of Israel was on the side of His people. In the New Testament it was different; its divine history was hidden and understood by only a few. Who believed in Christ? In the redeeming power of His death? In His resurrection? Who perceived anything of the continuing power of the Holy Spirit, the power that guided and protected His congregation? This was the history of faith. From this grew the second distinguishing mark of God's people: Faith in Christ became all-determinative. The term "God's people" was now transferred entirely into the spiritual realm. The people of God is the communion of the believers in Christ.

But this pure, early Christian view did not long remain unalloyed. A great change took place. From two directions alien spiritual powers broke into primeval Christianity: first, from the realm of the Greco-Eastern mystery religions. To them the most profound essence of a religion was a mystery penetrated by an occult religious act, sometimes by a baptism with water, wine, or blood; sometimes by a frenzy, for example, a wildly exciting dance or a slumber haunted by dreams and visions in the temple of a deity. In such a religious act, accessible only to the initiate, mysterious, supernatural powers flow into man, deifying him and making him immortal. These beliefs of the mystery religions affected Christianity. Baptism and Holy Communion often appear as mysteries to be considered just as sacred as the most solemn rites of other cults and likewise withheld from the unbidden. Soon the idea of immortality medicine (φάρμαχον ἀδανασίαζ) made its way into Holy Communion from the Isis mysteries. As early as the second century many theologians considered it more important for Christ to bring powers of life than to bring words of life. Thus the people of God soon became the people who possessed the true mysteries.

Second, a new invasion of Old Testament ideas took place. While the effects of the mystery religions are more pronounced in the Greek and Eastern churches, the Old Testament mode of thought, in addition to other strong influences, brought about an alienation from Christianity in Roman Catholicism. Old Testament thinking and that of the Roman Church are related in their legalistic forms. Judaism and Roman Catholicism are distinctly legalistic religions. The free grace of the Christian faith is expressed by the Roman Catholic system in legal forms and safeguards. Elements of the mystery religions and other influences may also have insinuated themselves into Roman Catholicism, but they did not attain right of domicile in the early Catholic Church until they had been associated with the Old Testament tradition.

Self-evidently the organized church also appropriated the beautiful name "God's people." But on what does it base its claim to this title? It is significant how forms of Old Testament thought again come to the fore in the Catholic Church: First, the Catholic Church lays claim to the correct mode of worship. The Catholic Mass is not only a mystery, it is at the same time a development of the Jewish temple service, it is a sacrifice. The memorial and Communion service of the early Christian church was transformed into a sacrifice, an expiatory sacrifice. Soon matters came to such a point that the sacrifice on Golgotha had to be presented and offered anew every day in an unbloody manner to atone for the daily sins of mankind. Only where this is done is the true church to be found. Second, the priest is indispensable to the sacrifice. In the second and third centuries the dignity and the power of the priest grew in proportion to the increase of the mysterious and sacrificial aspects of Holy Communion. The clergy was soon elevated above the level of the congregation and invested with ever-increasing sanctity. This clergy was considered irremovable because the rite of ordination gives it an indelible character (*character indelebilis*). It advances in social life. It has to remain celibate because the natural state of marriage would desecrate the holiest, the sacrament. Just as late Judaism was based on the sacerdotal caste, so the church was now founded on the hierarchy. As early as the second century, it was zealously and stoutly proclaimed that the church is where the bishop is; whoever breaks with the bishop parts company with the church. Heated spiritual battles were fought, especially during Augustine's day, over the question of whether there could be a true church of Christ outside the body centering in the hierarchy. The Roman Church has staunchly replied in the negative at all times. Finally the church becomes a huge graduated structure, culminating in the monarchial pope. The prototype of pagan and Jewish priesthood is clearly discernible. Even today the pope bears the title of the chief priest of the old Roman religion: Pontifex Maximus. Third, as in Judaism, the claim of the Catholic Church to be the people of God is predicated on sacred tradition.

This tradition is not restricted to a holy Law (nor was it confined to that in Judaism), but it is more comprehensive. It is intimately related to the position of the priest, which is safeguarded and guaranteed by the uninterrupted succession of the bishops. The notion of the apostolic succession is really the cornerstone of the great Catholic fiction that the rite of ordination can transmit the possession of truth. This idea is consistently carried to its climax, reaching, as it were, into heaven. The pope enjoys the cooperation of the Holy Spirit in a special way and is, therefore, infallible in his solemn decisions on questions of belief and morals. Finally, tradition culminates in one person. At the Vatican Council, Pius IX declared correctly: "I am tradition." In this tradition, ancient sacred history—the life, the death, and the resurrection of our Lord—are admittedly preserved, but no less is the Law preserved there. For in the Catholic Church, Law and grace are inseparably linked. It is true that the Gospel is perpetuated in the Catholic Church, but it is equally true that it is radically altered by the revival of Old Testament traits: the differentiation between greater and lesser commandments or, more accurately, between commandments and counsels; the distinction between the position of the clergy and the monks and that of the laity; and the concept of satisfaction to be rendered by expiatory acts, merits, and indulgence formerly acquired by monetary payments, now by prayers. All this stems from the character of a legalistic religion. Armed with this tradition, which is vouched for by the hierarchy, the Catholic Church poses as the guardian of all religious and moral truth. In this she claims superiority over the often vacillating, groping, and discordant Protestantism. She bases this superiority on the postulate often voiced by Catholic Christians: After all, there must be some area where truth absolute appears on the scene; there must be one supreme arbiter of truth in the confusion of opinions.

After this cursory survey, we shall have a better understanding of Luther's view that the holiness of the church consists in "the Word of God and true faith." This is a return to early Christianity. Luther was quick to adopt the New Testament expression "body of Christ" for the church. It does not mean what the Catholic Church is wont to designate as the *corpus Christi mysticum*, which is based on the mysterious presence of Christ in the Sacrament and on the unity in the hierarchy. Luther means the body in which the Spirit of Christ lives, the body permeated with His Spirit, namely, the believers in all the world.

To this concept of the church Luther adhered to the end of his life. He began exactly where, more than a thousand years before his time, the question regarding the church of the New Testament had been stirred up again and never answered: with Augustine. Augustine had conceived of the church as the communion of the Spirit, created solely by God, who bestows faith and elects for Himself the citizens of His realm. But side by side with this view we find that Augustine was also convinced that the Catholic Church, visible and tangible, with her bishops, sacraments, and dogmas, was the only saving church. Augustine did not solve the problem of reconciling these two views concerning the church. Luther clearly perceives the contradiction. Only for a few years did he endure the vagueness and the half-measures of Augustine. In his first lecture (lecture on the

Psalms) we find the substantial and basic features of his doctrine on the church. The dividing power of the Word eliminates the multitude of nominal Christians from the true believers, that is, the church. The church is not a visible organization; it extends over all the world. But it is a real communion, which rallies around Christ, its common head. It no longer finds its unity in the Catholic episcopal succession (*successio episcoporum*) but in the hidden yet uninterrupted continuity of believers (*successio fidelium*). Only for a short time after this do we still find an unrelated, external acknowledgment of the hierarchical church in Luther; then he executes the critical work for which Augustine had been too faint. The Ninety-five Theses marked the first step: There is no difference within the clergy. All are, on principle, of the same rank. The pope is, spiritually understood, no more than a priest; and both have no prerogatives beyond those of intercession for the believers. The second step is initiated in the theses and is consummated in and after the Leipzig Debate: No ecclesiastical vocation enjoys any religious advantage. There is no clergy (*Klerus*). The pope possesses no power of the keys over the souls of the believers. The councils are subject to error. The individual believer has the prerogative to interpret the Scriptures; this means that he is a priest. For Luther, a heretic threatened with excommunication, it was simply a question of existence whether he, the excommunicate, was nonetheless still a member of the Lord's church. Yes, he faced the question whether he, an individual, had been called to protect this church against a world power that bore the name of the church wrongfully. With unparalleled spiritual courage, Luther answered this question in the affirmative. "He who teaches the Gospel is pope and Christ's successor; he who does not teach it is Judas and Christ's betrayer."[3] This denial of every spiritual character of the legalistic institution with its usurped prerogative aids Luther toward the attainment of his coherent doctrine of the church, the doctrine that he henceforth proclaims unswervingly and to which, in the year 1528, he gives clear confessional expression for the event of his death:

> Accordingly, I believe that there is one holy Christian Church on earth, that is, the communion and number or the congregation of all Christians in the whole world, the only bride of Christ and His spiritual body, of which He is the only head; and the bishops or priests are not the heads or lords or bridegrooms of the church but servants and friends. . . . And this same Christendom does not exist solely under the Roman Church or the

---

3. "Ad librum Ambrosii Catharini responsio (1521)," WA 7:721.32.

pope but in all the world . . . and Christendom is, therefore, bodily scattered among the pope's followers, among Turks, Persians, Tartars, and everywhere, but is gathered spiritually in one Gospel and one faith under one Head, which is Jesus Christ.[4]

That Luther adhered firmly to this concept of the church is evidenced by the passage from the Schmalkald Articles quoted in the beginning of this chapter and, above all, in the famous third section of his great writing *Of Councils and Churches* (1539): The church is "the communion of saints, that is, an assembly or gathering of such people as are Christians and holy, that is, a Christian holy assembly. . . . A Christian holy people believing in Christ . . . and possessing the Holy Spirit." This is God's people (*Gottes Volk*).[5]

This is Luther's view of the church. It is a coherent and unambiguous concept of the church. For Luther there are neither two groups in the church (believers and unbelievers) nor is there a church in the narrower and in the wider sense (as Lutheran orthodoxy held in a later age) or a church in a primary and in a secondary sense. For him there is only one definition of the church.

But is there really nothing visible about this church? Is it, as in a fairy tale, only an invisible kingdom of faith? Most assuredly there is something visible about the church! If this church is really alive, much of it comes to view. Luther enumerated her visible signs on occasion: There God's Word is preached and believed purely and ardently; there children are accepted into the kingdom of God through Baptism; there hearts assailed by sin and temptation find solace and strength in Holy Communion; there sinners unburden their conscience in confession; there ministers are commissioned in orderly fashion for preaching the Word, for administering the sacraments, and for other pastoral ministrations; there a prayerful Christian people offers God praise and thanks in public worship; there people are opposed and persecuted for the sake of Christ; and there they must bear the cross of their Master.[6] All these external signs and activities betoken the presence of the church. All are inseparably connected with the essence of the church, with the life of faith derived from the riches of the divine Word. Therefore one may draw a conclusion from

---

4. "Vom Abendmahl Christi (1528)," WA 26:506.

5. "Von den Konziliis und Kirchen (1539)," WA 50:624f.

6. "Von den Konziliis und Kirchen (1539)," WA 50:628–43.

the effect to the cause and say that where these signs and activities are present, there the church is. "Where God's Word is, there the church must be; therefore, where Baptism and Holy Communion are, there God's people must be."[7] Because it is God's purpose to gather unto Himself a real people on earth through His Word, it follows that the church is not only a gathering of believing individuals who are separately united, so to speak, with Christ by faith (like the dots of a circle by radii with their center), but it is also a brotherhood, united by a common bond of love, a love that radiates a power perceptible far beyond the confines of Christendom. Wherever there are true Christians—and this means wherever the real church exists—there a warm and radiant love is present that also touches the heart of the unbeliever. Thus wherever the spirit of sincere affection and mutual forbearance dwells in a home; wherever one comes to the aid of the other in physical or spiritual need; yes, wherever a person takes up and bears his own burdens of life courageously; wherever people mutually comfort and strengthen one another with God's Word; wherever parents train their children by Christian precept and example; wherever one diligently avails oneself of Word and Sacrament—there is the church, for Christ is there. And where Christ is, there the church is.

There is something wonderful about the church. It is something real. Wherever it is strong, it can transform a whole nation. It is capable of altering the life course of an individual completely; it can do away with unbridgeable rifts among men. The church cannot be exterminated. Even if all media of power were applied to suppress every external ecclesiastical form and to dissolve all Christian congregations, the church would still live on. Even if it has been pronounced dead, it will make its presence felt again, youthful and indestructible, at the hour appointed by God.

But the church is not amenable to statistics; one cannot take the church's census. Luther realized that God alone knows His own. Our shortsighted vision cannot discern the membership of Christ's body. To this body belong many about whom scarcely another person knows or would believe that they are members and who themselves imagine least of all that they belong. Many do not belong who doubtless would like to count themselves members and are regarded as such by others. Nor are the signs of the church—Word and Sacraments—dependable insignia of membership in the body of Christ, that is, in the church. The fact that

---

7. "Von den Konziliis und Kirchen (1539)," WA 50:631.27.

someone has been baptized signifies that God has opened to the baptized the door leading to the communion with Christ, the church. Such a person may confidently rely on his Baptism in hours of doubt and *Anfechtung*. But it does not mean that he now belongs to the body of Christ without believing or desiring to believe. The visible signs of the church—the Word and Sacraments—are, as it were, the lines of demarcation of a church's area. Within this area is the church. But unfortunately this area also contains much that is alien to the church—unbelief, erroneous belief, hypocrisy—but most assuredly also the church, that is, Christians who hold membership in the living body of Christ.

Thus the true church is a part of God's hidden glory, hidden under much that is worldly and human, remotely comparable perhaps to the revelation of God in the plain and unassuming form of Christ. Whoever wishes to behold some of the church's beauty must not fix his gaze on ceremonial pomp or on any visible display of power but on the unpretentious but revolutionizing miracles that God works quietly in the human heart through the Word and the service of the church. Because self-renunciation and self-denial, which run counter to human nature, are requisites for membership, it is apparent that the church, taken in the most profound sense, will always be confined to small numbers and will often seem lost and smothered by the large number of mere camp followers or even enemies. But in this it merely suffers the fate of its Master, whom the world crucified and whose victory was affirmed by that very act. Thus His church is also the bearer of this promise of victory. Whoever has an eye for the hand of God in history can see that the world is already overcome. Whoever remains standing beneath the cross will experience by faith that the enemies of God—devil, sin, and death—have been shorn of their power. "His doom is writ; a word shall quickly slay him." This confidence in victory, all appearances to the contrary notwithstanding, is not founded on human accomplishments and on triumphs in the course of the church's history nor on the fact that the church has proved itself indestructible in persecution throughout the centuries but on the fact that it cannot be destroyed, for "God is in the midst of it." His Word and Sacraments and the love engendered by Him lie embedded (like blocks of granite from a distant, yonder shore) in the midst of this world. They vouch that God is greater than the world and the heart of man and that His work cannot perish. For this reason Luther hid ensconced from the tumult of the world in this mighty fortress of God and exulted: "*Ecclesia* shall be my castle, my fortress, my chamber."[8]

This is the one great truth proclaimed by Luther on the church: The church is the people of God living from the Word of God. This communion of believers in Christ is the one holy Christian church on earth. Again and again the question has been raised: Is this not saying too little? What about local congregations and state churches? Are they not also church? Here Luther differentiated logically. He always chafed a bit under the term "church," first, because, as the name for a building made of stone, it is misleading and ill-suited to the communion of believers, the *communio sanctorum*; second, because it had become customary to apply the term "church" also to the properly constituted congregations. Luther follows this custom only reluctantly because many congregations bear little resemblance to the body of Christ. He expresses surprise that St. Paul uses the word *church* when speaking of the congregations in Galatia, which grieved him so much. He explains this by saying that Paul does so because of the fraction of church hidden in them, because of those divine gifts of Word and Sacrament and the life inevitably flowing from them. God never remains unattested. Wherever Word and Sacrament are found, there faith, as a part of the body of Christ, is also found. Therefore these congregations are called churches with the same validity with which a coin may be termed a gold piece though it is not 100 percent gold. They contain church as an ore may contain gold. Thus there is always a dividing line running through the congregations or through the hearts of those who want to be Christians. With one part of their heart they belong to the church, but with another part they still belong to the world. It cannot be otherwise because Christ is always the center of controversy, even in the heart of a Christian. Therefore the church is never a triumphant and perfect quantity; it is always a hidden and struggling power, a power that is often regarded as extinct but suddenly comes to life again. The words spoken by Luther of the individual Christian also apply to the church: It is not in the stage of having become but of becoming ("Sie steht nicht im Gewordensein, sondern im Werden").

But this did not go far enough for people who were anxiously concerned about the reality of the church. They thought it was a disparagement of the church. This was already apparent in Melanchthon. He fretted

---

8. "Lectures on Genesis (1535–1545)," WA 44:713.1.

over the Catholic sneer that the Protestant church was only a *civitas Platonica*, a cloudland. It can be observed how little by little a second idea insinuated itself, at the side of Luther's, into Melanchthon's consciousness. The church is also an outward sociological institution as are, for example, the state, cities, guilds, etc. At first this second concept occupies a secondary position, but gradually it is thrust forward. Finally, a second, equally justifiable, concept of the church was adopted by the Lutheran orthodoxy determined by Melanchthon: the visible church at the side of the invisible. This division into two parts is never found in Luther. It stands to reason that the visible church is of far greater interest to theologians, church politicians, and particularly to the jurists. Finally, the Lutherans followed in the train of Calvin: The invisible church is disposed of with the elaboration of a few principles, and with a reverential bow it is ushered into heaven. Then exclusive attention is directed to the tangible problems of the so-called visible church. In this way a new legal form of the church developed. It is an institution of public life and may be defined as such according to form, purpose, personal relationships, etc., as other sociological entities are. Thereby Luther's profound and unified concept of the church was destroyed.

Thus something irreplaceable was forfeited in the course of history, and our usage of language (church as local congregation or as state church) makes it impossible to retrieve this loss. Even in Luther's day, linguistic usage made it difficult to clarify his view and give it adequate expression. But his objective grasp of the matter must be brought to mind and emphasized again and again. His was the momentous return to the view of early Christianity and the decisive liberation from the secularized Catholic view of the church. We want to make only two of its consequences clear.

1. Luther's genuine concept of the church implies a strong striving toward the goal. An organized congregation is always church in the nascent state (*Kirche im Werden*); nothing ensures that it really is body of Christ. God has reserved judgment on this question to Himself. It must always be in pursuit of its goal, but it has no guarantee that it really is church neither because of apostolic succession and the resultant hierarchy nor because of a particular form of church government nor because of any mode of worship nor because of so-called pure doctrine nor because of the possession of orthodox confessional writings nor because of outwardly flourishing works of

charity, etc. Even a church with the most orthodox confessional writings may be dead, and the same thing pertains to other warrants. Luther's concept of the church shatters every arrogant and overweening ecclesiasticism that has found its way into every church and often also into the evangelical church. It discourages all satiety. The church is not in the stage of having become but becoming.

2. Luther's view of the church helps to overcome the dilemma of denominational divisions. All external church fences fall before his concept. True belief in Christ may exist in all Christian denominations, for God's Spirit blows where it wants to. This opens the portals wide. Who can know where God has His true believers? This makes us modest; we need not engage in competition among ourselves. Every church that styles itself Christian may be concerned that it really does become body of Christ, that faith and love dwell richly in its midst.

On the other hand, however, Luther's concept of the church also opens our eyes to the true differences. Whatever is part of the church's essence according to Catholic doctrine—ceremony, hierarchy, papacy, tradition—contravenes the church's true characteristics: the Gospel, a living faith, and a life in Christ. The Gospel marks the point of divergence clearly and sharply. All guarantees of church, also in the Catholic sense, run counter to the Gospel and the New Testament. No sector of the church possesses a monopoly on the body of Christ. All tend and strive toward that goal. For this reason war must be waged in earnest against a false churchism, both within our own borders and against the claims of the Catholic Church. The reality of the body of Christ in the world is at issue.

We have examined the internal nature of the church as Luther perceives it. In conclusion we must, though briefly, also view the external form Luther gave his congregations. In Luther's eyes this was a simple matter. The congregation occupied a most natural position in community and nation. Every citizen occupies a dual position—the one in the political order, the other in the Christian congregation. Citizens of the state and members of the Christian congregation are identical, the same people, only viewed from a different angle. A town is coextensive with the Christian congregation in that town, all inhabitants of the latter being members of the former. Luther could not envisage a time when this would change. He lived in a day of a self-evident Christianity in all political entities. At that time Christianity was practically synonymous with Europe, with the

WHAT IS THE CHURCH?

Occident in its historical-political form. Luther regarded his congregations as Christendom reborn and purged of papal abuses. For this reason it seemed quite self-evident to him that in this Christendom only one faith could prevail: the true faith, not the faith distorted by the papacy. Therefore he considered it the government's duty to abolish a manifestly false worship, such as the Mass, and also to take severe measures against the rebellious doctrines of the Anabaptists. This was not to imply any coercion of conscience for an individual. Luther considered it the proper function of the government to make provision for properly regulated worship in the country.

This, however, did not mean that Luther regarded church administration as an affair of the civil government. For centuries after Luther, the evangelical church underwent an unsound development that deviated widely from Luther's intentions. A church government administered by a prince or another ruler of the state was never part of Luther's plan. He did appeal to the princes in their capacity as Christians to assist in the necessary inspection and reform of the congregations. Only because he himself is a Christian is a prince under obligation to aid within a Christian congregation, not by reason of his governmental position. Later a prince was properly designated as the principal member of the congregation (*praecipuum membrum ecclesiae*). Because he is the only member in the congregation in possession of the necessary means, the power, and the money, it devolves on him to employ these means in helping the church when it is in need. "The hand should not help even if the eye is in great distress? Is it not unnatural, not to say unchristian, for one member to fail to come to the aid of another, to ward off his ruin?"[9] The prince has the same obligation to use his gifts of government that others have to employ any talents with which they may be endowed, such as theological or musical gifts. This does not concede any preeminence to the prince; his service, like that of any other member of the church, is a service of love. This was expressed unequivocally by Luther in the preface to Melanchthon's instructions to the visitors in 1528: They were only adhering to the office of love when they petitioned the elector to entrust a number of competent men with a visitation. He adds expressly that the elector is not obliged to render the church this service in his role of government. Luther recognizes neither a duty nor a prerogative of the government as such to assume control and

9. "To the Christian Nobility (1520)," WA 6:409.13. Cf. pp. 213ff.

127

administration of the church; he recognizes only a service of love, which the individuals comprising the government are in duty bound to render as Christian brethren. In this question, too, Luther hewed consistently to the line. He always regarded the princes as emergency bishops (*Notbischöfe*), as surrogates, to serve until the day when truly evangelical bishops could replace the former Catholic bishops. The installation of an evangelical bishop in Naumburg in 1542 is indicative of the trend and the further development as conceived by Luther. That a prince could someday lay claim to church government in an undenominational or confessionally neutral state lay beyond Luther's horizon. And a church government administered by a prince of a different faith, a situation that obtained, though in modified form, under the Catholic electoral and royal houses of Saxony and Bavaria, would have been unthinkable for Luther. Today we no longer have the state of Luther's day. For centuries the state has departed from what Luther, in his day, took for granted: a state in which government and governed shared the same faith. Therefore it follows that today the evangelical church in a state that is neutral on principle not only with regards to the various Christian denominations but with regards to all other religious bodies as well must necessarily determine its own external and internal form.

Luther's ideas on the church are basically simple, but they must be understood and appropriated anew by each generation. We distinguish three chief points.

1. According to Luther, the church is the people of God on earth, which owes its being not to any external characteristics but to the Word of God and lives by faith and by love.

2. The congregations are nascent church (*Kirche im Werden*) called to become church. They possess God's great gifts of grace, His invitation and His means, with which He wants to gather all believers of the world.

3. With a view to the goal to become the genuine church, all congregations must choose their external and internal form. That is their own peculiar task; it is not the duty of any extraneous authority, for example, the state. For everything, even the church's external forms, must serve the effective proclamation and the authentic attestation of the Gospel, nothing else.

This is Luther's broad and sweeping picture of the church. It traces its origin entirely from the heart of God, from the body of Christ, from the

Word, and thereby it places us squarely into the world and before life's tasks. It is a safe lodestar that will illumine the way for the evangelical church in all vicissitudes of history.

GOD'S GRACE OR MAN'S EXPIATION?

LUTHER'S REPLY
TO THE QUESTION OF CONSCIENCE
POSED BY THE VARIOUS RELIGIONS

Sin and expiation—this is one of the great basic themes of all religions. It is not the only theme. Suffering, death, deliverance from the world's evils, eternal life, and many other things number among these fundamental questions posed by religion. But aside from the question of death, I suppose there is none that is drawn like a thread through the warp and woof of all religions (from the primitive nature religions to the advanced forms of spiritual piety) as is the question of sin and atonement for sin. The encounter with death and an awareness of commandment and of sin are two inescapable human experiences. A profound earnestness of conscience is reflected in the different types of guilt experience, both in the naive, primitive religions and, in penetrating self-analysis, in their more refined forms. Whoever has seriously pondered this fact is deeply shocked by modern speech so nonhuman and so unworthy of humankind: "There is no such thing as guilt or sin; a feeling of guilt is a morbid degeneration of the human intellect." All religions of the world raise a thousand voices in testimony against this falsehood and in the unanimous declaration that man is endowed with a conscience.

Almost all the religions of the world answer the question regarding deliverance from guilt thus: It must be expiated. In the various religious types we find innumerable modes of expiation. One tries holy waters for purification; another penalizes himself for sin by fastings or other privations. Still another offers sacrifices of all kinds, even human sacrifices, in atonement. Expiation may be made in solemn public worship or by penance in private. Primitive peoples believe in the possibility of laying their sins on an animal, a bird, or, as the Old Testament relates, a ram, which is then driven into the desert. Or one may load one's sins aboard a boat, which then drifts out to sea with its evil cargo, shunned by other ships as if laden with a contagious pestilence. Innumerable prayers and special festivals or days of atonement (pagan days of penance), at which time a nation's sins are to be expiated for a whole year, testify to man's earnest determination to atone for sin and escape the righteous anger of the gods.

What is true in relation to the gods also applies to human associations. Law owes its existence to the inviolable sequence of guilt and punishment; it has its origin in religion. The gods of all religions insist on punishment for guilt. This is demonstrated forcefully by the duty of blood vengeance that even our Germanic ancestors shared with countless other peoples. "An eye for an eye, a tooth for a tooth" is the sacred, divine commandment of atonement for the ancient nations. No matter how odd, ridiculous, or terrifying all these manifold forms of atonement may seem to us, he who understands them aright perceives in them a profound reverence for the majesty and the inviolableness of divine commandments.

Out of the countless expiatory prescriptions in the Persian religion, there rises the great myth of the eternal judgment over the soul. When the deceased sets foot on the world mountain, his good and evil deeds are weighed in the "balances of the spirits, which do not deviate a hairbreadth in anyone's favor." By the penalties imposed on him, he must atone for his evil deeds immediately. Then he steps on the great wind bridge that spans the universe. If he is destined for hell, this bridge shrivels and shrinks beneath him and becomes as thin as a hair, and he plunges into the yawning abyss. But if he is found worthy of heaven, this bridge expands before his eyes into a broad thoroughfare that he can cross without any difficulty. Thus the stern gods decree.

The great Greek tragedies also revolve around the commandment of purification and expiation. It is not a coincidence that Apollo is the chief god in all the great works of poetry. He was the god who sat in judgment on questions pertaining to guilt and innocence; he was, above all, the god of blood atonement and blood vengeance. In the spirit of this god, Aeschylus, the oldest of the great Greek tragedians, fashioned a powerful and stirring family trilogy to which theme Goethe contributed in his *Iphigenie auf Tauris*. In the first drama, Aeschylus tells about Agamemnon's return home from the long campaign against Troy. In his homeland he is murdered by his wife, who, during his long absence, has found consolation in the arms of another man. The chorus announces the law that now becomes effective:

The slayer of today shall die tomorrow—
The wage of wrong is woe.
While Time shall be, while Zeus in heaven is lord,
His law is fixed and stern;
On him that wrought shall vengeance be outpoured.[1]

In the second tragedy, Orestes, Agamemnon's son, wreaks vengeance on his mother and her paramour in accordance with the command of Apollo. Now the chorus exultantly proclaims that atonement has been made and that the honor and the happiness of Agamemnon's home have been restored:

Lo, freedom's light hath come!
Lo, now is rent away
The grim and curbing bit that held us dumb. . . .
And Time, the great Accomplisher,
Shall cross the threshold, whensoe'er
He choose with purging hand to cleanse
The palace, driving all pollutions thence.[2]

But this new bloodguilt also demands revenge. The Erinyes, goddesses of vengeance, confuse Orestes's mind. Again the chorus pronounces the merciless law:

Of Justice are we ministers,
And whosoe'er of men may stand
Lifting a pure unsullied hand,
That man no doom of ours incurs,
And walks thro' all his mortal path
Untouched by woe, unharmed by wrath.
But if, as yonder man, he hath
Blood on the hands he strives to hide,
We stand avengers at his side.[3]

Orestes is not delivered from the operation of this cruel law until the gods themselves intervene and terminate the gruesome events. But it is significant to note how this takes place. He dare not approach Athena until he

1. *Agamemnon*, 1823ff.
2. *The Libation-Bearers*, 1068ff.
3. *The Furies*, 364ff.

has been purged from sin by being sprinkled with the blood of a beast. And Apollo, who himself had charged him to avenge his father, unravels the plot by showing that the right of the father takes precedence over that of the mother. Finally, Athena decides in favor of Orestes and appoints the Erinyes the peaceful guardians of the law, that is, she converts blood vengeance into the state's judicial power over life and death. But the law of expiation is not abrogated. It lives on in the countless rites of atonement, and the pious Greek of a later day believes that he cannot approach his gods without these.

Among the old Germanic peoples the relation between guilt and expiation was equally inviolable. We know little about the degree to which they regarded moral delinquencies as an affront to their gods, but their sacrifices, especially many of the human sacrifices in sacred groves (sacrifices reported in a terrifyingly graphic manner), prove irrefutably that they knew something about the wrath of the gods that had to be placated. A still more immediate and direct association between guilt and expiation is found in the earthly realm, in the weird power of blood feuds that held sway among Germanic peoples until the end of their pagan days and, in fact, was not extinct in Iceland until long after the island's adoption of Christianity about A.D. 1000. This is, in every instance, an expression of the juridical-moral order according to which bloodguilt can be expiated only by the shedding of blood. To what extent the avenger fulfilled a religious duty with his deed and attempted to propitiate the gods we do not know definitely, for the sources have come to us from a time when the original motives were no longer clear. Moreover, the writers usually indulge in descriptions of the wild and elemental emotions and passions under which the original motives of the event were smothered. But when women, too, participate in these deeds of violence with unparalleled fury, and when brave and noble men often carry out the revenge by cowardly surprise attacks or by assaults with far superior forces, one may explain this by saying that they are serving a law that supersedes all commandments of chivalry and honor, a commandment that, in the final analysis, is rooted in a religious soil. In their sight the human legal order is really not an earthly provision either; it is an expression of the will of the gods. This is also evident from the fact that the ancient Germans have no distinct word for religion, but in Old German, as in Persian, *law* and *religion* are designated by the same term.

It would be an easy matter to continue the enumeration of examples by way of proof for the ever-recurring "Guilt demands expiation; this is divine law" in the religious thought of mankind. This stern and earnest conviction does mankind honor. And wherever the message of Jesus was proclaimed: "Son, be of good cheer, thy sins be forgiven thee," it encountered this earnest and stern religious viewpoint. It encountered it in the wearisome legalism of the pious Jews, who really toiled before God; in the many varieties and off-shoots of the ancient Persian religion; in the ingenious rites of the Greek mystery religions; in the religion of the Germanic peoples, etc. Thus it has remained up to the present time. Whether the Christian message comes face-to-face with the primitive tribal religions with their sacrifices and expiatory rites or with Islam (which is founded on strict prescription with respect to purity and rites and on minutely defined meritorious works) or with the religions of India (with their all-embracing doctrine of karma, the inevitable retribution for all deeds in future reincarnations of the soul and ever-new forms of existence), everywhere the Christian message of grace confronts the conviction of inevitable and necessary expiation. This is no less true with regard to the church's message to the modern apostate from the Christian religion. In his common rejoinder to the Christian doctrine of forgiveness, "If I have made a mistake, I stand ready to make amends, and I shall see to it that it will not be repeated," we find a picture, though rather faded, of that primitive human conviction that is voiced by all religions. Even this does honor to man, though his idea of restitution may be erroneous and his resolve to make amends may be weak.

In view of all this, it should not surprise us that the Christian religion is again and again reproached for a lack of conscientiousness by the other religions when the message of a forgiving Father who goes forth to meet His lost son and embraces him is proclaimed. We have heard many a voice, not only Jewish but also Greek, declining Jesus' message of mercy with moral indignation. Modern man, too, who still manifests at least a feeble readiness to make amends for his guilt, regards himself, with his rejection of grace, as morally superior to the Christian.

Another point must be considered. If one ponders what a deep imprint this fervent resolve to expiate—reflected in the worship, the customs, and the mores of the multistratified religious world of antiquity, in its Jewish, Eastern, Greek, and Roman forms—is apt to make on the mind, then the observation that even the Gospel at one time became steeped in this world of ancient expiatory religions need not surprise us. In the early days of the

Catholic Church, one can detect how these thoughts penetrated the church, which at the same time possessed the Gospel of Christ. The ancient expiatory washings find a revival in Catholic holy water; a purging effect is imputed to countless rites and ceremonies; the sacraments become acts of atonement; the Mass becomes a sacrifice; and the priest is transformed, in imitation of the ancient sacrificial religions of Judaism and paganism, into a higher being, a mediator between God and man who absolves the latter from sin. Above all, man's good works are again viewed as meritorious, as they were in the legalistic religion of the Jews. Now man is again assured that he can render satisfaction to God by special good works, such as fasting, prayers, alms, pilgrimages, various ecclesiastical services, and mainly by means of the powerful sacrifice of monasticism. It was but logical when one ascribed the mightiest expiatory effect to the greatest sacrifice—the entry into a cloister—and declared that a monk, after the performance of his vows, was as pure and innocent as a newly baptized child.

This viewpoint inspired the congratulations extended to Luther by his monastic brethren when he made his solemn vows to his prior in the Augustinian church at Erfurt. Now there began for Luther a terrible struggle with the contradictory elements in the Catholic Church. For here he was brought face-to-face, in a snarl that could not be untangled, with the assurance of mercy on the one hand and the stern command to expiate on the other. The church offered him more than a modicum of mercy. Indeed, it offered him all of Holy Writ, the prayers, the hymns, the liturgy of the Catholic Church, in which the gracious words of forgiveness re-echo. It directed his eye to the suffering and to the cross of Christ and taught him that the crucified and risen Christ had throttled death and overcome the world. But at the same time it taught him that all depended on him. Confess, do penance, mortify your flesh, perform as many good works as possible, for you can never know how your accounts stand before God. Believe in the Roman Church, in the meritoriousness of your monastic office and your good works; read Masses in holy places, for example, in Rome; kneel before statues and pictures of mercy; creep up the holy steps in Rome; abase yourself on your monastic mendicant missions; give alms; perform works of satisfaction before God. This internal contradiction put a terrible strain on Luther. What was his fate in this system in which one view repealed the other, in which God's grace and man's expiation were so adroitly distributed that the two always counterbalanced each other? One can readily understand Luther's profound perturbation when his belief in God's free grace was again challenged by demands to expiate his sins, demands issued in the name of the church, yes, in the name of Holy Writ. It is significant that it was not, as we might suppose, the moment in which he realized that the church's message also contained the fine old Gospel of grace that clung to his memory for years. No, even long after Staupitz had led Luther to his Savior, the words that he had read in his Bible about "God's righteousness" still rushed at him like a foe: What is to become of me if God deals with me according to His righteousness and His Law?

> Denn so du willst das sehen an,
> Was Sünd' und Unrecht ist getan,
> Wer kann, Herr, vor dir bleiben?

> If Thou rememb'rest each misdeed,
> If each should have its rightful meed,
> Who may abide Thy Presence?

If God, who knows me thoroughly, wishes to exercise justice, where, then, does the comfort of His mercy remain? Therefore it seemed to Luther like a return to paradise when he became certain that the righteousness of God in the New Testament and in passages of the Old Testament important to him, especially in the Psalms, is merely another expression for God's free grace.

Luther's anguish of soul would not have endured so long if the Catholic Church had not presented such a maze of the religion of grace and the religion of expiation. With the one hand it takes away what it gives with the other. The priest absolves the penitent sinner in confession and simultaneously imposes expiatory penalties for his satisfaction before God. How deeply this destroys the import of grace can be seen clearly in the reasoning advanced in the Catholic Church in support of it: God has decreed two types of penalty for sin, first, eternal punishment, which God remits in His mercy; second, temporal punishment, which man must expiate under the church's guidance here on earth or in purgatory. A dismembered grace, a contradictory and divided God. If the Catholic Church has objected vociferously to the accusation of works-righteousness and has pointed to the countless words and statements in which she, too, has taught "justification by grace," then the Lutheran Christian must counter: Yes, you too! But never an either/or: grace or expiation.

On many an occasion this either/or was on the point of breaking a path through the Catholic doctrine like a lava stream. Augustine had approached it. To him, as to no one since the days of Paul, it had become impressively clear that man remains indebted to God for everything and is wholly dependent on His grace. The great medieval theologian Anselm had declared with overpowering earnestness that man's sin is far too heavy to be counterbalanced by good works and that, as it is, we owe to God all the good deeds we are able to do and for this reason cannot atone for past guilt with them. However, the successful penetration of such volcanic thoughts had always been contained by the adamantine crust of tradition. Both Augustine and Anselm had stopped short of abolishing the entire system of works-righteousness in the Catholic Church. They permitted the Catholic Church's practical religion of expiation to exist side by side with their own doctrine of grace. Thus this system of half-truths, of internal contradiction between grace and expiation, because of which Luther almost bled to death, was perpetuated. Luther alone broke through and found the way back to the unqualified and absolute Gospel: "Therefore we conclude that a man is justified by faith without the deeds of the law" (Romans 3:28). He put the whole ardor of his life into the word *without*.

In the course of this chapter we have recalled the religions of the world. We have heard the earnest voices of the Persian world judgment, the voice of the Greek tragedian, and the voice of our Germanic ancestors. Now we behold the isolation and the aloneness of the message of grace, rediscovered by Luther, in the history of the human mind. It is surrounded, as it were, by a double ring of enemies: by the Catholic perversion of the Gospel (compounded of half grace and half expiation) and by the stern expiatory law of the religions of the world. Is it surprising that Luther was often terror-stricken as he asked whether he alone could be correct with his interpretation of the Gospel?

With two revealing truths Luther opposed the erroneous belief of mankind that we can expiate our guilt before God. First, we cannot make restitution for a single past deed. It is unnecessary to inform the great, serious religions of this. For the most part they are aware of this, and they do not presume to be able to undo any past deed by expiation. But it is necessary to tell modern man this, who appears so respectable in his own eyes when he declares: "I do not want your Christian mercy. If I have made a mistake, I make amends for it and see to it that it is not repeated." The fact remains, however, that one cannot make amends, not even among men. If one has deceived a person, the pain caused by betrayed trust and confidence cannot be, and is not, healed by a confession, no matter how honest. If I have treated someone unfairly or only misjudged him, how can I ever undo or delete the days or years of bitterness I have caused him, even if I overwhelm him with kindness? He must forgive me freely, otherway I cannot expunge my injustice. Proof for the necessarily imperfect human judicial system is clearly seen, among other things, in the fact that the law can in no wise make restitution for imprisonment innocently endured. It is unavoidable in our judicial system that an innocent man is occasionally charged with an offense and is acquitted after he has been jailed for investigation. His liberty and his civic honor can be restored to him, but he had been in possession of these before. How can amends be made for all the torture of soul, and perhaps also for the physical harm, caused by the suspicion resting on him? At that, there was no evil intention involved. In some instances no ill will result, and the affected person will also be sensible enough to realize that an experience of this kind may be unavoidable. However, the alarming element is neither the consequence in the individual case nor the gravity of the consequence; it is the fact *per se*. It is proof that we human beings must remain in debt to one another for many things without any possibility of making full reparation. How much more is this the case when real guilt is involved! Just as the penitence of a murderer cannot bring the slain person back to life—this is the gravest and clearest example—so I cannot make amends for a deed or a thought with which I have sinned against a person. I cannot undo what has been done.

So matters stand between man and man. But the decent man of today who finds the acceptance of mercy below his dignity is entirely oblivious of the main factor: Every sin is first and foremost a sin against God. Both the commandment and the conscience I have violated come from Him. How can I make amends for even a single sinful thought before Him who searches the inmost recesses of my heart? We human beings, and especially the respectable ones among us who are honestly ready to make amends, evade this question in a cowardly manner, this question that takes the ground away from under our feet.

With the recognition of a second fact, the Gospel, as Luther understood it, shatters man's false belief in expiation for our guilt. We may resolve to make reparation for past wrongs by a future bestowal of twofold love on our wronged fellow man, or we may essay to settle past accounts with God by a decision to redouble our efforts to do good in the future. But we are mistaken. Our future has already been disposed of; we no longer own it. Our future days belong to our neighbor as it is, and not only with a twofold or a threefold love but with all the love of which we are capable. As it is, our future belongs to God with all the good words, deeds, and thoughts in our power. We cannot settle a debt by promising or giving either to our neighbor or to God something that belongs to them in any case. We are not our own, but we belong entirely to God and thus also to our neighbor. For this reason we have no hand free, as it were, for dispensing the special gifts of expiation demanded by all religions, including Catholicism. Therefore future good deeds cannot enter into our calculations for the settlement of past debts. The debts we have made remain. (This is what *debt* means.) For these there is no expiation before God and man.

For Luther this realization was so terrible and tormenting because he was a man with a delicate, stern conscience. He wanted to make amends. More accurately, he knew that he had to make amends. Every decent, sensitive child feels an innate urge to make recompense by some token of love for any wrong committed against parents, sisters, or brothers. It finds no peace of mind until it is persuaded that all is again in order. The delicate, earnest conscience of an adult has the same experience. Luther never despised man's impulse to make amends; he regarded it as the best thing in us, for it is our conscience that makes us truly human. Luther expressed contempt for the man who did not manifest this desire to make amends. He viewed indulgence as something altogether inferior, not merely because of the filthy financial transaction and the crude conception of sin but also because it tread the best in man underfoot: the urge to make amends. Indulgence is an agency for changing heavy penalties into lighter ones. To Luther this was both unscrupulous and incomprehensible. Therefore the most profound and most remarkable of his Ninety-five Theses reads: "True penitence desires and loves punishment," that is, the man who is truly aware of his sins wants to atone and make amends to the best of his ability.[4]

However, man cannot really make amends; he cannot undo anything that he has done; he can square no accounts with God or with man. No morbid qualms of conscience drove Luther to despair in the face of this *no* and *not*, but only a childlike, delicate conscience, which had evolved into a wonderful, manly tenderness. "If you do not become as little children"—in these words of Jesus we seek not only the wholesome mind, the well-adjusted oneness, the happy, ready love of a child (not to mention its innocence), but we must also include its childlike, earnest conscientious-

4. "Resolutiones (1518)," WA 1:597.6ff.

ness, which we unfortunately lose lamentably fast and for which, in consequence, adults have only scorn and a lack of understanding. Just as a noble-minded child becomes perplexed and upset if the word of forgiveness is withheld and it finds itself unadjusted in the world, so Luther was distraught in every fiber of his being when he again and again ran his head against this wall: We can make amends for nothing. And we human beings who say that we have a conscience—above all, we Christians—should share this despair with him.

We should have a deep understanding for Luther's experience when, as it were, the portals of paradise opened for him, when he detected the only escape from this hopeless situation, God's own way of escape, when he was called back by God from this insurmountable wall with a thousand voices, both harsh and tender, and learned to surrender himself unconditionally to Him. Luther was intimately acquainted with all the dangerous powers bent on restraining us from this final step: pride and shame, recklessness and unbelief. But he also knew the hellish tortures of a troubled conscience, and he experienced daily that these torments of hell subside and heaven opens as soon as man ventures to seek refuge in the mercy of God. No word was expressive enough for the jubilation over the change that had been wrought. John Franck's words, and still more Bach's musical setting, reflect his heart's exultation:

> Weicht, ihr Trauergeister,
> Denn mein Freudenmeister
> Jesus tritt herein.

> Hence, all fear and sadness!
> For the Lord of gladness,
> Jesus, enters in.

Then Luther also realized that God must lead us over a thorny path, that He must plague us through our conscience, that He must let us ram our heads against the walls of expiation before we can finally comprehend the magnificent either/or and learn to rely solely on God's mercy. With a wonderful word, he designated the work God does in us as God's foreign, God's alien (*alienum*) work. "When God begins to justify a person, He first condemns him; when He wants to build up, He first tears down; whom He wants to heal, He first batters to pieces; whom He wants to bring to life, He first kills."[5] Not until then is God able to initiate His real,

---

5. "Resolutiones (1518)," WA 1:540.8ff.

His true work: to pour out His kindness on us, to make us His children. But "all this purely out of fatherly goodness and mercy"—without works, without expiation, without making amends.

Men who claim to be versed in morality have at all times rebelled against this Lutheran doctrine of justification. They shout: "For heaven's sake, not without good works! What will become of man's moral life if he is taught that he is saved by grace alone?" This was and still is the cry of Catholic theologians: Thus Erasmus spoke and many humanists; thus strict and pious princes said, for example, Duke George of Saxony. The man who had almost bled to death storming the impenetrable wall of human expiation, who had emerged from those hellish tortures amid which he had groped for the right way to God, could listen to these objections only with bewildered astonishment. Whoever spoke thus did not know what it means to meet God. To Luther this meant being dedicated and devoted to Him. Anyone dedicated to God can no longer live immorally in His sight. Furthermore, those who object to Luther's doctrine of justification do not know the meaning of faith. Faith not only means the acknowledgment of this or that biblical teaching as truth nor does it merely signify trust in God, but it means to belong to God wholly. Luther tried to give his opponents a simple answer in his wonderful essay *On Good Works*. In it he declared that it is just like telling one who is sick: Get well first, then you will also have strength to use your arms and legs. How nonsensical it would be on the part of the patient to maintain that he had been told that he need no longer move and use his members! After he has regained his strength, he will move them automatically and voluntarily, and this will no longer be a hardship for him but will be his joy and his most natural life. This is also the story of faith. Faith means health through God. Then an active life, a life of good works, follows as self-evidently as a healthy person moves his limbs.

That faith requires no definite prescriptions and instructions for a life of good works Luther illustrated with another example, an example equally simple. If husband and wife love each other, no directions are necessary for their proper conduct toward each other. Love dictates this to them far better than any moral law can teach them. Their hearts tell them what to say, what to do, when to keep silence. They do not have to search and check whether this or that occasion calls for a great or a small deed; every deed, without exception, is an expression of the same love. Nor are they anxiously puzzled about whether the other is pleased or would have expected something else. They live in the knowledge, in the confidence, that the other person is pleased and will receive everything in the same spirit of love in which it is given. "Therefore a Christian," Luther says,

> who lives in this confidence toward God, knows all things, can do all things, makes bold to do all that is to be done, and performs it all happily and freely, not in order to lay up a store of good works and merits but because he delights in pleasing God. He serves God without expecting payment and is content to please God. On the other hand, he who is not at one with God or entertains doubts regarding this begins to seek and worry how he might render satisfaction to God and move Him with many good works.[6]

The fruit of the belief in God's free grace, as described by Luther, is the glorious ministering spirit of freedom that finds its mainspring in love. The fruit of the religion of man's expiation is an ever-present uncertainty of conscience, constantly in doubt about its record with God and therefore unable to lead a life to the glory and praise of God. In place of the expiatory acts with which the world's religions and also modern moral man want to make amends for past sins, the Lutheran Christian presents his entire life. This is the fruit that grows from the either/or of the Lutheran doctrine of justification. This is not the demand; no, it is the gift of the Gospel to him who believes in it.

In conclusion we must cast another light on all that has been said thus far. This will not alter the facts; however, without this new light the picture would not be seen in its proper perspective. As Luther saw it, the two scenes in a Christian's life—the end of man's expiatory attempts and the gift of God's free grace—are enacted before a curtain, as it were. Now this curtain must be drawn aside, and we discover that what we have considered thus far is only a shadow of the scene behind the curtain. What we saw in the first place as the lot of the individual Christian is at the same time the lot of Christ.

When Luther portrayed that terrible helplessness and despair of a soul confounded and harassed by the expiatory demands of conscience, he often declared that in such moments the soul is crucified with Christ. "Then the soul is nailed to the cross with Christ so that all its bones are being broken and its every recess is filled with the bitterest bitterness, ter-

---

6. "Von den guten Werken (1520)," WA 6:207.26ff.

ror, anxiety, sadness."[7] Conversely, he declared that on the cross Christ had drunk to the dregs the whole cup of man's woes, distress, temptation, and abandonment by God. Luther regarded the outcry "My God, My God, why hast Thou forsaken Me?" as an expression of the bitterest truth and the sorest trial of Jesus' abandonment by God. He is wont to say that Christ became like us and that we become like Him.

What does this mean? Was this a comparison for Luther? Is Christ an image of the tempted and tried man? Is man an image of the tempted and tried Christ? No, in Luther's mind this relationship between Christ and man is completely real. Luther held that on the cross something happened that pertains directly to all mankind, that something happened there to mankind. What does this mean?

We can best catch a glimpse of this secret—one cannot treat the matter more extensively—if we recall what we discussed at the beginning. The mighty law of sin and atonement for sin that is found in all the religions of the world was a testimony for us of the basic and profound conscientiousness of true humanity. The entire legal order and all moral life of mankind are founded on this law. Did God abrogate this law when He, through Jesus Christ and later through His disciple Martin Luther, called mankind away from its attempts to expiate and directed it to God's grace? Has this moral sense of humankind become untrue? Is not conscience, too, the voice of God that abides in us today?

Luther replies with the New Testament: God did not abrogate this primitive law of sin and expiation, but He Himself fulfilled it. He had Him who came in the Father's name not only teach but also die on earth. This is the most terrible guilt with which mankind ever burdened itself; at the same time it is the most terrible punishment all of humanity's sins were punished with at one time. A greater penalty could not be inflicted on mankind, for after incurring this guilt by the infliction of death on God's Ambassador, on God's Son, man's conscience can never again find rest—or it dies. When mankind no longer feels the sting of the cross of Golgotha, it becomes conscienceless, and man again becomes the first animal of creation. But wherever mankind does feel this sting, it realizes in all eternity that with every sin it commits it is carrying nails to the cross.

But God be praised that faith knows more than conscience does. It knows that God Himself, the Father, had His Son die. It knows that in the

---

7. "Resolutiones (1518)," WA 1:558.5ff.

"alien work" the real and true work of God lies embedded. It knows that this most terrible punishment was ordained from the beginning as a punishment to lead to freedom. For this reason the cross, where the paths of God and of man seem to separate completely, becomes the junction for their final and enduring meeting.

On the one hand, the cross confirms our conscience, corroborates our moral consciousness, and strengthens the human legal order of guilt and expiation. On the other hand, the cross is the irrevocable end of all our expiation before God; it is the abode of our reconciliation. At the place where it becomes conclusively and irrefutably clear that man can never come to terms with God, God came to terms with man. There He established the eternal terms on which man can at all times come home to Him.

Therefore all that happens in the Christian life is really only a shadow of that which is enacted behind the curtain. It is always repeated anew. To come to the end of the path of conscience, to the end of all human expiation and making amends, means "to be crucified with Christ." And the life that springs from the glorious liberty of grace is the life of the risen Christ in us.

Many of the world's religions have instituted special days of atonement on which they give definitive expression to the stern law of conscience alive in man. The Christian church has, at various times in its history, set aside especial days of penance. In Germany it was customary to observe these days particularly during the distressing years of the Thirty Years' War. But we observe such days of penance in a truly evangelical spirit only if they become days of faith for us and when our cry rises from the depths to the comforting conviction that God wants to be at our side and to the freedom of a life in God. The call to repentance and the Gospel of joy will ring as clearly and as harmoniously in our proclamation as in the great penitential songs of the Reformation era:

> Wach auf, wach auf, du deutsches Land,
> du hast genug geschlafen.
> Bedenk, was Gott an dich gewandt,
> wozu er dich erschaffen.
> Bedenk, was Gott dir hat gesandt
> und dir vertraut sein höchstes Pfand,
> drum magst du wohl aufwachen.

> Gott hat dir Christum, seinen Sohn,

die Wahrheit und das Leben,
sein liebes Evangelion
aus lauter Gnad gegeben.
Denn Christus ist allein der Mann,
der für der Welt Sünd' g'nug getan,
kein Werk hilft sonst daneben.

THE PICTURE OF NATURE

In the sixteenth century and its peripheries, two genuine revolutions broke through the cover of Occidental intellectual life. They were real revolutions. They contributed something new to the history of mankind, and unlike humanism, they signified more than a return home to ancient wisdom and to the measured and adjusted humanity of bygone ages. The one is the revolution of Christian faith through Luther; the other is a revolution consisting in a new conception of natural science, which was introduced by Nicholas of Cusa and extending through Paracelsus and Copernicus to Bruno, Kepler, and Galileo. The former is the accomplishment of one person—necessarily so in the realm of faith—with an outcome entirely unpremeditated, born solely of truthfulness, which gave direction to the conflict between two worlds in him. The latter was premeditated and prepared in many ways—necessarily so in the realm of science—and is the collective work of human genius, in which a discovered truth, a truth attested in life as well as in death, was transmitted from one to the other. At times a conscious effort was made to avoid confusing the two. Paracelsus declined the appellation "a Luther of medicine" by declaring: "I shall let Luther answer for his own affairs." On principle the Reformation of Luther, who wanted nothing less in the world than to be known as a philosopher, did not interfere with the freedom of the new knowledge in the field of science. From 1586 to 1588 Giordano Bruno found refuge in Lutheran Wittenberg, and in his farewell address he paid tribute to the heroic spirit of Luther and to the land of his birth. But the exact-methodical science accommodated the various religious persuasions: the pious Catholic Copernicus and the faithful Protestant Kepler, as well as the religious individualists Bruno and Galileo.

Despite all this, intellectual revolutions cannot be entirely divorced from one another in the hearts of the same era. It is true that Luther's religious faith also embraced a picture of the world, the picture found in the Bible. This was always tensely alive in him; it was arduously defended when he felt called upon to strike a valiant blow against hated and arrogant reason, and it was magnificently set forth on the basis of words from the Word, that is, the God of the Gospels. But in the clumsier hands of his successors and fused by Melanchthon with the Aristotelian system of science, this picture became the antithesis of the new picture of nature. Conversely, in the mysticism of the Renaissance, culminating in Giordano Bruno and in countless Protestant disciples of Paracelsus, the new view of nature became the essence of religion. Small wonder that these two intellectual movements crossed swords in unnumbered encounters in the dark decades toward the end of the sixteenth century and at the beginning of the seventeenth, a time pregnant with the future. They remained strangers to each other until far into the nineteenth and here and there into the twentieth century, a source of endless spiritual distress to the heart of modern man. In these battles something far more essential and significant was at stake than the front-line trenches of rational doubts and misgivings: the question whether the Lutheran faith had room for an experience of nature to which no one can shut his eyes who has said with Hölderlin: "Da erschienst du, Seele der Natur" ("Then thou, O soul of nature, didst appear").

This introduces a question of the greatest importance in intellectual history. Its answer determines essentially whether Luther is to be regarded as a citizen of medieval or of modern times. We can decide the issue only by addressing the question to Luther himself and by searching his works for words bearing on his view of nature.

On the surface it might seem that this question is readily answered by Luther's vehement rebuke of an astronomer, unknown to him by name, who wanted to prove that the earth moved and that the sun did not revolve about it. Luther charged him with an attempt to turn all astronomy topsy-turvy just to say something novel. For, after all, Joshua had commanded the sun, not the earth, to stand still![1] This utterance of Luther, famed as a statement hostile to natural science, assumes a somewhat different aspect when we recall that it was made before anything by Copernicus had appeared in print and that one of the earliest adherents of

---

1. WATr 4, no. 4638. Cf. Heinrich Bornkamm, "Kopernikus im Urteil der Reformatoren," *Archiv für Reformationsgeschichte* 40 (1943): 171ff.

Copernicus, Erasmus Reinhold, was permitted to teach in Wittenberg at Luther's side without the slightest molestation. It is seen in a different light when one reflects that Luther could not but envisage the effect of the new viewpoint "as if one were seated on a moving ship or wagon but supposes that he is sitting still and that the earth and the trees are moving." It almost seems as if he had to force himself to visualize this rejected theory and to picture to himself a reversal of previous conceptions of motion. But even these statements, taken from a table conversation and thus naturally inadequate for a judgment concerning Luther's attitude toward natural science, reflect his strong faculty of observation of nature.

This enabled Luther to derive a profusion of metaphors from the realm of nature. In his last year he wrote in a volume of Pliny: "All creation is the most beautiful book or Bible; in it God has described and portrayed Himself."[2] In the various phenomena of nature Luther felt the presence of God vividly. The clouds are on the wing like birds; they are God's pinions. Out of His impregnable fortress of clouds God shoots His lightning. Mountains melt at His approach.[3] A vast panorama is unfolded before Luther at the sound of thunder: The devils have planned a disputation, but an angel has swooped down and has torn a hole in their theses.[4] On another occasion Luther termed a thunderstorm "eternal prophets," meaning that even in this time of grace the terrors of God's Law may overtake us in our conscience. The dew that falls at the dawn of day and particularly in the spring, the merriest season of the year, is an image of the Holy Spirit, who delights in creating Christians.[5] The break of day pictures the Christian, who is sinner and saint in one person, who is neither night nor day but changes more and more into day as the shadows of night recede.[6] The red morning sky (*aurora*) itself resembles the comforting, joyful proclamation of the Gospel. Summer and winter are comparable to periods of peace of mind and to periods of trials and temptations by sin or sorrow.[7]

From this portrayal of an irreconcilable antagonism between the seasons of the year and the seasons of the mind, one might be tempted to

---

2. WA 48:201.5. Cf. Hans Preusz, *M. Luther, der Künstler* (1931), 229ff.

3. "25 Psalmen (1530)," WA 31/1:328f.

4. WATr 3, no. 3507.

5. "Sermon (May 29, 1535)," WA 41:163.4.

6. "Commentary on Galatians (1519)," WA 2:586.9ff.

7. "Psalm 147 (1532)," WA 31/1:447.15.

infer that Luther, like the Manichaeans, accepted two hostile gods who govern the world. Yet it is one and the same God who controls both the change of the seasons and the variations in the inner life of man. Even from the winter of trials we should learn "what a precious time summer is and what praise and gratitude it deserves. However, we are as accustomed to it as we are to the sun itself. Our daily enjoyment of God's gifts renders them too commonplace, paltry, and insignificant for us." A mild breeze becomes an image of the Gospel, which melts the winter of the heart. The ever-discontented world is "a head of a thistle; no matter which way it is turned, it invariably directs its prickles upwards."[8]

For years on end Luther did not miss an opportunity to preach about the birds under the heavens and about the lilies in the field, blooming there to our shame, for we have no eye and no ear for their message. The healthy and well-fed birds—which have clothing, trousers, jackets, and kitchens and cellars so extensive that they cannot fly across them—call to us: "Well, are you in need of the Frankfurt Fair to acquire clothing? If you disdain to accept our God as your Father, you must have the gulden as your lord."[9] Thus the birds are like living saints. They work, and they fly hither and yon, as they must; but they merrily let God provide for them.[10] Forest and garden, field and yard afford Luther a rich sphere for observing God's dealings with men and man's conduct toward his fellow man. The honeybees, their little paunches filled with honey, are troubled by the bumblebees, which steal the honey and devour everything the pious little bees produce. They are a picture of the sectarians and the factious spirits who invade the church, also of the gentlemen at court who are a burden to the people.[11] Luther's description of the diet of the jackdaws and the crows at the Coburg is both charming and graphic.[12] The birds convene under the mighty vault of heaven, which is solid and firm without columns.[13] The miracle of Christ's presence in the Eucharist is explained by means of the miraculous sunlight, which is there for all without being divided. Luther's supply of such imagery is inexhaustible.

---

8. "Psalm 101 (1534–1535)," WA 51:246.3.

9. "Sermon on Matthew 6:24ff. (1528)," WA 27:346.9.

10. "Sermon on Matthew 6:24ff. (1534)," WA 87:531f.

11. "Psalm 101 (1534–1535)," WA 51:228.13, 236.3.

12. Letters of April 24 and 26, 1530.

13. Letter of August 5, 1530.

Luther made such abundant use of imagery not only because of the freedom of poetic imagination but also because he was aware of a deeper right to do so. He believed that nature is to be explored not for its own sake but because it is a sign. It is a sign in a twofold sense: first, a sign of a more deeply hidden wisdom of God, which is to become manifest through this sign; second, a sign of the purpose nature serves. Of course, Luther is still ignorant of the modern scientist's passionate devotion to science for science' sake. He wants to know the purpose and the objectives of nature, how life springs from life, and how nature's forces constantly engage in a wonderful play and counterplay of action. Any interested person, Luther declares, will perceive that there is still "much secret activity in nature. And whoever is able to apply this performs more wondrous deeds than those who do not possess this skill."[14] All medical skill is based on this knowledge of associations and interrelationships, that is, the function of each single particle in the whole of nature. This was the magic art of antiquity, which Luther again recognized in the physiology of his own day. To be sure, he lamented with Paracelsus that the peasants were better versed in this than the scholars at the universities. Only experience, not abstraction, can bring one to this knowledge. But because the secret associations of nature, which at the same time are also associations in and with God, manifest themselves here, it is more than a playful symbolism when he finds that this also points man from the things in nature to Christ and to the questions of human existence. If only one recognizes nature in its real naturalness, one can reasonably regard it as a symbol of things invisible.

For this recognition of nature in its naturalness, devoid of all preconceived ideas and of purposes not served by nature, Luther had the necessary talent, the prerequisite for a proper study of nature: a sense of genuine, primal wonder and awe. How amazing is the spawning of the fish, the propagation of the birds by means of an egg! "If an egg were no familiar sight to us and someone brought us one from Calcutta, how astounded we would be!"[15] "We possess such beautiful creatures; but we pay little attention to them, because they are so common."[16] Who, after all, marvels at the miracle of the human organism? "This is due solely to the fact that

---

14. "Kirchenpostille (1522)," WA 10/1.1:560.9.

15. WATr 3, no. 3390.

16. WATr 5, no. 5539.

people have never scrutinized a creature closely."[17] "If you really examined a kernel of grain thoroughly, you would die of wonderment."[18] A true faith must have clear eyes for the miracle of creation as it is celebrated in Psalm 104. This psalm "sings and takes great delight in God's creatures, so wondrously fashioned and so beautifully coordinated. But who pays any heed to this and views them thus? Only faith and the spirit."[19]

Most people are ignorant of these works of God.

> They are so accustomed to them; they are as permeated with them as an old house is with smoke; they use them and wallow around in them like a sow in an oats sack. Oh, they say, is it so marvelous that the sun shines? That fire heats? That water contains fish? That hens lay eggs? That the earth yields grain? That a cow bears calves? That a woman gives birth to children? Why, this happens every day! You dear dolt Hans, must it be insignificant because it happens daily? If the sun ceased to shine for ten days, then its shining would surely be regarded as a great work. If fire were to be found only in one spot in the world, I judge that it would be esteemed more precious than all gold and silver. If there were only one well in the world, I suppose that one drop of water would be priced at above 100,000 gulden and that wine and beer would be considered filth by comparison. If God created all other women and children of bone, as He did Eve, and but one woman were able to bear children, I maintain that the whole world, kings and lords, would worship her as a divinity. But now that every woman is fruitful, it passes for nothing. If a magician could make a live eye, one able to see for the distance of a yard—God help us, what a lord he would become on earth! Yes, anyone who could fashion a real leaf or a blossom on a tree would have to be elevated above God and receive the admiration, the praise, and the gratitude of the whole world. But is it not vexing to see the accursed ingratitude and blindness of mankind? God showers man with such great and rich miracles, but man ignores them all and thanks God for none.[20]

Only the eyes of "the upright" (*der Aufrichtigen*), as Luther translated the term at the time in Psalm 111, only they who accord God the honor, recognize God's wonders.

---

17. "Sermon von dem Sakrament," WA 19:487.25.

18. "Sermon von dem Sakrament," WA 19:496.11.

19. "Summarien über die Psalmen (1531–1533)," WA 38:53.15ff.

20. "Psalm 111 (1530)," WA 31/1:407.28ff.

For whenever they behold a work of God, they imagine how conditions would be without it. Death ennobles life, darkness praises the sun, hunger kisses the precious bread, sickness teaches the meaning of health, etc. The word "not" prompts them to praise the "being" [*Wesen*], and this implies that they search, explore, and ponder the works of the Lord, esteem them, and imagine what the world would be like if these works had not been created. Then they rejoice over them and behold them as real miracles.[21]

Therefore Luther could proudly boast—as compared to both the papacy and the ignorance of nature to be found in the writings of the humanists—of having awakened a new interest in the works of creation.

> We are now living in the dawn of the future life; for we are beginning to regain a knowledge of the creation, a knowledge we had forfeited by the fall of Adam. Now we have a correct view of the creatures, more so, I suppose, than they have in the papacy. Erasmus does not concern himself with this; it interests him little how the fetus is made, formed, and developed in the womb. Thus he also fails to prize the excellency of the state of marriage. But by God's mercy we can begin to recognize His wonderful works and wonders also in the flowers when we ponder His might and His goodness. Therefore we laud, magnify, and thank Him. In His creatures we recognize the power of His Word. By His Word everything came into being. This power is evident even in a peach stone. No matter how hard its shell, in due season it is forced open by a very soft kernel inside it. All this is ignored by Erasmus. He looks at the creatures as a cow stares at a new gate.[22]

Luther's open delight in reality and the sincere awe with which he viewed even the most insignificant miracle in nature not only reveal an astonishing observation of details—in his final compliment paid to Eck at the Leipzig Debate, he said that Eck penetrated the Scriptures just as little as a water spider does the water[23]—but behind all this one also discovers views of far wider scope, pertaining to all of life in nature.

On no other branch of nature study did Luther have so much occasion to express himself as on astrology, the ill-bred child of the science of astronomy. His entire century—including nearly all the humanists—shared in the belief in astrology. Copernicus and Kepler clung to it. In

21. "Psalm 111 (1530)," WA 31/1:408.22ff. Also consult Luther's interpretation of "Psalm 118:1 (1530)," WA 30/1:69ff.

22. WATr 1, no. 1160.

23. WA 2:382.20.

Luther's own circles horoscopes were cast and constellations were studied. Melanchthon kept dinning his evil forebodings and dismal prophecies into Luther's ears. Luther mockingly said that Melanchthon pursued the study of astrology "as I take a drink of strong beer when I am troubled with grievous thoughts."[24] Thanks to thorough instruction in natural philosophy in Erfurt, Luther cast the superstition of his time aside. He admittedly also believed that comets, rainbows, and other phenomena in the heavens could be signs and hints from God, as everything in nature was a sign to him. But it seemed ridiculous and impious to him to try to make this a science. Events are not dependent on the stars but on God. "Our God does not consult the sky."[25] To regard astrology as "an exact science" is depriving man of the comfort granted him by an unconditional trust in the unknowable and inscrutable will of God. With a faith-inspired defiance that surrenders unconditionally to an unsearchable God, Luther opposed the superstitious attempt to attain a feeling of security by means of astrology amid the uncertainties of human existence. However, he marshaled not only his faith against the evil of superstition, he also enlisted reason and good judgment in his cause. They afforded him an insight into the legitimate domain of the study of nature. Astrology has no proof to adduce in its support as astronomy and mathematics have. It is not based on symptoms and experience as medicine is. Luther rejected astrology primarily because it has no basis in experience. This brands it as impossible for his conception of nature. No one is able to test and check the claims of astrologers. Therefore Luther jeeringly quoted the proverb: "It is safe to lie about distant lands."[26] There is a deep gulf between astrology and Luther's concept of science: "Science consists in differentiating and sifting, but astrology deals only with generalities."[27] It presumes to apply general statements to what is specific. All people born under the same sign of the zodiac are consigned to the same fate. Luther posed the age-old question: How, then, do you explain the case of twins whose lives take a radically different course?[28] Furthermore, one can never determine which star of a

---

24. WATr 1, no. 17.

25. WATr 4, no. 4846.

26. "Kirchenpostille (1522)," WA 10/1.1:566ff.

27. WATr 2, no. 2120.

28. WATr 4, no. 4846; WATr 5, no. 5573.

constellation exerts its influence upon a life. Luther inferred from this that all true science must sift and must pay heed to what is concrete.[29]

Astrology's real weakness is its materialism. It speaks about the effects of the celestial matter on the fate of man and forgets that this matter is unformed and therefore no definite influences can be claimed for it. As a board lends itself to the manufacture of a table, a blackboard, or some other object, so also the material influence of the stars is entirely indeterminable.[30] In nature, form prevails, and that means purpose and will; only from these can concrete and definite effects issue.

Furthermore, it is exceedingly stupid to try to maintain such definite claims of astrology in view of the vastness of the cosmos. If the earth is as small in the family of the celestial bodies as the astronomers declare, then it must be the intersecting point of countless lines of influence of the stars. This quashes every claim of astrology.[31] Luther is firmly convinced that the immeasurableness of the cosmos stamps astrology's calculations for the benefit of puny man as ridiculous.

Thus in Luther's polemic the application of a profound understanding is evident everywhere: natural science as a science of experience and proof, as skill in sifting facts; the cosmos ruled by forces of form, will, and purpose in a space so vast that it defies any practical human application. Nature is based on the immutability of the species, as is amply demonstrated by the animal and the vegetable kingdoms. Dissenting from most of his contemporaries, Luther also rejects alchemy because it disregards insuperable barriers.[32]

Despite the fact that all these views were sound, keen, and astonishingly untainted by his century's prejudices, Luther was no natural scientist. His views on nature are not the measure of his scientific knowledge; they are, intrinsically, the reflex of his religion. Is Luther not the father of such a personalized God and of His creative activity that no bridge can be built from there to the new and vigorous perception of nature? Without any doubt Luther clung to the biblical image of God with the ardor of a deeply disturbed and tried soul and with the despair of a person who again and again sought his way through to assurance and peace of mind. But

29. WATr 1, no. 857.

30. WATr 5, no. 5734.

31. WATr 1, no. 589.

32. WATr 5, no. 5671.

remarkable circumstances forced Luther to rethink the image of God and to reflect on the relationship of this God to nature. He was driven to defend the reality of Christ's presence in Holy Communion against Zwingli, the humanists, and the enthusiasts. Hard-pressed by his adversaries, he revealed, little by little, the most magnificent lineaments of his picture of God. How can the eternal Christ, who sits at the right hand of God the Father and participates in the rule of the world, appear in the poor little morsel of bread in Communion? How can He, who ascended into heaven outside space, again be present in space? Those were some of his opponents' pointed questions with which he had to cope.

This unavoidably poses the question regarding the existence of God in and outside nature. According to Luther,

> it is vulgar and stupid to suppose that God is a huge, fat being who fills the world, similar to a stack of straw filled to the top and beyond. . . . We do not put it this way. We do not say that God is such a distended, long, broad, thick, tall, deep being, but that He is a supernatural, inscrutable being able to be present entirely in every small kernel of grain and at the same time in all, above all, and outside all creatures. Nothing is so small that God cannot be still smaller; nothing so broad that God cannot be broader; nothing so narrow that God cannot be narrower.[33]

These words involuntarily bring Nicholas of Cusa to mind. No matter how far removed Luther's thinking was from the Christian Platonism of Cusanus, it must be said that Luther contemplated and experienced the coincidence of the infinitely biggest and the infinitely smallest in God just as vividly. Luther's dynamic concept of God and of God's infinity externally and internally stem from the same elemental feeling that broke through the scholastic system in Cusanus.

> The divine power cannot be contained and measured, for it is incomprehensible and immeasurable, outside and above all that exists. But at the same time it must really be present in all places, even in the most insignificant leaf of a tree.[34]

> God is substantially present everywhere, in and through all creatures, in all their parts and places, so that the world is full of God and He fills all, but without His being encompassed and surrounded by it. He is at the same

---

33. "Vom Abendmahl Christi (1528)," WA 26:339.25ff.

34. "Dass diese Worte Christi . . . (1527)," WA 23:132.26. See also the quotations on pp. 57f.

time outside and above all creatures. These are all exceedingly incomprehensible matters; yet they are articles of our faith and are attested clearly and mightily in Holy Writ. . . . For how can reason tolerate it that the Divine Majesty is so small that it can be substantially present in a grain, on a grain, over a grain, through a grain, within and without, and that, although it is a single Majesty, it nevertheless is entirely in each grain separately, no matter how immeasurably numerous these grains may be? . . . And that same Majesty is so large that neither this world nor a thousand worlds can encompass it and say: "Behold, there it is!" . . . His own divine essence can be in all creatures collectively and in each one individually more profoundly, more intimately, more present than the creature is in itself; yet it can be encompassed nowhere and by no one. It encompasses all things and dwells in all, but not one thing encompasses it and dwells in it.[35]

Luther also philosophizes on the question of space. Christ, who is seated at the right hand of God the Father, is not confined to a space outside space, as the enthusiasts, Zwingli, and even Calvin naively imagined. The idea of space is eliminated altogether. God, with whom Christ is consubstantial, is inside and outside space simultaneously. He is independent of all concepts of space. But this may mean that He is only in one single spot and everywhere at the same time. Luther portrayed the immanence of God in all creatures most vividly. At the mention of "God in all creatures," reason always envisages straw in the sack or bread in the basket. "But faith realizes that the preposition 'in' used here includes over, outside, under, through, through once more, and everywhere."[36] This God is everywhere and nowhere, thus Christ, who is identical with God, is far, far outside the creatures, just as far outside as God is outside and just as far in, and close to, all creatures as God is. To be sure, Luther did not think he was pronouncing a profound article of faith with these words; after all, they relate only to questions belonging in the forecourt of religion. More wonderful by far than this immanence of God and Christ is the fact that Christ enters our bruised and sin-laden hearts. This miracle transcends all others. "But God retains the smaller miracles that through them He may remind us of the greater ones."[37]

Thus Luther spoke of the fervid indwelling of God in nature in terms as impressive as those used by, for example, Giordano Bruno: "Not with-

---

35. "Dass diese Worte Christi . . . (1527)," WA 23:134.34–136.36.

36. "Vom Abendmahl Christi (1528)," WA 26:341.13.

37. "Sermon von dem Sakrament (1526)," WA 19:493.24.

out reason has it been said that God fills all things, that He is immanent in all particles of the universe, that He is the central point of all existence, One in all, and He who through all is one. Since He is all and in Himself contains all that exists, one may finally say: Everything is in everything."[38] The picturesque language employed by Luther to describe God's presence is the same as that used by Bruno. We have an idea of God's omnipresence in the voice that fills space and in the omnipresent qualities of the sun and light.

Yet we find Luther's concept of God radically at variance with the pantheistic mystics of Bruno's type. This seemingly manifest God is concealed for Luther because no one is able to recognize His will merely from His presence. "For although He is everywhere, in all creatures, and although I could find Him in a stone, in fire, in water, or even in a rope (for He surely is there), still He does not want me to look for Him apart from the Word. . . . Search for Him where the Word is. There you will surely find Him. Otherwise you only tempt God and establish idolatry."[39] Thus nature is not the revelation but only the mask of the omnipresent God, a mask thoroughly permeated by Him. "Therefore it must be our skill to distinguish between God and His mask. The world cannot do this."[40]

Another reason for exercising this skill is found in the fact that nature is also subject to the fate that oppresses the whole world. This does not refer to the transitoriness common to all, for the alternation of life and death is God's order.[41] But according to the words of St. Paul (which never lost their mysterious sound for Luther), the vanity to which the creature remains subdued is the sin-laden human race, which nature must serve unwillingly. Luther paints a vivid picture of nature's repeated attempts to shake off this accursed dominion by means of hail and floods, sickness and earthquakes. He declared that sun and moon would rather surrender their light than be forced to illuminate robbery and other shame. Weeds and vermin, sickness and the debility of the aged still betoken something of the curse sin has cast on the world. In Luther's paean on nature, we hear an

---

38. *Opera ed. de Lagarde*, 1:279. Cf. Heinrich Bornkamm, "Renaissancemystik, Luther und Böhme," *Lutherjahrbuch* 9 (1927): 156ff. Bruno has in mind Nicholas of Cusa; cf. *De docta ignorantia*, 2:5.

39. "Sermon von dem Sakrament (1526)," WA 19:492.19.

40. "Commentary on Galatians (1531)," WA 40/1:174.3.

41. "Sermon on Romans 8:18ff. (1535)," WA 41:307ff.

undertone of sadness—a tone different from that of the contemporary Renaissance mysticism or even of Bruno's new pious religion that jubilantly announces the harmony of the cosmos. Luther's viewpoint does not have a mythological tinge, as some might be tempted to judge; no, it finds its being in a conviction, flowing forth with poetic force, of the loneliness and the forsakenness of sinful man in the world. With terrible and ever-growing animation, Luther describes the despair of a conscience that has not only become loathsome to itself but sees itself surrounded by enemies on all sides, "all creatures, together with God, against it." Through the circle of nature's menacing powers, the terrified conscience flees back and forth like Cain and many other murderers for whom heaven and earth "have assumed a different face"; even a rustling leaf may frighten it.[42] Luther did not give way to gnostic speculation about a possible fall of the world. Creation itself is not contaminated by sin; no, it is good. "The nature of animals has remained as it was created."[43] But it is subject to man's abuse. According to Luther, God's self-evident order to man to rule the world resulted in a curse for nature. Through man's restiveness and dissatisfaction, the order of creation was disturbed. Thus God was obliged to chastise man with the very possession entrusted to him, that is, nature. Therefore man is pathetically alone in the world with his guilt. It is only God's boundless mercy that tolerates and preserves him and the earth. This profound feeling of Luther concerning nature finds its roots in his faith.

As we survey the essential elements of Luther's perception of nature and its relationship to God, we find that primarily he approached the new cognition of nature in two respects: first, with his keen eye for reality, with his awe and his attentiveness for the great and also the small and insignificant things in nature, of which the life of nature consists. In Luther there is something of that passionate zeal for painstaking observation and investigation that begat modern natural science. Second, Luther had a profound understanding of the infinity of the world. This is embedded in the boundless and all-pervading presence of a God who is so distant and at the same time so near.

Luther divested God's personality of all that is anthropomorphous and naive. In it we find the all-pervading fullness of natural life, but in a hid-

42. See Heinrich Bornkamm, *Luther und das Alte Testament* (Tübingen: Mohr, 1948), 50ff.
43. WATr 1, no. 678.

den manner that constrains man to find this God as a personality through faith in His Word. Luther by no means destroyed the idea of the person of this creating, consoling, and pardoning God; in faith he bridged the great distance between this God, personalized in Christ, and His hidden vibrant activity and life in all and through all forms in nature.

The question whether it was and is still possible to find a path from Luther's concept of God and the world to the modern perception of nature is hardly necessary any longer. For a time this task was neglected. No one was capable of the boldness of Luther's idea of God and his radical openness of mind toward the reality of nature. Melanchthon's baneful domination of Protestant theology by means of his textbooks went even less challenged in this theological-philosophical frontier than in other domains. Under Melanchthon it again became fashionable and ultrawise to reconcile the biblical concept of the world with the system of Aristotle, who was so genuinely hated by Luther. In this scheme, astrology was accorded abundant space. Thus a theological-philosophical fusion originated, which because of its alliance involved mutual obligations and by preconceived ideas handicapped any natural cognition. The natural system of the sciences, which strove to develop science according to universal and rational principles, destroyed for the time, through the philosophical-theological tradition, the immediateness and the realism of cognition of nature emerging in Luther. A punier generation again preached a God humanly conceived and far removed from the earth, who had, to be sure, once upon a time laid out His garden of creation and perhaps still occasionally manifests an interest in it. The nature-mystics of the time, above all Jakob Böhme, and the young intellectuals of the beginning of the seventeenth century contended against this viewpoint and, after much internal conflict and against opposition from without, overcame it. Until far into modern times, an uncertainty and indecision devoid of the magnificent freedom once displayed by Luther prevailed in Protestant thinking on questions of nature. His rich bequest to posterity had been dissipated. When the modern view of nature insistently rapped at the church's and at theology's door for admittance, there was no one who ventured to reach for the treasure that lay at hand in Luther's views for a true approach to the modern concept.

GOD AND HISTORY

The fact that we humans not only come into this world, grow, and die like animals, that we not only bloom and wither like plants, was emphatically brought home to our generation by the World Wars. A determinant power reaches into our personal life, a life affected by a long line of ancestors, and this power is a destiny we cannot escape. By birth we have been thrust into this warring century and into no other. We have been born into a particular nation, and we share its destiny whether we want to or not. All our plans of life are constantly thwarted and changed by the destiny imposed on us. War has reached its mighty hand into our lives. It has ruthlessly severed the thread of life of countless young people who, under normal conditions, might have enjoyed a long career. Yet we not only suffer this fate, we ourselves also shape it. Human decisions determine the distant future of individuals and of nations. This enigmatic activity that entangles us humans—whether active or passive, free or bound in its meshes—we call history. It is but natural that humankind has ever pondered this activity that distinguishes us from all other living beings. But there are times when historical happenings conglomerate and attack with such elemental force and fury that we stand aghast and shaken with fear, especially when these happenings pose not only a riddle of life but also an enigma of God. What is the meaning of this endless alternation of victory and defeat, of this hopeless snarl of compulsion and deed, of destiny and guilt, of great and terrible things, not only *per se* but also what do they mean in the sight of God? All thoughtful men brood over these questions today and usually peer into abysses that make us giddy. At such a time we look for a footing and for help from which we expect not only

161

satisfactory formulas for the present but order and clarification in our questioning and in our thinking. We shall attempt to have Luther render us this service.

Questions about the nature and the meaning of history are not peculiar to us Christians. They are common to all men and to all times. Therefore it may be well to interview Luther first with regard to his view of history as seen with his human eyes and later as beheld with his eyes of faith. Luther stressed three essential factors that shape history: the nation, the law, and the great men.

Luther possessed—especially when one considers that he never left Germany for more than the few weeks spent in Italy—a discerning eye for distinctive national characteristics. With delight he contemplated the richness of divine creation reflected in the human race. Clearly he perceived the traits distinctive of other nations, and he earnestly admonished his Germans to emulate their virtues. At the same time he gloried in his membership in the German race. With a precise brush he limned the various tribes comprising the German nation. It seemed entirely natural to him that God did not shape all the nations on the same last. Because of their dissimilarities, God also ordained segregating boundaries for each. In contrast to the humanists, who persisted in their medieval dream of German supernational dominion, Luther regarded empire and nation (*Volk*) as coextensive and identical. Each nation has a right, virtually a divine command, to live according to its own laws. French laws concern us just as little as the old Saxon law code concerns the French.

But Luther also recognized a caricature of this basic historical entity called a nation: the mob. He abhorred and feared the lawless and undisciplined rabble as much as he delighted in an orderly and well-governed people. Luther witnessed the spectacle of an unleashed mob on several occasions, especially at the beginning of the Peasants' War, when he himself attempted to mediate between peasants and government to forestall imminent bloodshed. At that time he found his deepest concern regarding the "mad mob," the "Mr. Everybody," confirmed. He shuddered at the thought that an unbridled rabble might someday be at the helm. Therefore he opposed it as passionately as he did the enemies of the Gospel. Ill-informed lectures and books often accuse Luther of having betrayed the common people's cause by his refusal to give ear to the peasants' petition. This is wrong. He set himself against the rebellion of the masses because he foresaw clearly and correctly that greater evil would ensue. The unleashed mob is a satanic distortion of the nation, an element of destruction, whereas the nation represents an element of life. A sharp line of demarcation separates the two. When a people regards itself as the only historical constituent, when it imagines that no barriers and limitations have been set to its wishes and demands, when it no longer respects law and order, it becomes a rabble, a mob actuated by desires and emotions.

Law draws the line that separates the nation from the mob. This is the second element of historical life. The peoples with their inherent national traits form its natural basis, but law is its indispensable power for order. Without this power, everything would be doomed to chaos. The state is law's visible form through which God Himself has erected a dam against the onslaught of human passions, avarice, and violence that otherwise would devastate the world. Only through the salutary restraint of the state, through law and punitive power, can order be maintained in the world. Thus the state is God's wonderful gift for humanity's own preservation. Therefore Luther called upon Christians to cooperate willingly and zealously in the maintenance of this divine order. Law and government are the innate strength of the state. They are God's gift and command to the world. Luther held that next to the office of the ministry there exists "on earth no more precious gem, no greater treasure, no richer alms, no more beautiful endowment, no more cherished possession than government, which creates and preserves order."[1]

Because the law is God's precious gift, we have to respect it. Men cannot dispose of it or evade it with impunity, neither as individuals nor as nations. Christians above all others are qualified to fill the God-given judicial offices that preside over the law. They are, as Luther was wont to say, "living laws or the soul of the law." It is the judge's duty to thread his difficult way between severity and leniency, between the letter and the spirit of the law. Who could be better suited to this than he who is not forgetful of the biblical reminder: "Ye judge not for man, but for the LORD" (2 Chronicles 19:6)? A judge "must subdue all passions, fear, love, bias, pity, avarice, hope, praise, life, and death; he must be a sincere disciple of unadulterated truth and of justice."[2] Who can do this without a sincere belief in God and without acknowledging that there is a judge above himself?

But the wonderful world of law and state are under the same curse as the nations. A demonic caricature raises its head also from this world:

---

1. "Psalm 82 (1530)," WA 31/1:201.16.

2. "Deuteronomy (1525)," WA14:667.1.

violence. Violence is usurped law, a law unrestrained and deprived of a sense of right and wrong. It either disguises itself with studied dexterity as law, or it poses with brutal openness as law. Thus it has always been in the world. The biblical words "The law is slacked, and judgment doth never go forth" (Habakkuk 1:4) have been proved true a thousandfold. These words reveal "the world's true colors."[3] Overweening pride often makes that which is great in history end in gross injustice. *Magna imperia, magnae iniuriae.*[4] In his insatiability man prostitutes God's wonderful gift of the state and of law and order. He abuses it, just as he disgraces and misuses the gifts of nature and transforms this beautiful world into a vale of tears.

The law-abiding people and the regulating power of the law constitute the normal life, as it were, of history. But there is a third, extraordinary, downright unpredictable factor: the great men. Only in them does the life of history really find its fulfillment. Not until one of these "miracle men or sound heroes" ("Wundermänner oder gesunde Helden"), as Luther splendidly calls them, is presented to a nation can one sense what government is. Without them, government is bungling and makeshift.

> The world is indeed a sick thing; it is the kind of fur on which neither hide nor hair is any good. The healthy heroes are rare, and God provides them at a high price. Still the world must be ruled if men are not to become wild beasts. So things in the world in general remain mere patchwork and beggary; it is a veritable hospital, in which princes, lords, and all rulers lack wisdom and courage—that is, success and direction from God—even as the sick person lacks strength and power. So here one must patch and darn and help oneself with the laws, sayings, and examples of the heroes as they are recorded in books. Thus we must continue to be disciples of those speechless masters which we call books. Yet we never do it as well as it is written there; we crawl after it and cling to it as to a bench or to a cane. In addition, we also follow the advice of the best people who live in our midst, until the time comes in which God again provides a healthy hero or a wondrous man in whose hand all things improve or at least fare better than is written in any book. Either he changes the law, or he overrules it in such a way that all things flourish and prosper in the land with peace and discipline, protection and punishment. Moreover, during his lifetime he is feared and honored and loved in the highest degree; and after death he is eternally praised.[5]

---

3. "Habakkuk (1526)," WA 19:361.14.

4. "Lectures on Isaiah (1527–1530)," WA 31/2:96.39ff.

5. "Psalm 101 (1534–1535)," WA 51:214f. Translation by Alfred von Rohr Sauer.

These are the masters, exactly as there are born masters among crafts-men, artists, scholars, indeed in every vocation. Even "among boys or apprentices" there are some who give promise of future leadership. No one can teach these miracle men the art of statesmanship; they have it at their fingertips. "Before they are taught, they have already accomplished what they are to do." These great men, these born leaders, are God's gracious gifts that He dispenses when it suits His purpose. God acknowledges them as His own in a special manner; they live under "a special star before God." They "also enjoy a good wind on earth and, as one says, good fortune or victory. What they undertake prospers. And though the entire world opposes their plan, it must succeed unhindered. For God, who has put the thoughts into their hearts and actuates their minds and their courage, will also enable them to carry out their thoughts and bring them to pass."[6]

However, into this wonderful scene its demonic caricature again intrudes itself, as it does into that of the people and that of the law. This picture is marred and distorted by those whose greatness exists only in their own imagination. Luther styled these the apes of the miracle men because they ape the latter in everything. The men of real genius do not stand in need of counsel; they are more adept in their calling than all their counselors. "The apes, however, should reasonably take advice, as they indeed stand in need of it. But they refuse to do this. They want to be the equals of the miracle men and to imitate them. For the devil rides and guides them."[7] So long as such aping is confined to any insignificant activity (such as a trade or domestic matters), the damage is not great. "But when it involves nation and people, kingdoms, principalities, and similar important affairs, both in war and in peace, so that one who is no more than a clown and undertakes a task for which he has not been created aspires to be a Hannibal—that is the cursed devil, and he causes misery and every misfortune." Only Satan can rejoice over these men; they are his "miracle men."

The same sharp line of demarcation we discover between the people and the mob and between law and violence separates the great men from those who ape them. But just as a nation can degenerate into a mob and law can be changed into violence, so the great men themselves can also go out of bounds. Luther observed the sinister fact in history that even great

---

6. "Psalm 101 (1534–1535)," WA 51:207.23.

7. "Psalm 101 (1534–1535)," WA 51:211f.

men may suddenly lose their footing and be irretrievably lost. This happens when they "become overweening and tempt fortune too severely." Then "the hour strikes in which God withdraws His hand because of their presumption and ingratitude. Thereupon they fall in such a way that neither counsel nor reason can help them any longer, and they must perish as Hannibal did." Luther was much perturbed over the danger that lurks in the heart of the man elevated above his fellows and that can change his rise into a rapid fall. These great men may be able to dispense with the counsel of men, but they stand all the more in need of the counsel of God's Word, "which teaches them to attribute all their good fortune and all their great accomplishments to God, according Him the honor as the Giver, and to desist from praising themselves for things which they cannot do or know how to do without God's Word. Otherwise, as all history testifies, these great men seldom come to a good end."[8]

This is, in brief outline, Luther's picture of historical life, a picture affording us a glimpse into the marked discord rampant in all phases of human-historical existence. He gained this insight both through keen observation of history and through experience. He beheld demonic caricatures and counterforces arrayed against the strength of the nations, against the law, and against the great men. These are mortal enemies. For this reason there is no tranquillity in history, but there is an incessant struggle between divine and satanic powers. God's great deeds and gifts make the devil restive. He whom God still permits to have space and power in this world plays his trump cards: the demons of the mob, of violence, and of arrogance.

But we have already passed beyond all that Luther perceives in history with his physical eye. With a little training, it is a relatively easy matter for us to discern this disharmony in historical happenings. But for the hidden struggle between the divine and the demonic, between the power of good and of evil, we require the sharpened eyes of faith. This sight alone beholds the proper perspective depth in the picture of history. Faith inquires into the invisible background of historical space. Where is God in these tangled happenings?

Luther's summary answer to this question was: everywhere. He not only resides in the good and noble forces, but He also imparts life to the

---

8. "Psalm 101 (1534–1535)," WA 51:207.30ff. "Si monarchae hätten das Ego feci auslassen, diutius" ("Stufenpsalmen [1532–1533]," WA 40/3:225.9).

evil and demonic. The devil and evil also owe their existence to God's omnipotence. Why God still does this and why He does not emerge from the darkness and lead His cause to victory is a tormenting mystery. Luther could not fathom it nor can we. However, we dare not ignore it either; otherwise we would be doubting God's omnipotence. Luther declared with extraordinary boldness that God is the life of all history, just as He is also the life of the whole realm of nature. To be sure, it is a hidden life in which it is often difficult to recognize the divine element.[9] In it God is disguised and concealed, as a man may hide behind a mask. All events of history, all men of history, and all forces of history are masks of God, who works all in all. He is just as present in the mask of the peacefully sowing or plowing peasant as He is in that of Hannibal or Alexander the Great, through whom He performed great deeds. "He Himself works through us, and we are only His masks behind which He conceals Himself and works all in all, as we Christians most assuredly know."[10] Therefore a nation should never rely on the strength of its armaments; it must know who is hidden behind these and who alone can achieve the victory.

> All such preparation and armament must be regarded as our Lord's mummery behind which He alone operates and carries our desires to fruition. . . . One may indeed say that the course of world events and especially the activities of His saints are God's mummery behind which He hides Himself and reigns and bestirs Himself in the world so wonderfully.[11]

> The soldier gains victory not only through his sword but by every word that proceeds from the mouth of the Lord. . . . Nevertheless God avails Himself of rider and mount, sword and bow. However, He does not fight with the strength and might of rider and mount, but He alone fights and does all from behind the curtain and the cover of rider and mount.[12]

Whenever the stronger has triumphed in war, it was God who fought through him. "Whenever a prince wins a war, it is God who has vanquished the others through him."[13]

But is this not a bleak picture? Even the unjust victor, even the destructive forces in history, are God's masks behind which He lives and acts!

---

9. Cf. pp. 61ff.

10. "Preface to Joh. Lichtenberger's Prophecy (1527)," WA 23:8.36.

11. "Psalm 127 (1524)," WA 15:373.7ff.

12. "Fastenpostille (1525)," WA 17/2:192.8ff.

13. "Magnificat (1521)," WA 7:585.33.

Does this not merely confirm and vastly aggravate the impression of absurdity that history, with its interminable series of alternating victories and defeats, creates, if we are to believe that all this would not happen without the breath of life given by God to all alike? This is indeed a sad truth if faith were not able to divine and to say more. Do we not detect in the confusing maze of history any of the footprints of the God in whom Jesus taught us to believe?

We repeat. With our physical eye we cannot penetrate the mystery. There is no reasonable explanation for the enigma of history. Whatever answers man might have contrived, such as progression to a higher type of civilization, steeling and hardening a nation through battle, victory of the just cause, etc.—all this will be found wanting in the face of reality. Not even the oft-expressed thought, borrowed from nature, that the wars of history result in the survival of the fittest holds true. Certainly there is a kernel of truth in this. The stronger generally, though not always, prove victorious. However, can that always be regarded as a survival of the fittest? Strength often consists only in a brutal superiority in numbers and in material. The idea of the survival of the fittest becomes nonsensical in this age of technical warfare, in which the outcome of a war is decisively affected by the supply of raw material. The struggle for survival of the fittest among animals of the same species is always determined with equal weapons—among mankind usually with unequal ones. And into the war of physical forces another factor enters, an unpredictable one, which, if viewed with human eyes, can only be called chance. This factor is the general of genius who is given to one nation and withheld from the other; or a revolutionizing invention, which may be made at the proper time for warding off disaster; or capricious weather, rain, an unexpectedly early and severe winter, which upsets all strategic plans. No, there exists neither a logical nor a biological nor a moral formula for an adequate definition of the meaning of history. Human eyes are blind and see nothing. But do we see more with the eyes of faith?

Luther would say: Yes—thank God!—faith does see more. It sees soberly and clearly not only the great turmoil and discord in all aspects of historical life, it not only senses God's stormy presence in them, but it also sees God act in them. God is not only the life of history, He is also its Lord and Master. But only faith discerns this, for it is able to confess: "I believe that God has made me and all creatures . . ." God's dominion over me and over history is predicated on the fact that He is my Creator. On that point Luther, who saw God concealed behind all masks without distinction, expresses himself concretely and directly.

Everything great and good in history is the gift of a merciful God: the great emperors of German history whom Luther dearly loved; the miracle men God presents to nations, such as David, Alexander, Hannibal, or his own faithful sovereign, Elector Frederick the Wise; just judges; able generals; wise and circumspect counselors; etc. To view history with the eyes of faith means, first, to view it with grateful eyes. Luther untiringly impressed upon his Germans how thankful we should be for all the blessings our Creator has bestowed on us through our beautiful country and our rich history. Sincere gratitude, always a most reliable guide to God, is also the best safeguard against presumption and arrogance. If imbued with gratitude, a nation will regard accomplishment and success not as its just due and merit but as alien gifts, that is, as gifts loaned by God. "Those people are truly God-fearing who regard all their possessions solely as gifts bestowed on the unworthy out of pure mercy . . . use them in a spirit of praise, gratitude, and awe, as if they were the property of others, and strive not for their own pleasure, praise, and honor but only for that of their rightful owner."[14] If we bear in mind that, according to Luther, arrogance and conceit must invite catastrophe, then it follows that humility and gratitude in individuals and in nations also play a major role in history. It would not be a difficult historical task to prove that such humility has prevented many great men from hurling themselves and their nations into reckless adventures and consequent destruction. The Christians among the great men of German history understood this truth. After one of his great political successes, Bismarck wrote: "May God in His mercy continue to guide us and not surrender us to our own blindness. In this calling one can learn very readily how one may be as clever as the clever of this world and yet at any time go into the next moment as a child goes into darkness." And Moltke, casting a retrospective look at the triumphs of his life, wrote: "One learns modesty when one considers how few successes can be ascribed to oneself and that God is mighty in the weak."

Whoever believes implicitly that everything great and good is the unmerited gift of the Creator (for which we can only thank with word and deed) will not find fault with the Lord of history for administering history with absolute sovereignty. Luther can express this in graphic pictures: "God has collected a fine, splendid, and strong deck of cards representing

14. "Magnificat (1521)," WA 7:585.3.

mighty, great men, such as emperors, kings, princes, etc.; and He defeats the one with the other."[15] It is God alone who acts in history. But is the way of history not natural? Is it not possible, in the end, to explain everything by its causes? The victor just happened to be the stronger and the more dogged. Luther saw this clearly. Granted. But God happened to be on the side of the stronger battalions. He employs the world's powers to attain His goal. "Thus God makes and destroys one creature through another. He who lies, lies; he who stands, stands."[16] One need waste no time exploring the reasons. Everything in history proceeds naturally. Yet what does this explain? History remains full of riddles nevertheless. We have already referred to those inexplicable happenings: the gift of great generals or statesmen, the whims of wind and weather, new inventions, etc. From the days of antiquity down to the present, non-Christian parlance terms these happenings luck or coincidence. Every general and every private knows about soldier's luck. But if even the Romans recognized the rule of the goddess Fortuna in history, how much more should we Christians revere God's hidden hand in it! "For why should we not be willing to accord to our God what the Romans, the greatest warriors on earth, accorded their false goddess, Fortuna, of whom they were afraid?"[17] To be sure, even this function of God moves within the confines of natural law. The birth of a genius, an earthshaking event such as the death of Gustavus Adolphus in the Battle of Lützen, or a decisive change of weather—all come to pass from natural causes; yet God acts in them with inscrutable sovereignty. When in 1582 King Christian II of Denmark was taken into captivity (which was to endure to his end) and his successor to the throne suddenly died at the same time—just as suddenly as seven years before this time Queen Isabella, the sister of Charles V, had died—Luther summed up these three unexpected events so incisive for Danish history and added: "And no one is surprised by them, although such things do not occur according to human but according to divine counsel."[18] If such sudden events happening in our lives accrue to our good fortune, we hail them as miracles; but if they redound to our misfortune, we term them a bitter fate.

But does the Lord of history not act arbitrarily at such times? The

---

15. WATr 6, no. 6545.

16. "Magnificat (1521)," WA 7:586.3.

17. "Ob Kriegsleute in seligem Stande sein können (1526)," WA 19:651.12.

18. WATr 2, no. 1761.

belief in fate, which has become such a power in modern thinking, would necessarily answer this question affirmatively. Its only recourse is a heroic defiance of fate and a determination not to be crushed by it but to bear it manfully. But that is not the Christian faith. It disavows the reality of all arbitrariness; it recognizes only a will. This will of God may remain incomprehensible in its associations and in its immediate aims, but its meaning is clear: It always signifies either mercy or judgment.

It has already been said that everything great in history—the gift of miracle men, law and state, victory and peace—is a mercifully bestowed gift of God. We have already spoken about this. There is, however, another side to this picture. Again and again the historian is obliged to expose to view the evidences of human guilt, of moral bankruptcy, of unfaithfulness to trust, of arrogance, of lawlessness that have led to the collapse of powerful states and splendid civilizations. The eyes of faith penetrate still further and behold the immutable sequence of guilt and punishment behind the external happenings. Luther, too, knew of the uncanny fact already recognized by the sages of antiquity: Whom the gods would destroy, they first make blind. From time to time, Luther declared, God dispatches his messengers into the council chambers of men:

> Dear Gabriel, go thither, take Isaiah with you, read this mysterious message to them through the window, and say: "With seeing eyes you shall not see, and with hearing ears you shall not hear, and with an understanding heart you shall not understand. Take counsel together, and it shall come to nought; for both counsel and deed are Mine." (Is. 6:10; 8:10)[19]

There is, furthermore, no dearth of signs of God's wrath. Nowhere is Luther's historical perceptivity mirrored more clearly than in the horror with which he contemplated the nations that have perished. For they did not die a natural death. Luther does not recognize that type of death in the history of the nations. The idea of a biological aging and dying of nations is still foreign to him; in fact, it would clash violently with his entire view of historical life. Nations do not perish of themselves, but God wipes them out because of their sins. The history of the nations is the history of an active God who metes out death as He wills. Because Psalm 2 draws such a striking contrast between rebellious kings and almighty God enthroned in His heaven, who mocks the former and laughs them to scorn, Luther finds among the psalms this "insolent fellow" (*Grobian*) who addresses princes

---

19. "Psalm 101 (1534–1535)," WA 51:203.35.

as though they were peasants, children, and servants—a song altogether after his own heart.[20] To this day the postscript to Luther's lectures on this psalm shows us the breathtaking earnestness with which Luther described how God makes a clean sweep of nations and kings. For the fifth verse— "Then shall He speak unto them in His wrath, and vex them in His sore displeasure"—he could hardly find enough words to depict how God's words and His actions merge and coincide: "When God speaks, He casts one kingdom or four away. When He utters a sound, the whole world trembles. . . . His voice does not sound like other voices and instruments; with Him word and deed are identical. No sooner does He speak than it comes to pass."[21] Therefore Luther boldly calls the nations God delegates to destroy other, godless nations God's word of wrath, His *verbum irae*. To be sure, the former do not escape their fate either. He paints a magnificent picture of God as one who shoots at the nations and whose guns are always loaded. He battered the Jews to pieces with the Romans, the Romans with the Vandals and the Goths, the Chaldeans with the Persians, the Greeks with the Turks. "Perhaps there will also be a bullet for us Germans which will not miss us; for we have conducted ourselves outrageously and still do so."[22] Perhaps the Turkish bullet is destined for us, for our coldness and indifference to God's Word cannot go unpunished. This fear wrests from Luther the cry of distress: "If they take the Gospel from Germany, the country will perish with it."[23] However, even if the Turks should destroy Germany, this will not be history's final chapter, provided the world continues. The Turks will also meet their "battering-ram" (*Stösser*).[24]

God's acts of judgment are preceded by a period of silence. Luther did not share the opinion often expressed today that God remains silent during history's great catastrophes. On the contrary, this is when He speaks. But before this time, while man supposes all is going well and becomes arrogant, God pursues a policy of angry silence. "There is no greater wrath than when God is silent and does not converse with us but lets us go our own way and do as we wish."[25]

---

20. "Enarr. Psalmi II (1532)," WA 40/2:276.10.
21. "Enarr. Psalmi II (1532)," WA 40/2:229.12ff.
22. "Psalm 118 (1530)," WA 31/1:126.13ff.
23. "Lectures on Isaiah (1527–1530)," WA 31/2:303.30.
24. "Habakkuk (1526)," WA 19:360.16.
25. WATr 5, no. 5554b.

When the hour of God's judgment threatens to envelop us in darkness, then faith, according to Luther, must direct our eyes upward into a sphere that remains bright and clear amid the encircling gloom. It remains clear: First, that God's judgment is consistently judgment of our sin and, *nota bene*, always of one and the same sin: presumption and ingratitude. Because man no longer recognizes God's sovereignty but presumes to be able to shift for himself without God's Word and commandments, God reminds him again of His power and His supremacy. For this reason one should certainly not rely even on a just cause. "The fairer your cause and the better your rights, the less should you presume to boast of them. Rather fear God, who likes to put to shame the most just claims and to overthrow the best causes because of the arrogance with which you boastfully rely on them."[26] For this reason victory is never proof of the justice of the cause. And history is by no means judgment in the sense that it confirms the justice of the victor's cause. The latter was merely the tool in the hand of God for the execution of judgment, nothing more. God will find ways to strike him down, too, when his hour is at hand. God takes a long-range view of history. He is still entertaining far-reaching plans for the nations that always look only at the situation as it exists at the moment. The words of Scripture "Whom the Lord loveth He chasteneth" may also have historical significance.

Second, the eyes of faith perceive that God does not withdraw His gifts from the world even in the storms and the tumult of His judgments. "So long as the world stands, government, order, and power must endure."[27] Law and order are the dikes that God has built into this chaotic world. They will arise anew from every catastrophe and upheaval. God's anger is directed solely against their misuse. "Accordingly, the sword and the government always remain in the world; but the persons who rule will topple and tumble as they deserve."[28] These words not only corroborate the historical experience that a new order regularly arises from great upheavals, but they also show Luther's awareness of God's promise not to withdraw His hand from the affairs of men despite sin and judgment.

If faith derives great comfort from this knowledge, then it must, third, direct its eyes to the wonderful fact that God's judgments, rightly under-

---

26. "Psalm 101 (1534–1535)," WA 51:204.10.

27. "Magnificat (1521)," WA 7:590.5.

28. "Habakkuk (1526)," WA 19:360.27.

stood, must inspire confidence rather than fear. No matter how terrifying these judgments may be, they nevertheless contain a sweet kernel in a bitter shell: the nearness of the living God. This God is not only strong enough to execute judgment, but He is also powerful enough to help when it pleases Him. In the final analysis, God's judgment is nothing other for Luther than His agency of mercy and grace. Faith must take hold of this interpretation with both hands and must by no means let go, even if everything seems to speak against it. The awesome earnestness with which Luther described God's judgment in history was to him a part of the Gospel. In addition to His activity "through the creatures," whereby He employs the earthly powers, God often acts directly and contrary to all expectations. Then He shows "strength with His arm" (Luke 1:51). History demonstrates that "He has often done this and daily does it without man and without steed whenever need requires and He is not tempted."[29] Only the humble who do not tempt God are helped by Him in this wonderful way. Thereby "all proceeds so quietly and unobserved that no one is aware of it until it has happened."[30] For the presumptuous God prepares His judgment secretly. He permits them

> to become great and mighty. He withdraws His power and lets them become inflated with a sense of their own strength. For God's power leaves where man's power enters. And when the bubble is full and all imagine that they are on top and victorious, and they themselves have become secure and think they have succeeded, then God pricks the bubble, and that is the end. The fools do not realize that as they rise and achieve might, God's arm forsakes them and is no longer with them. Therefore their affairs endure for a season, and then all vanishes like a water bubble as though it had never existed.[31]

But what is judgment for the presumptuous is comfort and assurance for the reverent and the believing.

> He lets the pious become faint and suppressed, so that they all imagine that this is the end. But at this very moment God's might is strongest, though hidden and concealed. And they who suffer oppression do not feel this might, but they do believe in it. God's might and His entire arm

---

29. "Fastenpostille (1525)," WA 17/2:192.16.

30. "Magnificat (1521)," WA 7:585.4.

31. "Magnificat (1521)," WA 7:586.21.

are present there. For God's power enters when man's power fails, if there is faith and trust in Him.[32]

To be sure, faith must be able to wait patiently, perhaps must often wait so long that it never gets to behold the change in events as it expected to see them. But if faith persists and abides, God will open its eyes to behold His method of help.

> We unbelieving ones grope with our fists for the mercy and the arm of God. When we fail to feel it, we suppose that we are lost and that our enemies have won the victory, just as though God's mercy had deserted us and His arm were against us. This is due to our ignorance of His works. For this reason we do not know Him either . . . for He must be and wants to be recognized with the eyes of faith.[33]

Astonishing words of trust and confidence spring from Luther's view of God's hidden activity and His terrible judgments. "Without hesitation and doubt you must fix your gaze on God's will and purpose with you, that you may firmly believe that He wants to and will accomplish great things with you. Such a faith is alive and active; it permeates and transforms the whole man. It compels you to fear if you are haughty and to be of good cheer if you are humble."[34] Times of judgment preach an eloquent sermon on the topic of God's omnipotence. However, faith may rely on God implicitly. He will not be mocked; He wants to be revered, loved, and trusted.

Thus Luther's discourse on God's terrible and inevitable judgments in history does not tend to arouse fear in us but to transport us from the terror that befalls a creature at the sound of God's angry voice into trust and confidence. To be sure, "He puts down the mighty from their seats" before they are aware of it; but contrary to all appearances, He also has strength and help for believing and humble hearts.

Did Luther treat this subject too lightly? Were his days so bare of terror as to cause his words, despite their earnestness, to breathe so much trust and confidence? It must be conceded that the world's situation has grown alarmingly worse since Luther's time. Human sin and divine judgment loom so enormous today that we no longer hear the familiar voice of God in the storms that break over us. He is entirely incomprehensible to us.

---

32. "Magnificat (1521)," WA 7:586.6.

33. "Magnificat (1521)," WA 7:587.11.

34. "Magnificat (1521)," WA 7:553.31.

Still fear is fear, and trust is trust, today as it was more than four hundred years ago. Luther's faith had to pass through the same experiences—though perhaps with dimensional differences—that we have today. After all, is the difference actually so great? The Peasants' War, too, was a gory affair, and in 1529 the Turks laid siege to Vienna. At that time Luther, who listened with horror to the steps of God in judgment, did nothing but admonish the people to confide in this God and fortify their hearts against fear and faintheartedness. "But they that wait upon the LORD shall renew their strength"—this, too, whether one understands it or not, is a historical fact of the first order.

This view and this faith of Luther answer the tormenting question regarding the meaning of history for us. The popular "meaning of history," in which many believe with a well-nigh desperate fervor and which they try to pour into a mold of idealism or economy, is nonexistent. No thinker has ever been able to express it. Nor will anyone ever be able to do so.

Since days of old many people have conceived of God as one who called the game of history into being, then left it to itself while He withdrew. Since that time we brood over the unknown rules of the game. But this is folly. The game has no rules, but it does have an invisible coplayer who, strictly speaking, is really the only player, while we all are only supers. Our one task is to find Him and to learn what He wants from us.

God speaks to us not through words but through acts—this is the meaning of history. God cannot be reduced to an abstract formula; He is happening (*geschieht*) daily and vigorously. This meaning of history is not to be fulfilled at some indefinite future time, but it is being fulfilled this very day and always when men listen with terror and faith to God's voice. Each can hear Him only in his circle of life, in his weal and his woe, in the fate of his nation; but there He really can be heard by everyone. Every happy experience, every instance of protection from danger, every victory is mercy in which a hidden judgment is enclosed. Every sorrow, every trial for the individual or for a nation is judgment in which secret mercy lies concealed. The measure of historical happenings has today assumed proportions defying our mastery. In view of this we must again turn our ear to where God confronts and addresses us. The message for our individual lives is the same as that for the world in general: "I am the LORD thy God. Thou shalt have no other gods before Me," neither thyself nor other men nor any earthly goods or powers.

The struggle for God's dominion is, according to Luther, the meaning and the content of history. Therefore the history of the nations and the history of faith are not two distinct entities for Luther, they are an indivisible whole. The outward course of history is at the same time the reflection and image of the innermost transformations of the human race: of the observation of the natural regulations that God has written into the heart of the nations, of His commandments, and of His gracious Word; it is the history of obedience and of rebellion, of long-suffering and of judgment, of the destruction of complacent pride, and of wonderful help for an unswerving faith. God's message amid the tumult of history is the same as that preached in His revealed Word: mercy and judgment. Even today we find these two incomprehensibly interwoven, as they will also be on the Day of Judgment. History is merely the prelude to that great day, a day on which God will not only destroy what is deserving of death but will also deliver what He has accepted unto life. Behind the thin wall of time, the wall separating us from God, Luther, with a longing that had conquered all fear, heard Him approaching.

But without the divine Word, without Jesus Christ, we could not understand the voice of God in history. Without Him we would remain in search of those unknown rules of the game. For this most profound mystery in history, this hidden but decisive process—"Where man's power enters, God's power departs" and "Where man's power departs, God's power enters"—only the cross offers the key: "Behold, therefore Christ hung feebly on the cross, and there He performed the greatest deed; He conquered sin, death, the world, hell, the devil, and all evil."[35] The cross of Christ is a pledge to faith that God's work begins where all is lost to the human eye. He can call forth life from death. At the very spot where men committed their greatest sin, He opened the gates to the Father's house from which they had fled. And wherever individuals and nations crucify Christ anew, not only God's punitive justice awaits them but behind His angry countenance the Father's beckoning voice as well. For Luther, Christ's cross was a pledge of God's wonderful, hidden rule in history; in it he found, as every Christian finds, the help not indeed to understand history but to bear it and to be victorious over it.

---

35. "Magnificat (1521)," WA 7:586.15.

THE NATION ("*DAS VOLK*")

The question can be raised whether we may relate our concept of a nation to Luther's thinking. In any case, we shall find that his terminology is widely different from ours. But surely this reality called a nation did move in his orbit. He must have had a concept of nationality united into a state both by nature and by history, as also of the natural differences among nations. By searching for a concept of a nation in Luther, we are not merely delving into a fascinating bit of civilization's history, but we are at the same time entering the field of theology. For the Christian message addresses itself not to anything abstract but to a living, one-time human being, who was created as a member of his nation.

This subject brings us face-to-face with a basic rule of Luther's theology: He was hostile to all speculation, and his theological utterances always bore the real human being in mind. The Word of God is not a doctrine to be learned by rote and recited thus; it is God's speech addressed to me, a promise in need, a definite assignment and command. Christ is God in human form for me; He is God with His commandment, which exposes my sin; He is God with His forgiveness, which refreshes the humble heart and endows it with renewed life.

And man is always a definite, distinct personality. To be sure, his is also a general nature, which makes him man beyond the differences in nations and times. But this nature always materializes only in individuals and in the thoughts, emotions, and acts peculiar to them. The individuality of a person is decisively affected by national ties. Therefore it is important for the proclamation of the Gospel to understand national traits and idiosyncrasies so it does not miss the mark by addressing a fancied person but

179

appeals to the heart of the real man. Man in his national identity is a part of creation, but he is differentiated from all other creatures by the law governing him. The law in its simplest features is as general as the fundamental traits that make man a human being. But in its concrete, legal, and moral ordinances, it is as manifold as the nationalities within humanity. The Gospel must take cognizance of this fact and adjust its message to man who is living under the general laws given him as a human being and under the specific moral obligations imposed on him by his national identity and by the historical hour in which he lives. This is what renders Luther's views on nationality, in their relationship to his world of theological thought, important to us.

It was essential for Luther's view on nationality, especially German nationality, that he was born into a time of an awakening national consciousness. Its first traces, to be sure, antedate Luther by far. Contact with the Romans made the Germanic tribes aware for the first time of the difference between themselves and the latter. The Romans as well as the Germans noticed the contrast. This for the first time inspired a stronger sense of oneness among the Germans. The figure of Arminius already began to lead to something akin to a universal Germanic consciousness; this was preserved and perpetuated by the heroic epics during the migration of the nations with its attendant extinction of large sectors of Germanic peoples. Among the tribes that withstood the allurement of late Roman civilization, tribal pride merged into national consciousness compared to the defeated Romans. But the Franks, the most important of these tribes, encumbered their national consciousness with a burden too heavy for it to bear: the tradition of Western culture, both ancient and ecclesiastical. The ambition to be the bearer of this universal culture became an essential characteristic of their tribal pride. Under a weak sovereignty possessed of little cohesive power, an awakening racial or tribal consciousness among the different segments of the Carolingian empire had to burst the East Frankish and West Frankish empires asunder. For the second time in medieval imperial history, we find incentives and obstacles to a German sense of nationality peculiarly intertwined. It was the splendor of a German empire assuming leadership of the West that for the first time led to a large-scale awakening of a German consciousness and an awareness of its own peculiar mission, which we meet in the literature of the Hohenstaufen era, in the *Deutschlandlied* of Walther von der Vogelweide, in the heroic epics, and in folk poetry. But at the same time, the idea of universal empire radically destroyed the national consciousness of the emperors. The German imperial dynasties change from tribal dukes to Mediterranean-universal emperors who expand their realm and their mission to the utmost limits of the Occident. This served to divorce the destiny of the German people ever more from the empire. The decisive political accomplishments of the late Middle Ages, the colonization of the East, the Hanseatic League, the flourishing of the free imperial cities, the development of the territories were all brought about by the people without the leadership of the emperors. The imperial idea and the German national idea opposed each other and fought their last battles under the great Hapsburg emperors in the beginning of the sixteenth century: under Maximilian with his opponent, Berthold von Henneberg, and under Charles V with his mortal enemies among the German princes, foremost among whom was Philipp of Hesse. The all-important question was: With which faction would German national sentiment coming to life in humanism side?

Among the humanists there was much fanatical enthusiasm for the imperial idea. But the latter was burdened by its ties with foreigners—despite the exultation over Charles V's election victory over the French king—with Roman law, and, above all, since the beginning of the Reformation, with the emperor's determined espousal of the cause of the old church. In comparison the territorial principalities seemed like the continuation of the ancient Germanic tribes. It was chiefly the territorial princes and their environs that contended for the freedom and independence of the territories within the imperial realm. After some hesitation and after the hopes reposed in Charles V, the "young, noble blood" ("das junge, edle Blut"), had been so bitterly disappointed and the emperor, in his dramatic declaration of opposition to Luther at Worms, had denied himself to the German popular movement, the stream of the new national feeling, in conjunction with the growing tide of the Reformation, poured into the paths of the *deutsche Libertät*, the freedom of the territorial princes.

In German humanism the new patriotic fire had been kindled by the German contrast to Italy. At that, the Romans themselves had provided the best fuel for this fire, namely, Tacitus's *Germania* and later his *Annals*, with which Hutten became acquainted in Rome in 1515. In them he rediscovered the figure of Arminius and made him the first German popular hero, whose fight against Rome he intended to resume. By doing so, Hutten significantly transformed the German idea of *Libertät* into a demand

181

for freedom from the outside, especially from Rome. To be sure, the shadowy form of the Cheruscan prince was now replaced in humanism and among the masses by Luther, the buoyant hero of the historical hour. Because the emperor failed to perceive the real pulse of the German people, Luther became the symbol of unity in the awakening national consciousness. All productive epochs of history require symbolic figures that represent the unity of national experience. The process that transfused the new national sentiment from humanistic circles into the masses was decided and accelerated by Luther. Since the beginning of the sixteenth century, the longing for German unity grew almost by leaps and bounds. Not only did a wealth of literature spring up that expounded and enlarged on Tacitus's *Germania*, but above all we now find the German folk song attuned to the all-German pitch:

> Frisch auf, ihr werten Deutschen!
> Frisch auf in Gottes Namen,
> Du werte deutsche Nation!

In the term "deutsche Nation," the feeling of unity is summarized. In the documents of the fifteenth century it still has a double meaning: It refers either to all the citizens of the empire (just as originally at the universities and councils even citizens of the empire who spoke a foreign language were classed as belonging to the German nation) or it was applied to German tribal and language unity, to which the concept was restricted since the Council of Basel.

Therefore we hear the term "deutsche Nation" loudly reechoing the national consciousness in Luther. He had become acquainted with it particularly in the complaints of the German nation, which had impressed him so deeply at the Diet of Worms in 1518, and now he himself disseminated it widely among the people in his treatise *To the Christian Nobility of the German Nation*. For it he found stimulating thoughts in humanism, especially in Hutten's *Vadiskus*. However, Luther's writing was infinitely superior to Hutten's diffuse tract because he did not attack individual excrescences but seized the evil by the roots: the precedence of canonical over civil law. By his restoration of the sovereignty of the state, he blazed the trail for the multitude of his own reformational proposals. His solemn term for this state was "die deutsche Nation." The nation's high secular estates were represented by the Christian nobility. But the term gradually begins to assume a decidedly popular (*stark volkhaft*) connotation. He pities the "poor people of the German nation" ("das arme Volk deutscher

Nation"). "According to the customs of the German nation" ("nach deutscher Nation Sitten"), the young sons of the nobility cannot take over the reins of government. He set off the *deutsche Nation* from the rest of the Christians. It is noble and in all accounts is praised as constant and faithful. Usury is the greatest misfortune of the *deutsche Nation*.

It conforms to this expansion of the term's meaning that the two traits of genuine national unity—namely, the natural racial bonds and their solidification by state and history—blend so well for Luther in the concept of the general term "nation," which he uses both in German and in Latin. He applies this term to the natural basic units of the German people (the tribes), as he does to the great national formations: the German, the French, the Italian, the Spanish nation. Thus these great national units also receive the character of a part of nature. To him a nation is a people contained within the firm structure of a state. Accordingly, his meaning approximates our present-day acceptance of the term "nation" ("Volk") in its truest sense.

But Luther's use of the word *Volk* (*populus*) cannot be sharply defined. Wherever the word does not simply represent a mass of people (*viel Voiks, so viel Adel und reiches Volk*), or wherever he does not use it in the particular meaning of the military (*Kriegsvolk*), it designates the subjects of a ruler, nothing more. It is vain to try to discover any fine and subtle shades of meaning of the term in Luther.

What are Luther's views of the German people?[1] He fretted and worried much about his dear Germany. He sees the rich, beautiful country greatly imperiled. His chief fear centers in his country's disregard for God's Word. The shower (*Platzregen*) of the Gospel will pass over it, and Germany will not be able to retain it. But he is also moved by political apprehensions. If it were ruled by one hand, it would be invincible. But handicapped by many and diverse sovereigns, it is not able to bring its homogeneous power together. The Germans are inept in the use of their riches. They lack the proper practical knowledge. "They have nothing because they do not know how to use things."[2] The worst national vices are gluttony and drunkenness. Thus the Germans are asleep, whereas the Turks are sober and therefore have a future. The German devil is "a wineskin, and his name must be Carousal [*Sauf*]."[3] He is an almighty god

---

1. Cf. WATr, index to vol. 6.

2. WATr 2, no. 1983.

3. "Psalm 101 (1534–1535)," WA 51:257.5.

among us Germans and seduces us to desecrate and despise God's Word. A comparison with other nations sharpens Luther's sight both for German virtues and for German vices. The Germans are more ingenuous and truthful than the French, the Spaniards, and the Italians. They are pious and therefore credulous in matters pertaining to religion and easily duped by the scoffers from foreign nations. They are loyal and brave, sincere and honest; but they are derided by other nations as vulgar and bestial. In Anton Lauterbach's collection of Luther's Table Talk we find references to German characteristics that the author probably copied from Luther's *Hand-psalter*.[4] Here Luther portrays the Germans' physical appearance far from flatteringly: "The German's demeanor is that of a swordsman; his gait is like a rooster's; he has a dissolute face, a voice like a steer's, vulgar manners, a sloppy bearing." In sharp contradistinction he points to the moderation, the amiability, and the easy elegance of the Frenchman; the imposing, solemn, and somewhat lachrymose manner and exquisite bearing of the Spaniard; and the vivacity, the grandeur, the poise, and the engaging speech of the Italian. It is particularly in his comparison with other nations that he makes observations on German foibles, though this comparison at times also affords him occasion to say something praiseworthy about his German compatriots. "All Germany does not take a matter very much to heart. When an Italian resolves to do something, he does not rest until he has carried it out."[5] Contrary to a common German self-characterization, Luther often laments: "Our constant craving for something new is our worst mistake."[6]

Luther is vividly cognizant of the German tribal divisions, and in his Table Talk he draws many a graphic picture of these tribes. Among the various dialects, he prized especially that of the Hessians because of its articulate and melodious qualities. The Westphalians appeared to him to be industrious and fit to govern. Because of their loquacity the Suabians intermeddle in all deliberative affairs, even those outside their own territory, but by nature they are candid, without guile, and they express their opinion openly. The Bavarians, too, are straightforward, honest, obliging, but they are less gifted than the Suabians. In both of these tribes Luther praised the virtue of hospitality. If he were to travel in Germany, his choice

---

4. WATr 4, no. 4857.

5. "Commentary on Galatians (1531)," WA 40/1:105.2.

6. "Commentary on Galatians (1531)," WA 40/1:311.12.

would be to sojourn among them. The inhabitants of Meissen and Hesse emulate the Suabians and the Bavarians in this regard, but they betray mercenary traits in their show of hospitality. The Saxons—Luther means the Lower Saxons—are honest and truth-loving, but they are cold, reserved, and decidedly unfriendly. If someone comes to their door, they answer: "Dear guest, I do not know what to give you. My wife is not at home; I cannot lodge you."[7] The inhabitants of the *Vogtland* have a tendency to pride with little cause for it. Luther reproaches the Franks with cowardice. When Emperor Maximilian was drawing up his army for battle, he discovered that he had lost the Franks: "Where are my Franks now? Yes, if it were a matter of finding booty!" The Hessians he calls chivalrous and valiant; they alone would be a match for the Bavarians and the Franks. He "was not so unfriendly [*entgegen*] to any other nations as to those of Meissen and Thuringia." The Meissners are dissemblers and dancing junkers; the Thuringians are cunning. For this reason he is happy to be a Lower Saxon, not a Thuringian.[8]

Despite its division into tribes, Luther felt that the German people, as opposed to the other nations and the foreign nationals on German soil, were one entity. His harsh judgment on the Wends ("the worst of all the nations God has cast among us")[9] reveals his feeling for racial contrasts. Especially does the thought of the Welsche (a term embracing all the Romance peoples) and of the Jews and the Turks awaken Luther's consciousness of German national unity. In part they seem to be tainted with the same failings. Just as the Wends remind him of the Jews, so he rebukes both the Romance peoples and the Jews for their arrogance.

Most conspicuous to Luther was the alien nature of the Jews. His judgment of these people (with whom he occupied himself from an early age and often) was not always consistent. At first his opinion was very unfavorable. In keeping with the prophecies of Holy Writ, he considered them unrepentant and incorrigible. With profound, lifelong emotion he observed in their fate what it means when a nation provokes God's anger and judgment with unbelief. He believed that part of the blame for this obduracy lay at the door of the Christians and their hatred and bloody persecutions during the Middle Ages because in this way the Jews must

7. WATr 3, no. 3473.

8. WATr 4, no. 4996.

9. WATr 4, no. 4997.

have been repelled from the adoption of the Christian Gospel.[10] For this reason Luther was hopeful during the early years of the Reformation that God's Word would now do its work in them. His first writing, *That Jesus Was a Born Jew* (1523), contained an appeal to bring them the Gospel. In the papacy they had been dealt with as dogs, not as humans. They should no longer be forbidden

> to work among us, to carry on a trade or business, and to mingle with us, which restraint drives them into usury. How could that reform them? If one wants to be of help to them, one must not use the law of the papacy but that of Christian love on them, accept them amicably, permit them to ply their trades and work with us, affording them both reason and room for moving among us, so that they may hear and see our Christian doctrine and life. And if some of them are stiff-necked, what of it? After all, we are not all good Christians either.[11]

They must be induced to recognize Jesus as the Messiah; then it will also be possible to lead them to the acknowledgment of His divinity. Luther's hope for great missionary success among the Jews was not fulfilled. A series of unfavorable impressions derived from individual Jews with whom he came into close personal contact and, above all, the reports since 1532 of Jewish propaganda in Moravia, the much-talked-about usury, and the Jewish defamations of Christ of which he knew substantiated more and more his original opinion of an impenitent people rejected by God. When the Jews were evicted from the Electorate of Saxony in 1536, he refused to intercede for them with the elector. He supported his position in 1538 in the "Letter of Dr. Martin Luther to a Good Friend against the Sabbatarians." All again revolved about the Messiah question. God cannot have broken His promise to send the Messiah for 1,500 years without special reason. Either the Messiah came into the world 1,500 years ago, or God lied and did not keep His promise. The most convincing testimony that the Jews are in error is the story of their sufferings for 1,500 years because

> they did not have to suffer more than seventy years for far more manifest, horrible, and murderous sins, during which period of time they, furthermore, were not deserted by prophets and consolation, but now in their present misery not even a fly buzzes comfort to them with a single wing. If

---

10. "Operationes in Psalmos," WA 5:428f.

11. WA 11:336.27.

this does not mean that they are forsaken by God, then the devil may also boast that he is not yet forsaken by God.[12]

Luther did not believe that he had now disposed of the Jewish question. His intention to write against them in detail was accelerated by a Jewish reply to his letter to the Sabbatarians, which was sent to him in 1542 with the request for a reply. The treatise *Against the Jews and Their Lies* (1543) was his rebuttal. He no longer writes for the purpose of calling for missionary work; instead, he calls for "sharp mercy" ("scharfe Barmherzigkeit"), by means of which a few might still be saved. To be sure he entertained no hope. If the blows of fate did not avail, what could be accomplished by words? The worst obstacle was the intolerable pride of the Jews. They boast of their descent from the patriarchs, of their distinction from others by reason of their circumcision, of their receipt of the Law directly from God (against which Luther interposed that only he who keeps the commandments, not he who possesses them, has reason to boast), and their erstwhile possession of the Holy Land. He levels his main attack against the Jews' perversion of Scriptures: They are still waiting for the Messiah. This gives rise to their hatred for the Christians, who believe the Messiah has already appeared. Their hostility is so intense that they are actuated to good deeds only by reasons of expediency because they have to live among the Christians. Their slanders and their accusations against the Christians show that God has stricken them with madness. Therefore only radical measures can still promise success. Even the harsh suggestions of Luther that seem so horrible to us today—the demolition of their synagogues, the destruction of their prayer books, the prohibition of the rabbis to teach—serve for Luther the purpose of putting an end to the Jews' blasphemy of Christ. In addition, he says that they should be stripped of the riches they have gained by usury, that some of this wealth should be given to the sincere converts from Judaism to make it possible for them to begin to do honest work, to use the money for the support of the old and the sick, and to enable the young and the healthy to earn a livelihood in agriculture or some trade. But if one still has reason to regard them as a menace and to fear that they will not become accustomed to work, then one should square accounts with them as to what they have gained by usury, assign them their honest share, then banish them from the country, as

---

12. WA 50:336.24.

has been done in the West-European countries. For all concerned it would be most beneficial if they were to return to their homeland.[13]

In the same year (1543) Luther's tract *Vom Schem Hamphoras und vom Geschlecht Christi* appeared. It is mentioned here merely in proof of the profound impression made on Luther by libelous Jewish books (and this one even after its reproduction in a Christian refutation of the fourteenth century). After various other severe utterances, especially in his Table Talk and in his lectures on Genesis, he also used his farewell sermon in Eisleben three days before his death for this topic, concluding it with a pulpit announcement, "Warning against the Jews." Again Luther gives the exhortation to deal with them in a Christian spirit and to offer them the Christian faith. "If they are converted, desist from their practice of usury, and accept Christ, we shall gladly regard them as our brethren." If not, they must be driven out, for it is impossible "to have communion and patience with the obdurate blasphemers and profaners of this dear Savior."[14]

After this survey it may be advisable to reexamine closely the premises and motives that distinctly come to the fore in his final utterances on the Jewish question.

First, Luther's accounting with the Jews involves a religious principle. The crime of the Jews is of a religious nature: blasphemy of Christ. Luther's goal, though he entertained little hope of attaining it even to a modest degree, is also religious: the conversion of individual Jews. Their fundamental sin is disobedience to Holy Writ; they do not believe in the promise that the Bible regards as fulfilled. They fail to comprehend the Old Testament in its purest and most profound sense; they pervert it again into the Law, though Christ is the fulfillment of the Law and though the hidden meaning of the Old Testament, which points to the Gospel, has become manifest. But they have not preserved even the Law in its purity. For the old Law has been choked up with additions (*Aufsatze*) of the Talmud, exactly as the Roman Church has suffocated the plain words of Christ with its abundance of decrees, customs, and precepts. The superstition of Jewish kabbalism finds its pagan counterpart in the Catholic practice of the sacraments. Judaism is matched in all this by Catholicism; both deprive God of His honor. Luther's profound love for the Old Testament may also be adduced as proof of the assertion that the Jewish question was

13. WA 53:522ff., 538.

14. WA 51:195f.

a religious, not a racial, one for him. His love for the Old Testament and an attempt to give his view of the Jewish question a racial aspect would seem contradictory. His conception of the Old Testament, to which he devoted by far the greatest part of his exegetical endeavors, harmonizes perfectly with his attitude toward the Jews.[15] They correspond to each other, only with the patterns reversed. He loves the Old Testament because it proclaims the advent of Christ; he contends against the later Jews because they crucified the incarnate Christ and still despise and blaspheme Him with their worship.

Second, in its official capacity the government has to proceed against such manifest blasphemy. Luther differentiated sharply between every coercive conversion to faith, which he rejected, and the prevention of public blasphemy, which devolves on the government. The Mass, which perverts God's act into a work of man, the public denial of the Trinity, the public preaching of the Anabaptists and the enthusiasts must be thwarted by a dutiful government if it does not want to invite God's wrath, hunger, and pestilence upon the country. Therefore it has to take measures against the defamation of Christ by the Jews, not for the purpose of a forced conversion of the individual but for the preservation of the country. This is the result of his combination of freedom of conscience, which does not tamper with private opinion, and intolerance in public life, which is such a departure from our modern, self-evident tolerance.

Third, the conversion of individual Jews remains the object of their public suppression. Even the severe suggestions in the writing *Of the Jews and Their Lies* were to serve their salvation. "With prayer and the fear of God we must exercise a sharp mercy in the hope of saving at least a few from the flames and the heat. We dare not be vindictive. Vengeance has seized them by the neck a thousand times worse than we can wish."[16] A converted Jew is to be accepted as a brother.

Fourth, the usury of the Jews also arouses Luther's ire and indignation. He censures this severely but not without including in this criticism the princes, whose constant pecuniary embarrassment has entangled them in the meshes of the Jews. The Jews

> live among us, under our protection; they use country and streets, market and lanes. And our princes and our government sit there, snore with their

---

15. Cf. Heinrich Bornkamm, *Luther und das Alte Testament* (Tübingen: J. C. B. Mohr, 1948), 1ff.
16. WA 53:522.24.

mouths open, permit the Jews to take, steal, and rob from their open purse and chest as much as they want. That is to say, they let the Jews flay and fleece them and their country and permit themselves to be reduced to beggary with their own money.[17]

However, we must not overlook the fact that it was not primarily the question of usury—clearly, this is only secondary—that provokes Luther's hostility toward the Jews. He has but one reason for his harshest counsel: "If we are to remain unsullied by the blasphemy of the Jews and do not wish to take part in it, we must be separated from them, and they must be driven out of our country."[18]

Luther's instinctive aversion to the Jews, like his dislike for the Wends and the Italians (for whom he had little feeling of friendliness since his journey to Rome), cannot be denied; but it is just as evident that his flaming battle cries against the Jews are not dictated by racial prejudice. Rather, they resounded against a nation that constantly offended God by unbelief and blasphemy. Such impenitence was aggravated by the fact that Israel had been chosen in preference to all other nations and had been in possession of God's Law and promise.

In passing we shall cast a hasty glance at the essential approaches heading from Luther's view of the people to his view of the state. His concept of the state is based on a definite relationship between people and government. On the one hand, Luther evolved (entirely in accord with his fondness for the old Germanic legal thought) the state entirely from the people (*Volk*). He regarded the political and the Christian congregation as a German community of freemen, equal before the law, who engaged and also deposed their agents, magistrates, and pastors. At the same time it was in harmony with primitive Christianity and with German law that he accorded the Christian congregation the authority "to judge all doctrine and to call, instate, and discharge teachers."[19] He always prized the sovereign rights of the nobility, of the provincial governments, and of the magistrates, which sprouted in the popular soil of the people, above "the far-fetched and circumstantial" imperial general law, the Roman law, and the new officialdom based on it. Therefore it was also one of the principal achievements of the Reformation that the concept of urban corporation

---

17. WA 53:482.29.

18. WA 53:538.8.

19. "Dass eine christliche Versammlung . . . (1523)," WA 11:408ff.

and commonalty gained currency. On the other hand, Luther never fostered the idea of a popular sovereignty that permitted active resistance or even revolution against the existing government. Even a tyrannical government must be borne. The people should not interfere with the designs of God, who uses tyrants for a while as His scourge and knows how to check them in due season. Only for reasons inherent in the constitutional structure of the empire did Luther finally concede the right of resistance against the emperor to the territorial princes. However, he held that a nation is in duty bound to oppose a wicked government with moral or spiritual weapons, with words of warning or accusation, with disobedience against a sinful command (e. g., refusal to serve in a manifestly unjust war or disobedience toward commands that involve denial of the faith), with patient suffering that might follow in the wake of such disobedience, and with a prayer for God's help in such a situation. For an extreme case God may, to be sure, delegate a man to be His special tool or sword, as He chose Samson in the fight against the Philistines. But such a contingency must be reserved for direct command of God.[20]

Luther did not link two paradoxical concepts of state together; his ideal was not that of the popular juridical state with an ancient patriarchal tinge. He wanted the people and the government envisioned as one. To be sure, the power of this state is unevenly divided, and the political limitations of the people are narrower by far. But the moral confines of the government are no less sharply delineated by Luther. Its absolute responsibility for the people renders its task no less consequential and dangerous. For it is not any political power but the verdict before God's judgment seat that is ultimately decisive; and Luther recognized this final verdict of God as the absolute reality behind all outward aspects and phases of life.

He could accept this contradictory juxtaposition of people and government, each vested with equal sovereignty, because both derive their rights from the same source: from divine creation. Not only the people but also the government is created by God. The government makes possible the attainment of God's objective in this fallen world and the preservation of a true human existence.

> Since God does not wish to see this world desolate and waste but created it
> that men may inhabit it and cultivate and populate the land, as recorded

---

20. "Von weltlicher Obrigkeit (1523)," WA 11:261.9ff.; "Lectures on Genesis (1535–1545)," WA 43:653.19.

in the first chapter of Genesis, and since all this is impossible without peace, He, as the Creator, is impelled, for the maintenance of His creation, His work, and order, to institute and preserve the government and to confer the law and the sword on it, so that it can execute and punish the disobedient as people who resist God and His order and are not deserving of life.[21]

For this reason government is a "divine" calling as are all other vocations in life (that of father, mother, master, servant). For "God's Word sanctifies and consecrates everything for its appointed purpose. Therefore such positions as have been instituted by God's Word are all called holy and divine vocations, although the persons are not holy."[22]

Both people (*Volk*) and state are a part of creation but in a different sense. A people (*Volkstum*) is, as it were, a part of nature. In it each person develops according to the law of heredity and environment. Luther, of course, envisages the nation as based on the family. A nation, therefore, stands in need of redemption the same as natural man. On the other hand, the state is created by God unto fallen mankind for the preservation of order. With it God shields His work of creation. For without the peace and tranquillity safeguarded by the government, man cannot earn his livelihood nor can the Word of God be proclaimed. This emphasizes the conclusion that Luther did not derive the state from any natural rights. Not to satisfy man's sin-affected wants and wishes, which stem from reason, did God create government but to save His work of creation from man's depraved nature.

All human life is subject to a double law: a natural law, which binds all mankind, and a national law, which has validity only within national confines. Insofar as the Law of Moses contains national law, it is the "*Sachsenspiegel* of the Jews" and is no more binding for other nations than German law is in France.[23] Even the Ten Commandments are generally valid only as far as they coincide with the natural law; the ceremonial law (images and the Sabbath) must be deleted from them. The state governs with both laws: the one that makes man a human being and the one that makes him a citizen of the state. Unless a state law defies God's commandments, the church's sermons on the Law and her educational program must embrace

---

21. "Psalm 82 (1530)," WA 31/1:192.25.

22. "Psalm 82 (1530)," WA 31/1:217.10.

23. "Wider die himmlischen Propheten (1525)," WA 18:81.14.

both of these. Church and state meet on common ground in their educational work. But even the proclamation of the Gospel, entrusted solely to the church, dare not lose sight of this double form of the law. The Gospel seeks man in his reality, consequently in the responsibility that is his as a member of mankind and also his responsibility as a member and citizen of his nation. The messengers of Christ are dispatched to all mankind without distinction but also to each nation in its distinctive individuality.

THE STATE

Luther was neither a statesman nor a political philosopher but a preacher of the Gospel. For this reason it is not easy to fit him into political history and to label him and his views. An investigation will, moreover, show a wide deviation of his principles from those of political philosophers. Luther's pronouncements on questions of political and national life are all spiritual counsel, the application of the Word of God to the activities of men sharing in the order of civic life. They do not lend themselves to being pieced together into a systematic whole.

To forestall any misconception, it must be said in the beginning that Luther recognized the impossibility of applying the Gospel directly to the different phases of civic life. But he also knew that though the Bible does not prescribe political rules, it does inculcate brotherly love and a sense of responsibility before God, which spell out moral forces making for correct political and civic attitude and conduct. Luther's distinctiveness can perhaps be seen best in the type of his writings. He composed neither a book *De regimine principum* or a commentary on the ethics and politics of Aristotle, as Thomas Aquinas did, nor a treatise on dogmatics, as both Thomas Aquinas and Calvin did, in which problems of state are also comprehensively dealt with under the topic of ethics. But Luther did write against the mad princes who opined "they could act as they wanted and command their subjects as they chose,"[1] could even dictate what their subjects should believe and what books (namely, the German New Testament) they should not read. He aimed principally at Duke George of Saxony. In 1523 Luther

---

1. "Von weltlicher Obrigkeit (1523)," WA 11:246.24.

counseled subjects whose consciences were assailed by these princes in *Of Human Government, How Far One Owes It Obedience.*

The Peasants' War finds him advising prince and peasant, admonishing the latter not to confuse social demands with the freedom of the Gospel but to advance his claims exclusively in the name of human justice. After his suggestion of moderation had gone unheeded, he informs the princes that they may combat the rebellion with a good conscience. He treats the question of war by answering a professional soldier's query: *Whether Soldiers Can Live in a State of Salvation* (1526). From the same religious point of view, his writings, especially the expositions of biblical passages and sermons, discuss questions of political economy, above all, the problem of usury. In all his utterances he is never anything but the pastoral adviser of his people. It would be far easier to catalogue Calvin, the learned jurist and statesman, among the political philosophers; he was strongly attuned to the ancient state theory, and he kept abreast of the problems of state.

However, within the confines of his dominant line of thinking and writing, Luther was such an ardent political being (that is, a man who was deeply moved by the fate of his people), and the influence of the Reformation was in so large a measure not only religious but also historical-political, that the question regarding Luther's political views—correctly understood—suggests itself spontaneously. It goes without saying that the counsel he gave his contemporaries as spiritual adviser must also contain some views on a proper political life. But only views—no more. In vain will one seek in Luther any teaching about the ideal state. One will, however, discover an extremely sharp eye for the motivating impulses and forces of political reality. Projected above all this we find all the demands he made for moral behavior in the service of the state.

Therefore it is wise to proceed not from any abstractions and concepts but from Luther's mode of viewing things. His thinking does not begin with the definitions of Aristotelian-medieval tradition but with the reality that is much closer to him, that is, with the people. Born of the people, living with and for the people, he is deeply imbued with their real life. He has a clear view of the German people, both collectively and individually. He perceives the common German traits, the differences between them and other nationalities, and with a keen eye and a good sense of humor he also detects the peculiarities of the German tribes.[2]

2. Cf. pp. 191ff.

The German nation is contained in the empire; the different tribes, in the principalities and other lesser governments. Luther did not play these two against each other but strove for a sound balance and an equable adjustment of the two. His desire for unity is unmistakable. Not even his religious antithesis to Charles V made him desist from demanding stronger political prerogatives for the emperor. He was not blind to the infinite wretchedness of division and disunity in the empire:

> Germany would be invincible if it were united under one head and controlled by one hand.[3]

> Germany is a beautiful, spirited stallion that has fodder and all it needs. But it lacks a rider.[4]

Luther comforted and strengthened his patriotic spirit again and again with a retrospective glance at the old German emperors. To be sure, he realized the fiction in the medieval notion that the Roman Empire was being perpetuated in the German *Reich*. The Roman Empire was destroyed by the Goths. Only the name and the title have come down to the Germans. Luther acknowledged without reserve the independence and the rights of the other occidental nations. He not only concurred with the humanists in their rejection of the Roman claim that the pope was the source of imperial power, but at variance with the humanistic ideology of empire, he also rejected the romantic universality that made the emperor the *imperator mundi* and the protector of all Christendom. Luther thought only of the unity of the German nation within the empire. But at the same time he wanted no imperial absolutism. The conferred and inherited prerogatives of the lesser governments should be honored and protected. That the emperor's position should be strengthened and acknowledged unconditionally in the proper area, the imperial cities, seemed just as self-evident to Luther as that Frederick the Wise was sovereign in his duchy. Luther regarded as a tyranny an absolute and autocratic state such as Turkey. Although he clearly perceived the advantages of the sultan's wealth and power, he still defended the hereditary fiefs in the empire against a centralized imperial power; but he impressed upon the nobility the duties entailed, especially the duty of military service![5]

Luther entertained no doubt regarding the desirability of the monar-

3. WATr 3, no. 3583.

4. WATr 5, no. 5735.

5. "Ob Kriegsleute . . . (1526)," WA 19:653f.

chial form of government, not only because it was the order of the day but also because history convinced him of the influence and strength of the individual personality. He was not led to this view, as Thomas Aquinas was, by an inference from the universal monarchy of God but by abundant historical experience. A wise prince is better than all laws; a "born jurist," for example, the electoral counselor Fabian von Feilitzsch, is better than any ever-so-learned professional jurist. Luther appropriately styled these masters of statesmanship and jurisprudence "miracle men of God" ("Wunderleute Gottes").

> Some have a special star before God. These God Himself instructs and raises as He wants to have them. . . . Such people I do not call trained and schooled but princes and lords created and impelled by God. These are so adept that they do not require much instruction and precept. Before one can teach them what to do, they have already carried it out.[6]

All government measures not emanating from this great aptitude and from this divine calling into office are "nothing but patchwork and trumpery."[7]

> To be sure, rules must be taught and observed, but in the manifestation of His power and wisdom God does many a thing counter to rules through especially called and qualified men, few and far between though they may be. The others must adhere to existing rules and regulations; for if they presume to emulate these heroes, who digress from the rules, they will fare badly. . . . In the political sphere we behold various types of regents and princes. Some observe laws and common privileges in their rule; others do not, as, e. g., Alexander, who was bound by no law but, because of his mental strength, broke through its restraint. With others this would have been impossible.[8]

Luther, of course, was well aware that those were exceptional times and that, as a rule, men of average ability preside over government affairs and that in many instances incompetents and tyrants have to be endured. But this prospect did not detract from his esteem of monarchial government. At the same time, however, he did not undervalue or disparage the advantages of representative-democratic government as it existed in the imperial cities and in the Swiss Confederacy. All governmental forms suffer in varying degrees from human frailties and shortcomings, most of all

---

6. "Psalm 101 (1534–1535)," WA 51:207.22ff.

7. Cf. pp. 172ff.

8. "Lectures on Genesis (1535–1545)," WA 43:62.35, 228.4.

those in which the masses, "Mr. Omnes," attempt to rule. He valued the blessing of the rule of wise and talented princes so highly that he was willing to risk the potential abuse of autocracy.

For Luther the proper unity of a nation inheres in the proper relationship between government and people, the latter falling into distinct vocational groups. The idea of the modern state, ruling as an abstract reality over the individual, is not found in Luther. He thinks entirely in terms of personal relationship and association: the government and the subjects. We must not lose sight of this. We must guard against foisting modern (or, in part, even ancient) ideas of the state on Luther's concept of the state, as has happened often enough.

This personal relationship between government and subjects by no means implies that Luther resolves the state into an equal union of subjective rights. The medieval doctrine of the compact (*pactum*) between ruler and people, and especially the modern contract based on natural rights, fails to find the faintest echo in Luther.

Governments and subjects are united by an objective and binding law, namely, by the will of God, who instituted the order of the state. From this divine institution flow cogently and inevitably the moral duties devolving on ruler and people, duties that in the modern philosophy of state are evolved from an abstract concept of the state. But personal as Luther's concept of the state is, it is not subjectivistic. The individual is not free to live according to his arbitrary discretion; he is committed to the norm of the highest objectivity, to God's order and command.

Thus the state does not emerge, as Aristotle believed, from man's natural social drive and impulse but from the plan and purpose of God to preserve a world torn and endangered by man's selfish passions. Luther might have cited the natural and inborn passion for power as a force and drive equally strong in man as the social or gregarious instinct. In view of this fact the latter cannot be accepted as a satisfactory explanation for the origin of state. Humanly viewed, the state is a nondeducible entity. For Luther it can be deduced only from the will of God. He would have regarded the question debated by scholasticism—whether the order of the state had already existed in paradise—as mental trilling and toying. In the Garden of Eden a harmonious and orderly freedom reigned. It did, to be sure, contain the family, the nucleus of later state power,[9] but not the state itself; for the

---

9. "Stufenpsalmen (1532–1533)," WA 40/3:221.3.

essence of the state is might or, more exactly, the law with coercive power. Its purpose is simple: to preserve life against destructive forces. The state is a miracle in a world that would, in its absence, be doomed to chaos. For this reason Luther was always ready to render counsel and aid in all concrete problems pertaining to civic life, such as education, public welfare, a wholesome family life, economic life, etc.

This conception of the nature and the mission of the state assumed special importance for Luther compared to the medieval view; for this reason he was a most zealous proponent of the liberation of the state from the tutelage of the church. He was proud of having restored to the state the sovereignty of which it had been stripped by the ecclesiastical powers. Government has its own peculiar divine commission; it is not the secular arm of the church. Just as every individual may regard himself divinely called into his vocation, so the government may also rest assured that it has been called and instituted by God. The prince is "God's magistrate" or, as Luther wrote his elector from the Coburg, his "gardener and caretaker" and the country's "father and aid," to whom God has entrusted especially His noblest treasure, His merry paradise, the youth, for protection and direction.[10] For this reason service in the state takes rank, in Luther's opinion, only second to service in the church. For the government is "the hand, the tube, and the means through which God channels all good things to us."[11] Thus participation in governmental service is a Christian's proper sphere for the practical demonstration of brotherly love. He must render this service not only because of compulsion and law but also out of "love and liberty."[12]

To be sure, this is and remains a secular service that can be rendered according to law and justice, not according to the rules of the Gospel or, let us say, of the Sermon on the Mount. The desire to rule in accordance with the injunction "Ye shall resist not evil" would mean converting the Sermon on the Mount into an impotent political Utopia that would founder miserably in the world of reality. For government without law and force would constitute, in effect, a charter enthroning evil. It would annul the order issued to the state by God: to preserve the world from chaos. Surely,

> if all people were true Christians, that is, genuine believers, then no prince, king, lord, sword, or law would be necessary. For what purpose would

---

10. May 20, 1530, WABr 5:326.45ff.

11. "Large Catechism," WA 30/1:136.

12. "Freiheit eines Christenmenschen," WA 7:37.4.

these serve if all people had the Holy Ghost in their hearts, who teaches and inspires them to deal fairly with all, to love everyone, and gladly and cheerfully to endure injustice, yes, even death, from all? Wherever there is a willingness to suffer injustice and to deal justly with others; there no quarrel is found, and no court, judge, penalty, law, or sword is necessary.[13]

As it happens, however, the world does not consist exclusively of genuine Christians; no, these are rare, even among the nominally Christian nations. Therefore, if necessary, order must be maintained by force. "If it were not for force, one man would devour the other, since all the world is evil and there is hardly one true Christian in a thousand; one could not marry and rear children, earn a livelihood and serve God, and in the end the world would become a desert."[14] The state is essentially an institution of force and coercion and, therefore, the antithesis of the kingdom of God, the kingdom of forgiving, of yielding, of loving, and of sacrificing. Nevertheless, the state is a divine institution. It is not essentially Christian. God preserves His work not only through a Christian but also through a pagan government, as ancient countries and the Turkish Empire demonstrate.

Thus the state, established by God, exists by reason of man's sin. If there were no sin, it would not be needed. But this, of course, does not imply that the administration of government or service in the state is sinful in itself. Nothing is farther from the truth than the oft-repeated canard that Luther regarded the state as sinful. It exists because of sin. Force is indispensable. Self-evidently, those who serve as officials of the state are sinful, but the order of the state *per se* is not. The old Anabaptist viewpoint, attacked by Luther, is rooted in this erroneous assumption of the state's sinfulness, and perhaps it has found its way into the Lutheran Church by way of pietism and in this way has done the church a great disservice. Luther has nothing at all in common with the pessimistic doctrine of Jakob Burckhardt that the might and force of the state are evil in themselves. "Licet potentes sint mali vel infideles, tamen ordo et potestas eorum bona sunt et ex Deo." ("Even though the mighty are sinful and without faith, their position and their authority are nevertheless good and of God.")[15]

---

13. "Von weltlicher Obrigkeit (1523)," WA 11:249.36.

14. "Von weltlicher Obrigkeit (1523)," WA 11:251.12.

15. "Epistle to the Romans," WA 56:123.20; cf. Johannes Ficker, ed., *Luthers Vorlesung über den Römerbrief, 1515/1516*, Anfänge reformatorischer Bibelauslegung 1 (Leipzig: Dieterich, 1908), 1:115.

But does the Christian in public service as judge or soldier not violate the commandment of love? Occasionally Luther has been understood as considering the commandment of love applicable only to a Christian's private life, not also to his public office. This is a disastrous misconception. On the contrary, Luther also regarded punitive jurisdiction and defense of country as works of love; they are services rendered to life and limb of one's neighbor. To be sure, one must realize that in Luther's vocabulary love is not synonymous with indulgence and weakness. God Himself can test and try man severely and lead him through death and hell to break his evil will; yet His goal in doing so is man's welfare and a new life. Therefore Luther knew that severity and kindness can be allies and that the helping hand of love cannot dispense with sternness. This truth he expressed repeatedly with reference to the government's dual office of the sword, its punitive power, and its right to national defense.

Justice is God's gift and commission. But for this very reason it is entrusted solely to the established government. Luther vigorously condemned every form of lynch law as demanded and practiced by the peasants and the Anabaptists. Whoever executes the office of the sword occupies an honorable and divinely instituted office. Therefore Luther also rescued the public executioner from the general contempt in which he was held. Luther emphasized that Christians must be the best judges, yes, that they alone are able to fill that position well. For law and punishment must not be manipulated rigidly and inflexibly. In view of this Luther contraposed the old dictum "Summum ius summa iniuria" and "Sheer clemency is the greatest inclemency."[16] Who is better qualified to be a judge than he who recognizes a higher judge over himself? Luther knew of scarcely another vocation so beset by inner dangers as that of the judiciary. For this reason he was unsparing with his harsh criticism of the legal profession. But on the other hand, Luther held that it is just this exalted and stern judicial office that is so suited to a Christian as a service of love and of protection of the weak.

Therefore the state and its service are "secular matters," determined by their own natural laws, subject neither to the precepts of the Sermon on the Mount nor to the dictates of the church; instead, its powers spring solely from its God-appointed mission to protect life and to safeguard the good citizen in the world. Because the state's function lies outside the con-

---

16. "Psalm 101 (1534–1535)," WA 51:206.1.

fines of the church, it listens to the dictates of reason. But does this imply that Luther evolved the state from a natural justice?

In this complicated question, it seems essential to me that we distinguish between natural law (*Gesetz*) and natural justice (*Recht*) in Luther. Although his usage of these terms overlaps, nevertheless the two domains are clearly separated. Luther was convinced that in our hearts we all have a natural law that tells us what to do. The universality of this law of conscience establishes the universality of human guilt. No one is exempt before God. Luther found the natural law excellently summarized in the Ten Commandments, in which, to be sure, the moral law, binding on all, must be lifted out of the national Jewish laws, for example, the Sabbath law. The Mosaic national laws, "the Jewish *Sachsenspiegel*," have been abolished for us. But the incomparable words with which Moses promulgates the natural law are God's commandment for all times. The quintessence of this moral law, the "two tablets" of the Ten Commandments, contain two distinctive features for Luther: the duty to worship God, for which the fidelity of the pagans to their idolatry offers him strong testimony, and the duty of regard for one another ("Therefore all things whatsoever ye would that men should do to you, do ye even so to them" [Matthew 7:12]), which Luther expressly equates with love of one's neighbor. The state is the natural sphere for the realization of both of these sections of the natural law. Self-evidently, it is obligated to proceed against atheism and blasphemy and to afford protection to divine worship, though it is not entitled to dictate to it. These are some of the state's most solemn duties; neglect of them will incur the wrath of God. The severe and punitive measures often demanded by the state are practical manifestations of love that befit a degenerate world.

We must distinguish between this natural law and what Luther calls natural justice (*Recht*). The latter is not a system of rules or of an established jurisprudence nor is it even patent to all; but it is the sum total of the vital rights that have developed from human intercourse and associations. Therefore only "God's miracle men" really have a thorough understanding of these. Luther approves the derivation of the written law from this natural justice. "But the mistake lies in the fact that everyone presumes to have this natural justice in his head. . . . This precious gem, called natural justice and reason, is a rarity among the children of men."[17]

---

17. "Psalm 101 (1534–1535)," WA 51:211.36.

For this reason Luther translates the ancient antithesis *iustum natura* and *iustum lege* ("that which is right by nature" and "that which is right by law") with "sound" and "ailing" law. "For what is done in conformity with nature proceeds well even without all laws, perhaps even in violation of all laws."[18] By natural justice Luther, therefore, means the unwritten measures demanded and suggested by a given situation, of which, to be sure, only the especially and divinely endowed judges and rulers have a full understanding. Just as God has implanted in the heart of man an enduring knowledge of His Law, the natural law, dimmed though it is today, so He has also imparted hidden internal rights to the historical forms of community life among men. Only to him who senses and perceives this will they yield their blessings. Otherwise only bungling and even disaster will result. When Luther essays to express in one word how best to meet this question of hidden and internal rights or justice, he is particularly glad to avail himself with special appreciation of the Aristotelian term of fairness (ἐπιείχεια), which must permeate all sound jurisprudence and government. But with Luther this fairness is nothing other than the love demanded by the natural moral law. Thus (still without any reference to the Gospel) natural justice and love converge into the same plane for Luther. They are not only placed in juxtaposition but are used synonymously when Luther says that one should always act in such a way "that love and natural justice always hover above. For if you judge according to the dictates of love, you will decide and determine all matters easily without law books; but wherever you disregard love and natural justice, you will never judge in a God-pleasing way, even though you had devoured all law books and lawyers."[19]

Thus the natural moral law and natural justice flow into love. It must be noted that Luther regards them as a natural demand. But it is just as clear that this natural justice, despite its direct contact with Aristotle, is something different from the traditional natural justice (*Naturrecht*). Luther has far more in mind than an equitable adjustment of the fair claims of all concerned, and he is less interested in the natural justice (for example, the subjective personal rights or the general principle of international law) than he is in the duty of love incumbent on all and operating through fairness (*Billigkeit*). Thus Luther deepens the ethos of the tradi-

---

18. "Psalm 101 (1534–1535)," WA 51:214.14.

19. "Von weltlicher Obrigkeit (1523)," WA 11:279.25ff.

tional natural rights. To be sure, he would never regard it as immutable, eternal law, as has often been done in what is taught about natural law; it is inevitably imperfect and fragmentary in this world. It remains natural justice for Luther. Therefore he would never call it Christian, for Christian justice says: Do not resist evil; endure injustice; repay evil with good. State and law are matters of reason, but reason is the basic chord of the divine commandment of love transposed to the earthly realm. One day it will be resolved into the full harmony of the divine law of love.

Now the question of the state's and of law's relationship to the area of spiritual life, the church, urgently suggests itself. This was one of the central themes of occidental history. It is a difficult question for Luther—first, from the point of view of the state because he had delivered the secular government from every vestige of ecclesiastical guardianship and had emphatically taught the difference between the spiritual and the secular spheres of life; second, from the point of view of the church. With this differentiation he had assigned distinctiveness and independence from the secular government not only to the church, which he regards as a purely spiritual though a real entity, namely, the communion of saints under its head, Christ, but also to the empirical Christian congregation. Although Luther does not yet draw a line of demarcation between civil and church community, he nevertheless had sharply separated the jurisdiction of each.

Surprisingly enough, Luther's attempt to separate church and state resulted in the church rule of each territorial prince. How did this come about? Its history reaches back to the independent Germanic church. The relationship between the lord of the manor and the priest, whom the former engaged for the church built on his soil, again made its appearance on a higher level in the investiture dispute. The bishops were, so to speak, the private priests of the kings. After long and hard struggles the papacy extricated itself from royal power and, in turn, laid low its adversary, the German emperor. However, in place of the one felled enemy dozens of competitors, the territorial princes, now arose for the papacy. As unnamed coheirs of the Worms Concordat (1122), they retrieved for themselves a large number of the lost royal rights over the church. They merely regained something that had been retained in other countries, for example, in France and in Norman England. In addition to this power of the territorial lords, based more on active influence than on laws, we have the comprehensive rights of patronage of the lower nobility. All these are roots from which the authority of the territorial princes over the evangelical churches of a later day grew. The church government of the territorial prince "is not the product of reformatory speculation at all . . . but an outcome of late-medieval public law fertilized by ideas emanating from the ancient Germanic *Eigenkirchentum*"—this is the succinct yet basically correct opinion of Heinrich Boehmer.[20] Modern research has revealed the extent of the princes' prerogatives even before the Reformation. Without further ado, they made bold to interfere with church matters in emergencies (and it is always easy to construe any situation as an emergency), to give ear to appeals against the abuse of ecclesiastical privileges, etc. "The strong development of church government by the territorial princes in various forms and for various reasons even before the Reformation offers ample proof that the deepest roots of these Lutheran views of ecclesiastical policy reach far back into the medieval past."[21]

But a second influence, dating back to the humanistic concept of the state, dare not be overlooked. This was a type of totalitarian idea founded on the *salus publica*. According to Erasmus, the public welfare is attainable only through the education of mankind. Therefore the state has a moral, even a religious, mission: It must educate the whole man. Because the church basically does nothing else than that, the duties of the two coincide. The public office of the state's educator and that of the true minister are really identical. It is no mere coincidence that Zwingli, the reformer who had the largest amount of humanistic blood in his veins, was also the most resolute contender for the Christian state. The moral idea underlying the humanistic welfare state and the reformatory liberation of the state to independent sovereignty merge for him into this goal.

Luther consistently followed the same line of thought on this subject from beginning to end. He always adhered to the idea of a temporary or emergency bishop (*Notbischofsamt*). He staunchly resisted the institution of government boards for ecclesiastical affairs, which the consistories even at that time were becoming and later did become. Their authority was to be confined to matrimonial laws, consequently, to a secular matter, which had to be redefined after the elimination of canonical laws. The princes and the visitors appointed by these were, in Luther's view, merely tempo-

---

20. Heinrich Boehmer, *Luther im Lichte der neueren Forschung*, 4th ed. (Leipzig: B. C. Teubner, 1917), 253. Heinrich Boehmer, *Luther in Light of Recent Research*, trans. Carl Huth (New York: Christian Herald, 1916).

21. Justus Hashagen, *Staat u. Kirche vor der Reformation* (Essen: G. D. Baedeker, 1931), 558.

rary substitutes for the true evangelical bishops who could later assume the office of church leadership. The course Luther wished to pursue is indicated by the installation of a bishop in Naumburg in 1542.

To be sure, the weight of facts and the use of language cannot be ignored here. At times Luther found it expedient to avail himself of the influence of city council or of prince, without again defining and delimiting an already clearly expressed opinion. With pious princes, such as the Electors John and John Frederick, he did not feel compelled to distinguish too closely. After all, everything depended on the person. A great emergency or a dearth of proper persons could occasionally necessitate connivance at a violation of the principle of separation of the two realms, that of the state and that of the church.

It seems particularly confusing that Luther clearly called upon the government as such to abolish the Mass as a public blasphemy and to provide for a uniform Divine Service. Prior to the introduction of the Reformation in the Saxon duchy, he admonished Duke Henry of Saxony to do away with idolatry in emulation of the Jewish kings and the emperors Constantine, Theodosius, and Gratian. But here the government was to act in its own interest to ward off the wrath of God from the country for rampant and unrestrained blasphemy. Likewise, he held that a uniform Divine Service must redound to the immediate welfare of a country, with discord and turmoil following in the wake of disparate forms. For this reason a government enlightened by God through the Gospel must take proper measures for its own sake and for the sake of the country. Thus he set the problems of the abolition of the Mass apart from the question of the proper relationship between the state and the Christian congregation.

When Luther assumed that he would not be misunderstood, or when necessity demanded it, he was often, as it would appear, incorrect in his choice of language and in his actions. But whenever it was a matter of defining the basic relationship between the government and the Christian congregation, he adhered clearly and definitely to his principle.

Exception has been taken to Luther's appeal for aid in the church's reformation to the prince as an individual, as *praecipuum membrum ecclesiae* ("chief member of the church") on the grounds that he [Luther] conceived the government as a member of the unified body of Christianity and, as such, authorized to help. The objection is supported by the formidable authority of Rudolph Sohm. This broaches the question concerning a unified *corpus Christianum*, which, however, cannot be treated in passing. Did this really imply a stronger union between church and state? Or does it not, in the majority of cases, refer to the *corpus mysticum* of the church, which embraces both spiritual and secular life, analogous to the church's head, Christ, who is Lord over body and soul? The proofs in Gierke, often cited for the *corpus Christianum* idea, apply, for the most part, to the church. Can it be said that there is a real concept of unity embracing church and state when both entities are placed side by side but with each in clear contradistinction to the other? Even the concordance doctrine of Nicholas of Cusa, adduced by way of explanation, merely points, after all, to the harmony between the two functions of the *corpus mysticum*, the church.[22] However, the question cannot be treated here in detail. I am convinced that Luther (even admitting certain dubious allusions in his address to the German nobility) surmounted the idea of a spiritual-secular body of Christendom in which the government as such is empowered to exercise an ecclesiastical function. Consistent with his conviction that faith is a matter of individual decision, Luther here had a person, not a body, in mind. To him, too, the Western world and Christendom are identical. But he conceives of this, insofar as it is church, entirely as a communion of individuals, not as the fusion of two organisms within a higher unit. This would have been a rehash of that intermixture of church and state that he had recognized and destroyed as the archevil of occidental history. Therein lies one of Luther's basic deviations from the medieval period.

Although Luther did not consider it his mission to evolve a complete theory of the state, his viewpoint nonetheless shows remarkable internal compactness. It is an application of his knowledge of God's Word to national community life. The most important item is the correct relationship between the secular and the spiritual realms. The state, the law, and community life are not subordinate to any superior canonical law but have their own divine commission and their own responsibility. Luther believed in the immediacy of God to each station in life, to every vocation. The secular and sacred spheres do not lie side by side, but service in the secular realm is also service to God inasmuch as it is service of love to one's neighbor. For this reason civil service can be performed properly only when the incumbent looks reverently to God, to His justice, and to His forgiveness for all shortcomings. When Luther thus freed the public offi-

---

22. Otto Friedrich von Gierke, *Das deutsche Genossenschaftsrecht* (Darmstadt: Wissenschaftliche Buchemeinschaft, 1954), 3:538.

cial's conscience from every clerical or ecclesiastical tutelage, he at the same time addressed the most exacting demand to it, namely, strict accountability to God. There is hardly a more Lutheran utterance by a German statesman to be found than the well-known reply of Bismarck to the critic who had reproached him with being an unscrupulous politician: He [the critic] "should first try his own conscience in this arena"; it was not easy "always to achieve that clarity on the soil of which trust in God grows."[23]

This training of the conscience for the proper use of reason is Luther's essential contribution to the German development of the state concept. With it he reared a government faithful to, and solicitous for, the public welfare, as well as law-abiding and devoted subjects, teaching them to observe proper moral bounds in every political act. In the German nation he instilled an aversion to an absolute imperialism, an aversion not forgotten until recent times, and then only by a relatively small number who were alienated from the Christian tradition. Luther acknowledged the government's power and its authority, but he differentiated between protective and predatory power. It was, therefore, more than incidental that Machiavelli remained practically unknown in Germany for approximately 100 years and that he was violently opposed later. On the other hand, even if Luther adhered to certain doctrines inherited from his day, he also left behind him a norm anchored in a conscience that believed and trusted in God, a norm that could divest itself of historical ties and meet the requirements of a later day.

Above all, Luther's awareness of the divine origin of the state ruled out any doctrine in which human rationalization no longer recognized the state as a power ordained over us and superior to us. For this reason the antagonism between state and individual, so prominent in the enlightened state doctrines of Western Europe, never took real root in German soil. "In the final analysis, it is the moral instinct of its Lutheran training which prevented this."[24] All German state doctrines, whether consciously or unconsciously affected by Luther, breathe the conviction that the state is something original, something nondeducible, an order established by God that cannot be explained from any natural impulse or from a historical

---

23. "Letter to Andrae, 26 December 1865," in *Collected Works* XIV, 2:709.

24. Günther Holstein, *Luther und die deutsche Staatsidee*, Recht und Staat in Geschichte und Gegenwart 45 (1926), 13.

purpose, let us say, the necessity to regulate human social life after humanity's arrival at a definite stage of maturity and civilization.

Any concrete political views handed down by Luther rank second to this legacy of moral influences on political life. As we know, he did not draft and devise an outline of an ideal state; he did not regard it as his duty to make revolutionary proposals, but in the main he worked toward an amelioration of the system that he found.[25]

The immediate political effect of Luther's position on the state is undoubtedly to be seen in an increase in territorial power. In view of the aforesaid it must be obvious that this was not Luther's intention. The force of historical circumstances brought this about. His own idea of a strong *Reich* and his predilection for corporate, cooperative societies was pushed aside by the victoriously ascending power of cities and territories and by their professional officialdom (little loved by Luther).[26] No one benefited more by Luther's elimination of canonical law and by the strong authority with which he invested the government than the territorial princes who worked their way to the fore between the emperor and the lesser feudal lords. It required no great skill on their part to attract the strong wind of the Reformation's religious and moral force into their sails. The government that proved strongest politically naturally harvested the fruits of this new schooling toward the state. Because of its weakness and its inability to capitalize on the situation, it was not the *Reich* that garnered the fruit. Above all, this must be ascribed to the fact that Charles V, in his last attempt to strengthen imperial power, misjudged the situation, trying first to bridge the religious problem with half-measures and finally to eradicate it by the use of force. These policies drove the Reformation and the princes definitely into each other's arms and sounded the death knell for the union of the empire. Accordingly, Luther's view of the state never crystallized into a definite political form. However, it maintained itself as a moral idea and force and was able to develop amid the most varying historical forms because Luther had endowed it with the requisite elasticity and flexibility.

---

25. Cf. pp. 224ff.

26. Cf. Heinrich Bornkamm, *Die Bedeutung der Reformation für das deutsche Beamtentum*, Schriften des Verbandes deutscher evangelischer Beamtenvereine 3 (1932).

THE GOSPEL AND THE SOCIAL WORLD

This theme is a segment of a larger unit, namely, of the topic: the Gospel and the World. It is impossible to understand Luther's position on the social world until we have familiarized ourselves with his views on the world at large. If we ponder the many words he spoke either in praise of this beautiful world or in sorrow over its evils and penetrate to the core of the question, we find ourselves, in the end, confronted by two simple contrasting statements. These are as simple and plain as all the seemingly wild contradictions and surprising outbursts of this mastermind are basically simple and clear. This world was created and fell into decay—created so order and progress were once identical in it, so the laws of nature and of the mind were automatically observed. For more penetrating eyes, the world even today bears, under the scars of decay, the marks of its origin in God, to whom it will one day return. At the same time the world has fallen prey to the powers to which God makes temporary concessions in His creation: sin, conflict (*Kampf*), insecurity, death. The present time marks the interregnum of the devil in the world. But God has not only fixed a definite time limit to the devil's reign in the world, He also is even now challenging his might with a dual counterforce: reason and love. These constitute the second pair of contrasts. Since the fall of man, the world stands in need of law, order, and a restraining hand. Reason, though vitiated and erring, can still perform miracles in the preservation of this decaying world. But even at its best, all the functions of reason are only makeshift by means of which the world contrives to exist. Reason falls far short of restoring the pristine beauty and freedom of creation. To re-create at least a fraction of this on the poor earth is the great prerogative of love. Without force, yet surpassing reason by far in efficacy, love grants us a faint glimpse of that pure naturalness of life that we forfeited. Where love reigns (and to Luther this means in true Christendom), there we find a restoration of proper order; there only justice is practiced and injustice willingly endured. There court, judge, punishment, sword, and law can be dispensed with.[1] One of pure creation's characteristics was the absence of possessions, freedom from worry and from cupidity. This is ushered back into the world by true love. Accordingly, the two pairs of contrasts reflecting Luther's worldview are closely allied. The world's decay can be stayed only through the agency of clear and rigid reason. But love alone can weld the sundered ring of creation together again. Love is the Gospel's great gift to the world. And this love owes its being to the love of God, which antedates it. However, Luther is at the same time painfully conscious of the weakness of this love in the world and of the scarcity of genuine Christians (whom he calls "rare birds") who are able to cure all the world's social ills.

Just as Luther's view of the world in general and thus also of the social world was nothing but a sober and objective reflection of reality, so he advocated no remedies for the world's ills except those of reality. Any abstract ideal according to which the world might be reformed was entirely foreign to him. Neither any system of ancient natural law nor any ecclesiastical-scholastic order or a secular social order determined his view of the social world.

Luther's clear and sharp differentiation between the secular and the spiritual realms, which rejected the dictatorship of any ecclesiastically approved order, separated him from the social ideal of scholasticism. "Christus non curat politiam aut oeconomiam" ("Christ does not concern Himself with the state or with political economy").[2] With this categorical statement, Luther forbade any trespassing from the spiritual realm into the secular, whether this was by way of a Christian natural law, as the scholastics demanded, or by means of a social reconstruction patterned after the Sermon on the Mount, as advocated by the Anabaptists. To be sure, Luther did not propose that the world should drift and fend for itself; otherwise he would not have concluded the aforementioned sentence with the words "sed rex est ad destruendum diaboli regnum et ad salvandos homines" ("but He is a King who wants to destroy the reign of the devil and save mankind").

1. "Von weitlicher Obrigkeit (1523)," WA 11:250.4.

2. WATr 1, no. 932.

He recommended stronger weapons for the preservation of the world than those contained in the admonitions of the Gospel: for the obdurate, the inexorable power of a reasonable law, and for those into whose heart God found entry, victory over diabolical selfishness through love.

Another more profound comprehension of the concept of reason separated Luther from natural law as a system of simple, unalterable rules. When Luther often refers to "natural" law or, preferably, to "natural laws," he has the deep organic laws governing growth and development in mind, laws that must be preserved in a sound political and social order. To be thoroughly conversant with them is a real art. This is the skill of the sound heroes (*gesunde Helden*) and miracle men whom God sends to a nation occasionally and whom He endows with special grace, so they require the written laws no more than a Christian imbued with love stands in need of the commandments.[3] They know that the world cannot be governed by rule of thumb because there are ten exceptions to every rule. They know that the world is "an ailing thing," constantly in need of mending.[4] Judges must be able to thread their difficult way skillfully between the letter and the spirit of the law, between severity and leniency, for they are "leges vivae seu anima legis" ("the living law or the soul of the law").[5] It would seem clear that Luther regarded as qualified for this difficult calling only him who believes the scriptural saying: "Ye judge not for man, but for the LORD" (2 Chronicles 19:6)—only him who recognizes a judge over himself and, as a result of this knowledge, is free from the personal inclinations and passions that altogether too easily dull and obscure fair judgment.[6]

Finally, Luther's keen understanding of national bounds and boundaries induced him to reject the humanists' dream of a world-embracing imperium. His sound concept of a national state would not permit him to accept such a universal state and universal law, though these are divorced from the universal church, as advocated by the humanists.

But what remained for Luther's structure of a social world if he discarded all these ideologies from which a social ideal may be evolved? What is the meaning of his desire to use the forces of actual life? Undoubtedly Luther adhered rather closely to the existing forms of social life. He cer-

---

3. Cf. pp. 149f., 172ff., 205f.

4. "Auslegung des 101. Psalms (1534–1535)," WA 51:214.29ff.

5. "Deuteronomium Mosi (1525)," WA 14:554.39.

6. "Deuteronomium Mosi (1525)," WA 14:667.1ff.

tainly feels no great urge to reconstruct a world that is fast approaching its demise, a world in which a Christian is not to insist on his own rights but should be willing to endure even an unjust fate. Therefore Luther has often been charged with having a narrow patriarchal view and with thinking only of preserving the status quo. To be sure, in the main Luther gave support to the existing order, but he did so only when this was in accord with his own judgment and with common sense. But even when he regarded change and revision as necessary, he demanded that this be done in an orderly manner and through the proper channels. For he was convinced that in general violent upheaval is more destructive than constructive.

Most of the phases of the existing social order that found favor in Luther's eyes were derived from the old German judiciary system, both as this pertains to the law in its narrower sense and as it pertains to principles governing civic life in general. He preferred the old popular forms of the civil code and jurisdiction, the peasant courts, the knights' courts (*Rittergerichte*), and the courts of the territorial government. Because each land and province has its own peculiar nature and character, it would follow that each should be governed according to its "own simple laws," not according to the "complicated and foreign" imperial laws.[7] The centralization of power to which the emperor aspired seemed to Luther a deprivation of the rights of the lesser governments of the princes, the counts, the lords, and the knights. He regarded Turkey, the only country with a rigidly centralized government with which Luther was acquainted (at least from hearsay), as a pure and simple tyranny. He held that the acquired and the conferred privileges must be honored and preserved. For this reason the corporate bodies that at one time played so prominently in German law were dear to his heart. He even viewed the Christian congregation as a body of equal freemen, which by reason of the universal priesthood of believers elects its ministers of the Gospel just as a civil community elects its magistrates. What Luther learned and received from German law he transmitted through his reformatory works to public life; for the most immediate effect of the Reformation on Germany's internal political life was, as the legal authority Alfred Schultze declared in a famous treatise, "the emergence of the concept of a public body, of the body corporate" in the cities.[8] Therefore Luther had an open mind for the idea of mutual

---

7. "An den christlichen Adel (1520)," WA 6:459.36ff.

8. Alfred Schultze, *Stadtgemeinde und Reformation*, Recht und Staat in Geschichte und Gegenwart 11 (Tübingen: J. C. B. Mohr, 1918), 49.

economic aid within various civic groups, and the later, similar aims of the Christian Socialist movement were surely in harmony with his views.

Luther's insight into the old German law was also reflected in his views concerning the problem of interest.[9] In any business transaction involving interest, Luther demanded a clearly defined security (for example, an acre of ground or a house) to which the debtor's liability was to be confined. He denied the creditor's right to demand payment at any time without the debtor's consent.

But Luther also found fault with the old German law. He decried the social asperities in the Old Saxon law, especially the harsh treatment of widows; however, he raised the question whether the literal and slavish interpretation and application of the jurors was not to be blamed rather than the old law code itself.[10] The incarceration of debtors seemed non-sensical to Luther because it implied that property was more highly esteemed than man, who has been destined for work.[11]

It needs be pointed out only in passing how much Luther contributed to an improvement of social conditions even in the absence of basic changes. In a prosperous peasantry he recognized the foundation of a sound political economy. Marriage at a relatively early age was advocated by him to give the sex impulse a proper and fruitful outlet. For all strata of the people, he desired an opportunity for healthy social and economic progress. Therefore he fought zealously against the guilds for isolating themselves with a moral mien, which he unmasked as professional jealousy, from the "dishonorable" have-nots in the cities. At the same time he was not blind to the value of corporate regulation of manufacture by the trades, and he vigorously opposed free trade, which even then had its proponents. He feared that capital would thereby gain control of the crafts and that the poorer classes, supposedly the beneficiaries of such a move, would be crushed by the ensuing unlimited competition.[12]

---

9. Hermann Barge, *Luther und der Frühkapitalismus*, Schriften des Vereins für Reformationsgeschichte 168 (Gütersloh: C. Bertelsmann, 1951), 47ff.

10. WATr 4, no. 4139.

11. "Deuteronomium (1525)," WA 14:714.31ff.; "Predigt uber das 2. Buch Mose (1524–1527)," WA 16:542.14.

12. Cf. Karl Holl, *Gesammelte Aufsätze zur Kirchengeschichte* (Tübingen: J. C. B. Mohr, 1928), 3:130ff.

Luther warred against lewdness and harlotry, against carousing, and against luxury in dress. He called for a proper relationship between employer and employee, a relationship based on sympathetic concern and on obedience. Even if we were to lengthen the list of Luther's social and economic suggestions, the picture would not change. He neither drafted a new program of social reform nor did he confine himself to the program of his day, but he strove and labored toward an organic improvement of existing civic and social forms.

Luther does not dispense such counsel on social and economic problems in his capacity as a theologian or according to biblical precepts. There is scarcely another idea that he drove home so tirelessly as this: that the spiritual and the secular spheres must remain strictly separated. With regard to this difference, he felt constrained

> to knock it, chew it [*einkäuen*], drive it, and wedge it in. . . . For the cursed devil does not desist from cooking and brewing these two realms together. The lords of the world always want, in the devil's name, to teach and instruct Christ how He should govern His church and conduct ecclesiastical affairs. Similarly the double-dealing clerics and the factious spirits want (not in God's name) to show and teach how the secular government should be managed.[13]

Any opinion Luther ventured on such social or economic questions does not lay claim to the authority of canonical law or to that of a New Testament social order. He spoke merely as a Christian who, as he was obliged to do, served his brethren in love by marshaling reason in support of his views. He did not shrink from preaching these opinions from the pulpit, but he always stated them only in the form of sound and sensible advice. For example, in his discussion of the Seventh Commandment in 1525 Luther inveighs against the guilds for their occasional abuse of their monopoly and suggests that if friendly negotiations do not avail, their defiance be broken down by entrusting the provisioning of a city to a single, reliable merchant.[14] He never transgressed the dividing line that he had drawn so sharply between the spiritual and the secular realms. Wherever he saw this line endangered seriously, he assailed the transgressor with a ferocity that can only be understood on the background of a centuries-old calamitous disregard for this line by the medieval church.

---

13. "Psalm 101 (1534–1535)," WA 51:239.22.

14. "Sermons on Exodus (1524–1527)," WA 16:518.4ff.

Only in light of Luther's recognition of this danger can his severity against the peasants in the Peasants' War, still regarded by many as a blot on his social attitude, be explained. The accusations that he had no sympathetic heart for the oppressed and struggling masses never cease. Luther's position will be intelligible only to him who realizes that the peasant movement was a social problem to Luther only at its inception. It was revolt, and he opposed revolt at all times like a wall of brass. More than this, it was rebellion in the name of the Gospel, thus it resolved itself into rebellion against the Gospel itself. So long as the demands of the peasants remained only social demands, they found a rather ready champion in Luther. Within the limits of his knowledge of the questions involved, and unless he saw fit to entrust these to expert opinion, he gladly cooperated with the peasants and earnestly pleaded their cause before the conscience of the government. But he did insist that the peasants' suit be submitted and discussed in an orderly fashion. Furthermore, he denied them the right to advance their claims in the name of Christ. So long as they supported their demands with an appeal to their natural and human rights, they met with no opposition from Luther. In that event one would have to wait how God Himself would settle the matter. In Luther's view those who adorn themselves with the name of Christ are invested with an entirely different type of right and prerogative, namely, that of suffering. "Suffering, suffering, cross, cross is the Christian's prerogative, that and no other."[15] Because of such expressions, Luther has been charged with a morbid delight in suffering, a delight that has no ear for the voice of social justice. This does not apply to him. He never objected to a peaceful and orderly negotiation for adjustment of social problems so long as these moved in the secular orbit; but, above all, the entire theme of suffering by Christians was encompassed for him by the promise: "Vengeance is Mine; I will repay, saith the Lord" (Romans 12:19; Deuteronomy 32:35). That promise was genuine and real for Luther. But whoever chose to carry out that vengeance himself—especially under the banner of Christian liberty—brought down the wrath of God upon himself. Luther abhorred the devastation and the endless bloodshed that result from rebellion. He often said that it is easy to initiate a quarrel, but it is beyond our ability to terminate it. Above all, he knew that God does not tolerate a rebellion. This conviction explains his harsh summons to resist the rebels. His reply

---

15. "Ermahnung zum Frieden (1525)," WA 18:310.10.

to any accusation of being unmerciful was: "Merciful—that is neither here nor there. That is not the question. We are speaking of God's Word. God wants to see the king honored and rebellious people destroyed. Methinks God is as merciful as we are."[16] He viewed his own attitude toward the Peasants' War as a service of "harsh mercy," which, as he said, heals body and soul.

Two examples for Luther's consistent stand with regard to the Peasants' War may be cited: first, his clear-cut no in answer to every question of a revolt of the Protestant princes against their sovereign, the emperor, no matter how insistent and solemn their assurances that the survival of the Gospel was at stake. Here, too, he counseled to preach the Gospel and to suffer if it was God's will. He exhorted the princes to obedience with the same determined zeal with which he admonished the peasants. Second, Luther forbade any resistance to the emperor if the latter should come to the country to imprison him or his adherents. In that event nothing but the duty of martyrdom remained.

Luther did not desert the peasants. Nor did he betray his former position proclaimed, for example, in his writing *To the Christian Nobility*. The opposite was true. If he did not choose to deny the core of his message and become untrustworthy, if he did not want to make the Gospel a political matter, he had to assume that position and no other. The peasants themselves forfeited Luther's strong voice of intercession. He saw that the fanatical preachers were mainly at fault; they had pressed the banner of revolt into the hands of the rebels in the name of Christ. That was the tragedy of this fateful hour, not lack of sympathetic understanding for the social position of the peasants. Luther was deeply sympathetic and tried his utmost to avert disaster. But all his pleas were futile. Therefore nothing remained for him but to sound a sad and fervent warning as he engaged in a struggle for the purity of the Gospel and the preservation of the divinely ordained order in the world.

Every statement made by Luther on civic and social life stems from the firm conviction that a corrupt world can be saved only by reason and force. This is in accord with God's plan for this world. Force, properly and fairly applied, is, in Luther's opinion, part of God's design for the world. His utterances on the state, on law, on war, etc., offer abundant proof of this.

---

16. "Sendbrief von dem hasten Büchlein wider die Bauern (1525)," WA 18:386.14.

The fact that this world is depraved leads to another result, which Luther mentioned in a most wonderful manner in his discussion of interest. With no other economic question did he occupy himself so much as with this one. He was bewildered not only by the gigantic business enterprises—the corporations, the monopolies which, with the growth of capitalism, were determining the economic life of the time in ever-increasing measure—but still more by the unscrupulousness and the ungodliness underlying all these enterprises. After all, the charging of interest was generally based on the want of the other person who needed money and was obliged to pay any rate demanded of him. It seemed unnatural to Luther that inanimate money should yield revenue like an acre of ground or like any productive labor. But his objections went beyond this. His most urgent objection was directed against man's attempt to safeguard and guarantee by means of lending capital at interest what God has placed into the category of uncertainty and insecurity. Property in this transient, changeable world is, after all, something insecure. Whoever lends his money to another at a fixed rate of interest shifts the insecurity to the shoulders of the debtor. But by no means did Luther reject all profit accruing from lending money at interest. He found no objection to this so long as the rate was modest and other reasonable conditions were met. He believed that the creditor is entitled to a share in any profit gained with his money, but at the same time he insisted that the creditor also share in any loss sustained. Many a well-considered suggestion was offered by Luther with regard to this problem, but his most important advice undoubtedly was this: The possibility of gain and of loss must be taken into account. The creditor as well as the debtor must participate in the risk that is unavoidable in this insecure world. At the same time Luther disapproved of any unsecured loan at interest; he demanded that the loan be secured in some definite way, for example, by a piece of real estate.

Luther's viewpoint has often been cited as proof of an outmoded and long since rejected attitude toward questions of political economy. Undoubtedly capitalism could not be checked. New principles of political economy brushed Luther's objections aside. But it is my opinion that the more the evils and the dangers of the capitalistic era are recognized and organically overcome, the more clearly Luther will emerge as one of the great warners on the threshold of this era, a warner whose fundamental ideas in a new form deserve attention.

Reason and love. This forceful pair does not represent two heterogeneous, mutually exclusive media for putting the world in order and healing it. The Christian—yes, according to Luther, any conscientious man—perceives the deep unity behind them. In the providence of God the regimen of reason, its law and its justice, is an agency of love. With it He vouchsafes continued life to mankind, which is addicted to sin and bent on self-destruction. It is a means of love conforming to the needs of this unregenerate world. This truth will be best understood by the true Christian who has experienced how God has drawn him unto Himself with the terrors of an aroused conscience and who is aware that the old Adam in us constantly requires the discipline of the Law. Therefore he understands that in human community life love must avail itself of the stern measures of the Law. Yet the Christian is the one who is destined to rend this earthly garb and guise of love in his own environs and to unveil its true form.

Our discussions thus far might have created the impression that the Gospel has no direct answers to questions bearing on social life but answers them only through the circuitous route of law and reason. Nevertheless, the Christian finds all the answers to social questions in the Gospel. For all the barriers and crutches required by reason for overcoming social need are eliminated for him who lives on the love of God.

So far as the Christian and the Gospel are concerned, the restraining arm of the state and of the law and the restrictions on interest rates could be abolished. In the life of the Christian the love that springs from the Gospel abounds. In this love alone we find the freedom of God's original creation restored. Christian love is cognizant of a better use of money than that of legally regulated loans on interest. When a Christian "beholds a man who has no coat, he says to his money: Come forth, Sir Gulden. Here is a poor naked man without a coat, You must serve him. Over there lies a sick man who has nothing to refresh him. Come forth, Sir Annaberger; come forth, Sir Joachimsthaler, you must go there and help him."[17] Among true Christians all social problems solve themselves. It is disgraceful for a Christian congregation if any of its members find it necessary to go begging.

But the power inherent in the Gospel for the solution of social problems is even more far-reaching than this. To ensure that the power of love does not lie fallow, the Gospel assigns a definite place to every Christian in

---

17. "Sommerpostille (1526)," WA 10/1.2:376.14.

the world. Among other things, two words, *calling* and *labor*, figure in Luther's contribution to the development of the German social life.

It was Luther who first gave the word *calling* (*Beruf*) the deep, full ring it has today.[18] In Catholic parlance from the Middle Ages down to the present, the word denotes being called to an ecclesiastical office. The priestly calling or the monastic calling are fixed in the popular mind as designating God's act of calling a person into these preferential vocations. Surpassing by far any linguistic attempts in this direction by German mysticism, Luther adjudged that the incumbent of any honorable occupation has been called to his office by God just as truly as anyone else. Thus Luther extended the term "calling" to all honest and productive vocations. Not only the ecclesiastical office but all honest work and every occupation is a calling in the best sense of the word in Luther's language. Thus our word *calling* (*Beruf*) has attained its deep connotation of obligation and duty. The view that all honest labor, performed in the fear of God, is hallowed is one of the cornerstones in the social history of Germany since the days of the Reformation. It expresses the basic equality of all classes and of all types of honest toil in the sight of God, the Supreme Judge.

Luther's contribution to the meaning of the word *labor* (*Arbeit*) is indissolubly allied to this.[19] This word, too, has a long history. Originally it referred principally to exertion, pain, struggle (*Ringen*). This is its meaning in the beginning of the *Lay of the Nibelungen*, and it was often applied to ascetic, meritorious work. Through Luther it received its decisive meaning. It lost its ring of privation and asceticism that still adhered to it and became the general expression for human activity. The Christian knows that this activity is the sphere assigned to him by God. Therefore he performs his work joyfully and with the confidence that it is God-pleasing.

Luther's influence on the social structure resulted in a secularization of the world. The state, the law, the community life received their own sovereignty and were no longer subject to ecclesiastical law. This, however, implied at the same time a hallowing of the world. For in the spirit of the Gospel it expressed the immediateness to God of every calling and of all work.

---

18. Karl Holl, "Die Geschichte des Wortes Beruf," in *Gesammelte Aufsätze zur Kirchengeschichte*, 3:189–219.

19. Hildburg Geist, "Arbeit: Die Entscheidung eines Wortwertes durch Luther," *Lutherjahrbuch* (1931): 83–113.

The genuine love in Christendom that is qualified to cure all social ills has only one inexhaustible source for Luther: the love of God, which has appeared to the world in Christ and is poured out into our hearts. Here lies the secret of an inexhaustible life. This is indicated by Luther in a sermon on the rich man and poor Lazarus:

> The believer sets no store by himself but takes comfort solely in divine mercy. This he regards as his riches. And even though he had much, even the treasures of all kings, still his heart is not attached to these; but he always looks down humbly, takes the troubles of all people to heart, and serves all those who are in need. And whatever face he has inwardly before God he shows outwardly.[20]

That represents, figuratively expressed, Luther's contribution to the question how the Gospel equips the Christian for his position in the social world: "Whatever face he has inwardly before God he shows outwardly."

---

20. "Predigt (1522)," WA 10/3:180.8.

Luther's Translation
of the New Testament

In December 1521 Luther had secretly left the Wartburg for a short sojourn in Wittenberg, where he wanted to check the turbulent innovations that had been introduced and work toward moderation. Upon his return to his quiet asylum, he embarked on a momentous undertaking that his friends had earnestly enjoined upon his conscience: the translation of the Bible. It was self-evident that he, as an individual and with the few aids at his disposal at the Wartburg, could consider only the translation of the New Testament, not that of the entire Bible. Yes, if he could live in hiding in Wittenberg and there enjoy the assistance of his friends, he would come at once and begin with the Old Testament! He asks the Wittenbergers to consider this thought "that it may result in a translation worthy of being read by Christians. I hope we shall present our Germany with a better one than that of the Latins."[1] It was the love for his people that pressed the pen into his hand for this great work. This was the motive he also mentioned in a letter dated November 1 written to the Strasbourg humanist Cerbel for the German essays composed at the Wartburg: "I have been born for my Germans; them I also want to serve."[2]

All his previous work impelled him with inner logic to the translation of the Bible. Through the Bible alone he had become what he was. Through it he had learned to rout scholastic theology, and in it he had

---

1. "Jan. 13, 1522, to Amsdorf," WABr 2:423.48; "To Melanchthon," WABr 2:427.128.
2. WABr 2:397.34.

rediscovered the core of the Gospel. The Bible was his only friend in his lonely hours, the sole weapon in his conflict against a thousand-year-old system. If he had a right to believe that up to this time he had won all his oral and literary skirmishes, he had to tell himself that he was indebted to the Bible for these victories. Although the plea of his Wittenberg friends gave the final impulse, yet he carried out his own work, his *opus proprium*.With this work he not only revealed to his people the source of his life, but in it he also found the fullest justification for his previous actions. Henceforth everybody could and should judge for himself and thereby exercise the first duty and the foremost privilege of the universal priesthood, for this was precisely what Luther had discovered in the Scriptures as the basic essence of the church.

Although Luther confined himself first to the translation of the New Testament, his task was by no means an easy one. The second edition of the Greek text by Erasmus (1519), to which the great humanist had appended his own Latin translation and his detailed explanations (*annotationes*),was the basis for Luther's undertaking. Some have maintained that Luther could not have used this text of Erasmus because in several passages he failed to avail himself of hints that were helpful for a proper understanding of the text.[3] Although this in itself is true, the explanation is to be found in the great haste (concurrently with his work on the book of Advent homilies, he completed the translation of the New Testament in the incredibly short span of eleven weeks), which precluded a constant consulting of Erasmus's translation and particularly of his annotations. However, many passages prove beyond all doubt that Luther did use this exegetical aid, which at that time was the most modern work of this kind. Furthermore, his intimate acquaintance—dating back to his lectures on the Epistle to the Romans—with the edition of Erasmus, which first appeared in 1516, would make it seem incomprehensible if he had foregone its help for the difficult work of translating. To be sure, in the beginning, this help of Erasmus was surely not available in its entirety to Luther at the Wartburg; at first he had only the reprint of the Greek text (without translation and annotations). Gerbel had published this in 1521 and presented it to him or, as Luther expressed it, had brought it to him as a wife who bore him sons (his Wartburg literary work).[4]

---

3. Wilhelm Walther, *Luthers deutsche Bibel* (Berlin: E. S. Mittler & Son, 1917), 58f.

4. "Nov. 1, 1521," WABr 2:391.41ff.

Thus in addition to the Vulgate, the use of which can often be estab-lished, Luther had a second Latin translation of the New Testament avail-able: that of Erasmus. The fact that Erasmus's Latin translation was printed in columns parallel with the Greek text makes it self-evident that Luther's eyes must have rested on it continually. Furthermore, one would overestimate Luther's knowledge of Greek if one believed him capable of translating the New Testament, with all the difficulties of Hellenistic Greek, in such a short time without the aid of other translations. After all, he had been schooled in the scholastic tradition, not humanistically; despite his Greek studies, which he did not pursue more seriously until 1518,[5] he always retained a greater familiarity with the Latin Bible. A study of Luther's knowledge of Greek reveals that despite the strong stimulation given by Melanchthon he never attained the mastery of Greek his philo-logically trained contemporaries possessed. This made the constant use of the two Latin translations he had before him—he knew most of the Vul-gate by heart—natural and imperative.

An impression of the use Luther made of the patterns before him can be gained by comparing a rather long passage of his own translation word for word with that of his predecessors. To pick words and phrases here and there suggestive of the one or of the other Latin translation does not enable one to penetrate into the live process of translating. But if one fol-lows sentence by sentence Luther's translation through a whole New Tes-tament book (for example, the Epistle to the Romans), one perceives with what mobility he selected expressions from this or that pattern. We are far from being able to explain all these decisions; one must often assume that a familiar phrase of the Vulgate simply flowed into his pen or that in his haste he did not consult the annotations of Erasmus. Romans 9:28–31 presents three classic illustrations that show how he could use them and immediately afterward disregard them. Nevertheless, one can see clearly how diversified his procedure is.[6] Often he translates the Greek text in accordance with the Vulgate, sometimes despite an express warning in the annotations, sometimes also in such a way that he instinctively corrects the faulty Greek text of the Erasmus edition. But as a rule he heeds the sug-gestions of Erasmus and corrects the Vulgate in conformity with them, at

---

5. H. Dibbelt, *Archiv für Reformationsgeschichte* 38 (1941): 300ff.

6. Cf. Heinrich Bornkamm, "Die Vorlagen zu Luthers Übersetzung des Neuen Testa-ments," *Theologische Literaturzeitung* 72 (1947): 23–28.

times even where Erasmus himself had not yet embodied his suggested corrections in his own translation. Often, however, Luther translates freely, sometimes according to varying impulses and stimulations, sometimes also according to his own understanding of the Greek text.

If one surveys these decisions, colorful and varied as they are, one is deeply impressed when observing how Luther chose and weighed despite the fact that he was working hurriedly. Self-evidently he always accorded the original text his prime consideration as he constantly tested and tried his texts, then incorporated all into a living language. Most of the questions regarding the aptness of a translation were settled by him. However, Luther undoubtedly did not, as is often assumed, translate exclusively from the original Greek; instead, he often took counsel with his two Latin aids. On the other hand, he did not consult only these almost to the exclusion of the Greek original, as has recently been claimed.[7] The source of his translation was the combined Greek-Latin text, not distinguishable in detail, lying before him in two parallel columns in the Erasmus edition. The annotations contained in the same volume and the Vulgate, lying at hand and fixed in his memory, must have impelled and directed him to a constant comparison of the two texts. One need only envisage this operation to realize that in this rapid play of eyes and thoughts a minute analysis was impossible. But this much is certain (attested by the passages in which Luther cast the safe crutches away and attempted to walk independently, though awkwardly at times) that he sought to grasp the sense of the original and availed himself of the Latin copies as an aid.

Although Luther always had recourse to the two Latin copies for an understanding of the original text, he was nevertheless entirely dependent on himself for the task of pouring the New Testament into a true mold of the German language. Even if one of the medieval German translations had been available, it would have helped him but little. These vernacular translations were all based on the Vulgate, consequently on a text that he was obliged to correct in innumerable passages. Moreover, they adhered too literally and clumsily to the wording of the text to serve him as a pattern. No matter how highly we may evaluate several of these translations as accomplishments in their day, the disparity between them and the more refined linguistic sense of the early sixteenth century and, above all, between them and Luther's conception of a good translation was nonethe-

---

7. Cf. H. Dibbelt, *Archiv für Reformationsgeschichte* 38 (1941): 300ff.

less too great to ascribe to them a vital influence on Luther. Despite a number of efforts in this direction, no proof has been adduced that Luther availed himself of any of these medieval German Bibles, for example, Gunther Zainer's Bible, which was printed in Augsburg in 1475.[8] Even the collected lists of alleged adaptations or loans from this book display nothing but insignificant trifles.[9] They fail to offer proof that Luther used them. In part they contain passages that Luther could not have translated differently. If one compares word for word longer passages from the two translations, any number of differences can be found between Zainer and Luther. This refutes the assertion that Luther used Zainer down to the minutest detail. Furthermore, if Luther made diligent use of Zainer at the Wartburg, then it is difficult to understand why the contacts and agreements should be confined to the Gospels and remain conspicuously absent in the New Testament Epistles and in the Book of Revelation. Luther would surely have welcomed any available help when translating these far more difficult texts. If one wants to gain an impression of how Luther constantly consulted an available translation, one must observe his use of the Vulgate and the Erasmus edition together with the latter's annotations. Naturally, Luther was acquainted with such older German translations as the Zainer Bible from former years. Sections from these Bibles, such as pericopes and plenaria, were often used in sermons and prayers, as well as in classroom instruction and in pastoral ministrations. Recollections of these passages, their frequent general correspondence to the Vulgate, and the limited number of possible translations explain the various similarities. But it is significant that such agreements are not traceable to any one printed edition or manuscript; they point to the various medieval German translations. Consequently, they reveal the traditional diction used in the church, not a literary dependence and connection.

If we are impressed by the difference between the eaglelike flight of Luther's language and the diction of his medieval predecessors, our admiration increases as we observe how in his translation at the Wartburg he

---

8. Cf. Heinrich Bornkamm, "Die Vorlagen zu Luthers Übersetzung des Neue Testaments," 23–28. See also Gerhard Bruchmann, *Verdeutschung der Evangelien und sonstiger Teile des Neuen Testaments von der ersten Angängen bis Luther*, Bibel und deutsche Kultur 5 (Potsdam: Akademische Verlagsgesellschaft Athenaion,1935), 21ff.; *Lutherjahrbuch* (1935): 111ff.; and *Lutherjahrbuch* (1936): 47ff.

9. A. Freitag in WADB 6:595ff.; 7:552ff.

has grown above his former stature, for this was not his first translation of Bible passages into the vernacular. His German writings, sermons, and postils abound in Bible quotations that he himself translated. It is astonishing how Luther ignored these, even those used in a recent Christmas homily, and how his uniform feeling for language created the entire New Testament anew. His former attempts still betrayed the idiomatic hue of the ancient language in many spots, especially of the Latin, but now everything is thoroughly German. Now he relates in the imperfect tense, no longer in the perfect; he places the predicate (aside from well-considered exceptions) at the end of the sentence; and he resolves noun combinations into sentences, for example, Matthew 12:34: "Aus Uberfluss des Herzens redet der Mund" (Postille); "Wes das Herz voll ist, des gehet des Mund über" (New Testament). Romans 8:7: "Die Weisheit des Fleisches ist Gottes Feind" (Postille); "Denn fleischlich gesinnet sein ist eine Feindschaft wider Gott" (New Testament). Almost all foreign words are eliminated, etc.[10]

Even if all this demonstrates conscious and methodical work, of which he later gave a somewhat detailed account, especially in his *Sendschreiben vom Doumetschen*, nevertheless his essential attainments were born instinctively from the depths of a great poetic heart. Gifted with a language that adapts itself to any mood, to the tenderness of the Christmas story as well as to the terrors of the Apocalypse, Luther does not work according to rules but according to inner laws. The incredible accuracy of expression with which he reacts to the depths of a text stems not merely from alert reflection but from a superconscious clear-sightedness. He hears and sees sacred history as though it were taking place at the present time; he transmits its sounds in such a way that the silent reader can hear it as living, spoken words. By means of sentence structure and meaningful punctuation, he makes the Bible a book to be heard, not to be read. With deepest sensitivity, he discovers poetic passages and responds to them with the poetic resources of the German language, with alliteration and rhythm. His use of the vowels merits a special study. Still, there is more at work here than the genius of a poet. His newly created biblical language, with which no translation on earth can compare, succeeded not only because he felt his way into it with perfect skill but because in countless hours the Bible message had reached into his own life. He read Holy Writ "as though it had been written yesterday," as though its words of admonition and of consolation

---

10. Wilhelm Delle, *Lutherjahrbuch* (1922): 66ff.

were addressed by God to him alone. Yes, his amazement at the fact that God is speaking and revealing the innermost recesses of His heart through the medium of the Word gave Luther full freedom to evolve his own language. His work was not merely the product of poetic intuition; no, in it we hear human words born from the Word of God. Luther did not beget this work during the quiet winter months at the Wartburg; he conceived it.

Thus Luther's work grew completely from his new understanding of the Gospel. It could not be otherwise. One clearly feels his heart vibrating to the Gospel's consoling message, pervading all his work like a soft undertone. He is resolved to preserve the Gospel in its purity and to protect it from misinterpretations. For this reason he translates the term "the righteousness of God" ("die Gerechtigkeit Gottes"), which had proved so ambiguous in his own experience, with "the righteousness which is valid before God" ("die Gerechtigkeit, die vor Gott gilt"). By inserting the word *alone* (*allein*) twice in harmony with the context, he engraves the Pauline meaning sharply: "Auf dass er [Gott] allein gerecht sei" (Romans 8:26); "dass der Mensch gerechtfertigt werde ohn Zutun der Werke des Gesetzes [since 1527: "ohne des Gesetzes Werke"], allein durch den Glauben" (Romans 3:28). In place of "aus den Werken," he says, more pregnantly, "aus Verdienst der Werke" (Romans 9:12, 32; 11:6). His effort to preserve the ring of the evangelical message is manifested most clearly in the painstaking care with which he reproduces one and the same word with consistent modifications. Thus he retains the word *gerecht* as an attribute of man only when it pertains unmistakably to God's gift of unmerited grace; otherwise he replaces it with the word *fromm*, a term replete for him with the content of the Gospel and devoid of any intimation of human attainment. Luther carefully divides (perfecting the division in subsequent revisions) the rather common New Testament word group σώζειν, σωτηρία into expressions of saving, helping, preserving, on the one hand, and on the other hand, into *selig machen, selig werden, Seligkeit* ("to save, to be saved, salvation"), achieving for the noun σωτηρία an especially ingenious differentiation: *Heil* for God's great deed for mankind, *Seligkeit* for its effect on human hearts in this life and in the life beyond.[11] With keen discernment, he avoids the word *Kirche* and chooses the word *Gemeine*; thereby he wished to avoid any transmission of the erroneous Catholic concept of the church to the days of primitive Christianity.

---

11. Emanuel Hirsch, *Luthers deutsche Bibel* (Münich: Christian Kaiser, 1928), 56ff.

Luther's translation of the Bible supplied the evangelical movement with the inexhaustible source of its message and the German nation with a perennial fountainhead for its new language. A wonderful providence had placed Luther, the greatest sculptor of the German language, into an area where a universal German language had long been in the making and could grow only at that time: the eastern German territory. Through the agency of the political and economic power of the extensive Wettin ducal state, culturally of greater importance to Germany than the mighty Hapsburg territories situated on the fringe of the empire, the unifying language of the Saxon chancellery radiated its influence also into most of the other German states. Luther was cognizant of this development: "I use the speech of the Saxon chancellery, which is accepted by all the princes of Germany." He knew that the methodical efforts to achieve a uniform German language were of recent origin; they dated from his own days. Emperor Maximilian and Frederick the Wise, he said, "have thus merged all languages into one."[12] By adopting this dialect natural to him, he could hope to be intelligible to most Germans. But by this act he, as no other German, opened the portals of the future for this High German dialect. "The new German language affords the Reformation the possibility of extensive operation; the Reformation gives the new German language a transprovincial impact."[13] Luther's language of the Bible and the resulting sermonic language of the Reformation were not only universal inasmuch as they spanned the farthest dialectal areas but also inasmuch as they became the language of the people, the language used in the studies of the scholars and the language spoken in the huts of the unlearned. By reason of their unparalleled dissemination through the printed page, they reached all strata of society. Whatever stock of raw material Luther received from his adoptive dialect, he gave back after qualifying it for the greatest role in the history of the German language. For not until there was a union of subject matter and genius was the common language of all Germans born.

---

12. WATr 2, no. 2758.

13. Theodor Frings, *Zeitschrift für deutsche Geisteswissenschaft* 1 (1938), 209.

LUTHER'S DEATH AND LEGACY

In the night from February 17 to February 18, 1546, Martin Luther entered his eternal home. Strangely enough, his life ended where it had begun: in Eisleben. At the request of the counts of Mansfeld, he had journeyed to the city of his birth for the purpose of adjusting a complicated legal dispute in which they were involved. The winter trip had been fraught with difficulties. Beyond Halle they had not been able to cross the swollen Saale. "We encountered a great female Anabaptist with high billows and formidable floes covering the ground and threatening us with rebaptism," he wrote to his wife on January 25. Not until a few days later were they able to cross the river. En route he received his first warning to husband his strength. On approaching Eisleben he had left his carriage and had walked quite a distance. There he suffered a heart attack (*angina pectoris*). He had had similar attacks several times before this. But he recovered, and the ensuing negotiations, which lasted nearly three weeks, found him hearty and in good spirits. On February 16 and 17, he was able to conclude the negotiations successfully; however, overexertion had exhausted him.

Justus Jonas, to whom we are indebted for the best report on Luther's last hours, related that he had no longer participated in the discussions on February 17 but had remained in his room.[1] His friends, who had found him especially cheerful and relaxed during these weeks, now had to hear him say for the first time: "Here in Eisleben I was born and baptized.

---

1. See Jacob Strieder, ed., *Authentische Berichte über Luthers letzte Lebensstunden* (Bonn: A Marcus & E. Weber, 1912); Christoph Schubart, *Die Berichte über Luthers Tod und Begräbnis* (Weimar: H. Böhlaus Nachfolger, 1917); WA 54:478ff.

What if I should remain here?" At table he uttered these words of absolute defiance of death: "If I reconcile my dear sovereigns, the counts, and, God willing, carry out the aims of this journey, then I shall return home, lie down to sleep in the coffin, and give the worms a good fat doctor to devour." In the evening the heart attacks recurred. After a short sleep he awoke toward one o'clock in the morning and in great distress went into the adjacent living room. Earlier in the evening he had still declined to see the doctors. They were now quickly summoned, and various restoratives were administered. Luther permitted this to happen to him as though he were no longer present. The feeble comfort of his friends that his perspiration was a good symptom he waved aside with the words: "Yes, it is the cold sweat of death; I shall give up the ghost." From now on he devotes himself solely to prayer. Jonas has faithfully recorded his simple dying prayer and the verses to which he clung in his last hours, above all, the oft-repeated words: "In manus tuas commendo spiritum meum; redemisti me, Deus veritatis" ("Into Thine hand I commit my spirit; Thou hast redeemed me, O LORD God of truth" [Psalm 31:5]), the same words with which so many Christians before him had walked through the door of death. He became more and more quiet, "as though he were sinking away." Only when his friends asked him: "Dearest father, do you confess Christ, the Son of God, our Savior and Redeemer?" he replied audibly once more: "Yes." Then he lay still, with his hands folded, and passed away between two and three o'clock in the morning.

"Der Tod ist mein Schlaf worden" ("Death has become my sleep"). Thus he had sung, thus he gently fell asleep, fully conscious. His death was not caused by a paralytic stroke but by a weakening of the heart, which was related to his old ailment and to the hardening of his arteries. One of the eyewitnesses reported: "All who were present relate that he did not die but went alive, as it were, from this life to the life beyond."

The fact that Luther died far away from his family and his accustomed environment accounts for the large number of reports and letters to his wife and friends during his last weeks on earth. Otherwise these reports and letters would not have been written.

Together with the intensified concentration that strange surroundings can bring about in us and, still more, with the collectedness that comes over a strong mind when death is near, these final utterances of Luther once again reflect the riches of this mighty life in rare abundance. Adopting the method that enables one to recognize the crystalline stratification of a homogeneous mountain range from a few fragments, we may be permitted to extract from these utterances the essential features of Luther's legacy to posterity. This legacy may be divided into three categories.

I: Luther's Legacy to the Political World

In the wider sense of the word, Luther's last act on earth was a political act. Today the quarrel among the Mansfeld counts may seem to us to be inconsequential and of a bygone age; it may be viewed as an example of the innumerable legal squabbles of sixteenth-century German petty princes. But to Luther it afforded an occasion for important practical decisions and, above all, for another declaration of his most profound convictions regarding questions pertaining to the eternal human quest for right and justice. The evil and deep-rooted legal quarrel among the Mansfeld counts (who had split into three lines since a division of inheritance in 1420) embraced a whole bundle of intricate problems—not only problems of a private-legal nature, such as the regulation of debts and the division of the mining property once held in common, but also those of a public-legal type, such as the bestowal of municipal privileges and bylaws on the *Neustadt* of Eisleben, with which the ruling count had trespassed on the prerogatives of the emperor and had provoked the resistance of the *Altstadt*. The dispute revolved around a social problem (a ruler's arbitrary reclamation of mines that had been conferred on certain families as hereditary fiefs) and finally about a problem pertaining to canonical law: the patronage of the Eisleben churches.

One must envisage the complicated legal dispute clearly to arrive at a satisfactory answer to the question: What, after all, induced Luther to assume the difficult office of arbitration? Did this not imply a renunciation of one of his fundamental principles: the strict and distinct separation of the secular and the spiritual spheres of life, the abstention from interference with each other's domain? To be sure, the fact that Luther had disentangled the well-nigh inextricable knot of secular and canonical claims and had returned the government and the church to the independent mission entrusted by God to each was his secular service to the history of the Occident. Was he not undoing this separation of church and state by accepting such a political-juridical office of arbitration, a separation that he had zealously defended again and again against emperor and pope, princes, city councils, and peasants? Did this not betray a medieval belief in the superiority of the ecclesiastical powers over the secular—after he had brought the spurious medieval union to a close both symbolically and effectively by burning the canon law before the Elster Gate of Wittenberg in 1520? By no means! Luther did not lay claim to such an office of arbitration for the church, as the popes had done in countless tragic disputes in every European country. But when it was offered to him not in his capacity of a teacher and a leader of the church but as a Christian individual, he did accept it for the purpose of rendering a simple civic duty. Thereby he emphasized the other side of the clarified relationship between church and politics, which dare not be overlooked when contemplating the principle of separation of their spheres: The Christian has been called to lend an active hand in the upbuilding of human society as reason and love, not canonical law, prompt him to do.

Luther's letters and other expressions of opinion give us an insight into the motives that persuaded him, despite his advanced age, to expose himself to the rigors of a wearisome journey in winter and to stake his last strength on this task so foreign to his nature and his calling. He wanted to reconcile his "dear sovereigns," to whom he, as a son of the land, felt under obligation. When his patience with the interminable problems gave way during the negotiations and he, in his anger, was on the point of having his carriage greased for departure, he was, as he wrote, deterred from leaving by the distress of his native land. Still another motive came into play: In this quarrel he again perceived to his horror the soul-destroying powers of filthy lucre. Jesus had compared riches to the thorns that choke the good seed. "Here is the school in which one learns to understand this." Human souls were imperiled. "For this reason I exercise greater patience in the hope that I may do some good with God's help" (in a letter to his wife on February 6). Both love of country and love of his fellow man inspired his decision to remain and arbitrate the difficulties.

Here again Luther found confirmation of his profound conviction that all legal and political questions are, in the final analysis, human questions that involve not only legal claims and title but at the same time human life, human happiness, and particularly also human souls. In this truth a Christian's inescapable duty to take his proper place of service in the secular realm is rooted.

Not only Luther's motives but also his last act itself deserves attention. On the last two days of his life he settled the questions at issue justly and courageously with two statements. The Berlin philosopher of law Rudolf

Stammler comments in an essay: "The decisions arrived at by Luther in those two agreements were excellent in their objectivity. . . . Every close scrutiny in the light of legality will only verify this."[2] But no matter how grateful Luther was for a successful adjustment of the difficulties, he was not yet satisfied. This event had pointed him to deeper questions of right and wrong. These questions disturbed him much during his last days on earth. On February 7 he wrote his wife: "I have now also become a jurist. But this will not redound to their advantage. It would be better if they permitted me to remain a theologian. If I live and come among them, I might become a hobgoblin who, by the grace of God, would check their pride." Luther was opposed to a merely formal and automatic verdict based on the norms of current laws. Consequently, he had demanded the withdrawal of a second juridical arbitrator who disagreed with him on this point. Luther had never defended a lawless justice based on a mere feeling of right and wrong. Now, however, he found new assurance for his oft-expressed conviction that true justice can never be derived exclusively from a blind compliance with the letter of the law but, in the end, can come only from the wisdom and sagacity of the judge. In one of his last Table Talks in Eisleben, he again appealed to an Aristotelian definition often cited by him in corroboration of his idea that fairness (ἐπείχεια), that is, sagacious discretion, must be the master of laws. This fairness in a legal judgment, as Luther now again found in a case open to him in its minutest details, can spring only from an alliance of justice and of love, not from one or the other alone. Because courts of law are usually oblivious of this, Luther wanted to pounce upon the jurists like a hobgoblin. Stammler concludes his essay with the beautiful words:

> The proper relationship [of justice and of love] is copied from the sentence contained in Rom. 13:10: "Therefore love is the fulfilling of the Law." The point is that one supplements the other. As all human science, so also the methodical contemplation of the idea of justice offers only possibilities of proper willing. The conversion of this possibility into reality requires the powerful cooperation of love. . . . This has its own peculiar and indispensable mission, which can be fulfilled only by means of the power of faith.

As a motto for his essay Stammler chooses the lines of Friedrich Rückert:
> Nur wo Gerechtigkeit und Liebe sich verbündet,
> Ist Menschenschuld gesühnt und ird'scher Sinn entsündet.

---

2. Rudolf Stammler, *Deutsches Rechtsdenken in alter und neuer Zeit* I (1938), 197ff.

This basic, lifelong conviction, confirmed and supported by his final act, is Luther's contribution to humanity's eternal question regarding justice. What further admonition could our world of today want as it thirsts for a new, genuine justice?

II: Luther's Legacy to the World of the Mind

If one were to search all Luther's writings for an expression on greatness and limitations of the human intellect, probably none more pertinent could be found than the profound Latin words that he wrote on a slip of paper two days before his death:

> No one who was not a shepherd or a peasant for five years can understand Virgil in his *Bucolica* and *Georgica*.
>
> I maintain that no one can understand Cicero in his letters unless he was active in important affairs of state for twenty years.
>
> Let no one who has not guided the congregations with the prophets for one hundred years believe that he has tasted Holy Writ thoroughly.
>
> For this reason the miracle is stupendous (1) in John the Baptist, (2) in Christ, (3) in the apostles.
>
> Do not try to fathom this divine *Aeneid*, but humbly worship its footprints.[3]
>
> We are beggars; this is true.[4]

This last memorandum from Luther's pen, also his final German sentence in a Latin discourse ("Wir sind Bettler; hoc est verum"), presents Luther's retrospective glance at his life; it is marked both by the deepest reverence and the deepest modesty.

What regard and respect for the work of others these words reflect! "No one who was not a shepherd or a peasant for five years can understand Virgil in his *Bucolica* or *Georgica*"! No one who was not active in important affairs of state for twenty years can understand Cicero in his letters.[5]

---

3. Quotation from the Roman poet Statius (died ca. A.D. 96): Thehaid.XII, 816f.

4. Ernst Ludwig Enders, ed., *Dr. Martin Luthers Briefwechsel* (Frankfurt am Main: Schriften-Niederlage des Evangel. Vereins, 1884–1912); WATr 5, no. 5677.

5. In this passage, I am gratefully adopting some thoughts of Friedrich Karl Schumann on these last words from Luther's pen.

Luther knows that long and silent toil is the prerequisite for true creative work. A real masterpiece does not grow from sudden inspirations; it is the product of humble service. For this reason it can he comprehended only from the same earnest and composed point of view from which it has grown. He will evince the deepest understanding for this who has reconstructed and recreated in himself, as it were, the conditions of a great poetic or reflective work. Understanding does not come from without; it comes only from within, only from like causes of growth. This is the contribution of Luther, one of the greatest interpreters of cultural history, to the age-old question of correct understanding. How great the disparity between this reverence and the superficial journalism that presumed to judge and criticize everything with ever-growing cocksureness during the last centuries! This arrogance has created the world of pretense, the world of sham values, in which the honest mind has to feel homeless. And humanity surely paid dearly for it. Because it babbles inanely on every subject, its words have become empty and meaningless.

Luther also places the Bible under this testament of reverence. "Let no one who has not guided the congregations with the prophets for one hundred years believe that he has tasted Holy Writ thoroughly." This, of course, is an extravagant expression because a hundred years are in excess of the span of life. No human life is long enough to exhaust the well of God's Word. Luther's words betoken a profound reverence, in fact, an adoration, before the fathomless riches of Holy Writ. Luther never presumed to be able to expound the Scriptures fully and completely nor did he arrogate to himself the right to force the content of the Scriptures into formulas. Here we find the strongest reason why he never composed a theological system, as did Thomas Aquinas, Melanchthon, or Calvin. He did not compress the Bible pedantically into textbooks as later orthodoxy did nor did he impertinently mutilate and hack it to pieces as the Enlightenment did. He never lost his sense of venerating awe before the riches of God's Word. His whole theology presents one long, never-ending grappling with the Bible's superior might. Again and again he sank a new shaft into a different side of this mighty mountain and unearthed treasures as no exegete before or after him. Until his last breath he regarded himself as a poor beggar before God's Word.

Germany has followed a different course since that day. She soon considered herself so much richer in wisdom and in intelligence than the poor Bible. Finally, she discarded it in haughty self-reliance. For this, too, we have paid dearly. No other prophecy was so horribly fulfilled in our nation as the plaintive cry of Luther, who saw unavoidable disaster approaching for his people by reason of their contempt for God's Word:

> If they take the Gospel from German lands, then the country will also perish.[6]

> Should God not be provoked by such contempt of His Word to strike with His fists?[7]

> O Germany, Germany, that you do not recognize the day of your visitation! How will you fare in the end?[8]

More terribly than ever before in any unhappy period of German history have we experienced the truth of these prophetic warnings. For never before has the relationship between godlessness and unscrupulousness, which have gained such a foothold in our nation, and the disaster that has befallen us become so palpably obvious. Because we no longer wanted to be beggars before God and His Word, we have become beggars before the whole world. We felt clever and mighty; now we have become paupers, materially and intellectually. May God grant that we find our way back to the position that was the center of Luther's life and that we may realize that God is infinitely richer and mightier than we are. It would be tragic if the impact of these shattering experiences merely led us to the limits of what is human and not also to the riches of God. God begins to act where man becomes conscious of his own impotence. Not a few Christians, tried in the fiery furnace of suffering and distress, have begun to marvel at the unprecedented truth and the incomprehensible riches of the Bible. It offered them comfort and guidance for every need and care. The higher the waters of adversity rose, the more reliable it was as a friend. To be sure (and this, too, is consoling), the Bible reveals itself only after long and humble serving. If Luther deemed one hundred years necessary for the acquisition of a thorough taste of the Bible, what, then, are we to say?

Luther does not say that one must have read the Bible one hundred years to understand it but that one must have guided the congregations with the prophets for that length of time. To understand the Bible is not an academic matter. Whatever scholarly, linguistic, and objective knowledge

6. "Lecture on Isaiah (1527–1530)," WA 31/2:303.30.

7. WATr 5, no. 5506;

8. "Of Pope Clement VII . . . (1525)," WA 18:265.5.

may be prerequisite (and no one is more insistent on this than Luther), the primary source for understanding it lies nevertheless in life itself, where the truths of faith are tested. An understanding of the spiritual conflicts of the days in which God's Word found a voice in the prophets, in Christ, and in the apostles grows solely from identical situations, identical longings and desires, and identical *Anfechtungen* of today. This part of Luther's legacy to theology is also his legacy to all learning. He had a low estimate of all abstract, merely theoretical knowledge. He challenged Erasmus and the rationalism germinating in him with the sentence "Cognitio non est vis" ("Knowledge is not power"). Thereby he anticipated and presaged the verdict on modern man's superstitious belief in learning. Perhaps we can again appreciate this truth today, now that the hollowness of all theoretical knowledge, which flits capriciously from one *Weltanschauung* to another, has been exposed. No matter how indispensable all knowledge is (Luther yielded to no one in his insistence on it in all fields and, therefore, espoused the cause of the schools so warmly), the true forces of the mind lie deeper and can be proved and seasoned only in life. Whoever does not direct his quest for knowledge thither will, in the end, remain a nonproductive scholar. For this reason theology and all other learning has an inexhaustible treasure house in God's Word and in His creation. All attempts to force life into fixed doctrines, into an orthodox or rationalistic, into an idealistic or materialistic dogma, or into any political *Weltanschauung*, etc., are futile rational attempts to lay hold of life in advance, whereas true and wise knowledge grows only out of long patient experience in life. This is Luther's legacy to the world of the mind: respect for every genuine work achieved and created in long years of service and toil; worshipful awe of the inexhaustible riches of God's Word, which touches every phase of our human existence; and a humble willingness to learn from real life instead of violating it with abstract rules of our reasoning. I can conceive of no grander conclusion to life than to hear one of the greatest geniuses of all times, one who as no other had shaken the world to its foundations, humbly confess as he viewed his work in retrospect: "We are beggars; this is true."

III: Luther's Legacy to Christendom

This legacy is the richest of the three. If we wanted to exhaust it, we would be obliged to spread out before us the wealth of his last sermons, letters, and conversations. This cannot be done here. From among the powers with which Luther struggled in these writings, I shall select only one, the power of worry, which he perhaps never before in his life battled so lustily and victoriously as he did in his last letters to his wife. Frau Käthe had every reason to accompany her weary husband with her worries on his fatiguing journey and into his taxing negotiations. The future was to prove those worries well founded. But she could evoke only a reproving laugh from her husband:

> You are worrying for your God as if He were not almighty; He could cre-
> ate ten Dr. Luthers if the old one were to drown in the Saale or in the
> stovepipe or on Wolf's [his servant's] fowling floor. Don't trouble me with
> your worrying. I have a better worrier than you and all the angels are. He
> lies in a manger and clings to a virgin's nipples; yet He sits at the right
> hand of God the Father Almighty. (February 7)

A few days later he informed her that, in consequence of her worrying, a fire in the room had almost burned him to death and a stone falling from the ceiling had almost slain him. "Unless you cease worrying, I shall worry that the earth will devour us in the end and that all the elements will pursue us." Then he grew serious: "Is this the way you learn the Catechism and the Creed? Pray, and let God do the worrying! You have never been ordered to worry for me or for yourself. It is written: 'Cast all your cares on the Lord, for He cares for you.'" In the last letter Luther commented on rumors regarding the emperor's and other princes' preparations for war and added: "But let them chatter [*sagen und singen*]. We shall wait to see what God will do." This was Luther's testament against worry, the sinister and weird guest whom we have learned to know so well.

The sum total of the concept of faith that Luther bequeathed to Christendom is found in his last confession, the simple prayer of a dying man, which was recorded for us by Jonas: "My heavenly Father! Eternal, gracious God! You have revealed Your dear Son, our Lord Jesus Christ, to me; Him I have taught, Him I love, and Him I revere as my dear Savior and Redeemer, whom the godless persecute, blaspheme, and defame. Take my soul unto Yourself." This life, full of unprecedented deeds and struggles and for this reason also filled with the most intense inner conflicts, now flowed into this simple childlike prayer. For a full understanding of the peace of mind reflected in this prayer, one must recall the incredible anguish of soul with which the young Luther in the cloister had torn himself away from the great Catholic distortion of the Gospel and the many hours that continued to come, hours "in which," as Leopold von Ranke says, "anxious melancholy arose from the secret depths of his soul, swung its dark pinions around his head, and flung him to the ground."[9] One must recall the glimpses that Luther had caught of the depths of a hidden God or hear again with him the footsteps of a God pronouncing judgment in the history of the nations. Now that he stood on the threshold of death, which he himself had so often called the last passage through the circle of *Anfechtungen*, this agony of soul had vanished completely. It had been dispelled in the security of the sheltering hand of his Lord, to whom he once more professed allegiance with his final yes in answer to the question put by his friends.

Thus Luther's confession of faith and his legacy are to be found not only in this or that word but also in his dying itself. He died in exact accord with the pattern he had drawn countless times for a Christian. Luther and his era were still cognizant of the fact that dying is a skill that must be acquired. First, one must learn not to avoid the thought of death as modern man does. The latter's perplexity and embarrassment concerning death have produced a wonderful aptitude for killing death by means of a conspiracy of silence. One no longer talks about death. Funeral processions are no longer seen on the streets. Death is banished to the hospitals, and even there every effort is made to conceal it, if possible, from the view of even the closest relatives. Above all, the dying person is lied to until the very last moment. Often, however, he is well aware of the falsehood and fraud perpetrated on him. This increases his feeling of utter loneliness. Luther, on the other hand, discoursed on death as naturally as he spoke about life. The one is inseparable from the other. To him the inevitability of death is the most natural thing on earth, and this makes every hour of life so inescapably serious. But the death of a human being is far different from the natural disappearance of plants and animals. It is the gateway into an unknown land. Whom does man face in this land? Can it be that he meets only himself? Is the assumption not more reasonable that he meets God, whom he has evaded during his whole life and to whom he now has to surrender unconditionally? Will not he, too, who regards death as the ultimate and absolute end be deeply disquieted by a consciousness of guilt, of fortune's denial, of life's miscarriage, of the hodgepodge he has made of his plans of life? Because Luther was aware of

---

9. Leopold von Ranke, *Deutsche Geschichte im Zeitalter der Reformation*, ed. Paul Joachimsen (München: Drei Masken, 1925), 1:213.

all these enemies, he knew that man must arm himself for death during his lifetime; in the hour of dying it is too late. With this in mind, he had written his sermon on the preparation for death, one of his finest German writings, as early as 1519. For this reason he prepared his parents for death in letters pervaded with filial love and at the same time with spiritual authority.[10] For this reason he had built his entire reformatory work on the first sentence of his powerful Invocavit sermon after his return to Wittenberg from the Wartburg in 1522:

> We have all been claimed by death, and no one will die for the other; but each one of us must be prepared and armed to contend against death and devil. We may be able to shout into another's ears, comfort him, admonish him to patience, to battle, to conflict; but we cannot contend or fight for him. Each one must see to his own redoubt and engage the enemies, death and devil, in combat himself and come to blows with them all alone. Then I shall not be with you, and you will not be with me.[11]

This is the core of what has erroneously been called the individualism of the Reformation but should more fittingly be termed the awareness of always being an individual before God. The fact that man faces God by himself without being able to appeal to and rely on others is documented by the solitude of death, where the individual is removed even from those closest to him. This hour reveals our true relationship to God; we always live face-to-face with Him alone. To strengthen the faith and the conscience of his hearers, Luther tried hard to inculcate this truth. Here we strike the root of the enormous transformation he wrought in the history of mankind. Together with medieval Christianity, Luther still knew something about an *ars moriendi*, an art of dying;[12] however, his mode of dying was unmedieval. It was without sacerdotal aid, without viaticum, without an appeal to the saints, without rosary or other consecrated objects; it was without a monk's cowl, which some laymen were wont to wear in death to step before God's judgment seat under the meritorious protection of a monastic order. In a constant preview of the final hour, which lays bare man's true character before God, the entire human-ecclesiastical apparatus had long since become unreal to Luther. Nowhere more than in Luther's dying do we find those beautiful lines of Dilthey substantiated: "As all

---

10. "Feb. 15, 1530," WABr 5:238; "May 20, 1531," WABr 6:103.

11. WA 10/3:1.

12. Cf. pp. 103ff.

individual objects recede in the darkness of night and man is alone with the stars and the invisible, so these great men perceived their relationship to heaven" ("Wie im Dunkel der Nacht alle Einzeldinge zurücktreten und der Mensch mit den Sternen und dem Unsichtbaren allein ist: so empfanden diese grossen Menschen ihr Verhältnis zum Himmel").[13] He died alone in the presence of his God.

For this very reason, not alone after all. As earnestly as Luther had prepared himself and others for the truth that we must appear before God entirely alone and without human help and mediation, so ardently he enjoined upon all: "No Christian should doubt that he is not alone in his final hour; on the contrary, he should be certain that . . . very many eyes are fixed on him."[14] God is there. When our thoughts regarding ourselves become confused and we view our own life in perplexity and bewilderment, then the words must be applied: "You must let God be God, persuaded that He knows more about you than you yourself do." This same God, "who loves us more dearly than we love ourselves," beholds us, so Luther wrote his father. And Christ is there, who, "together with all the angels, is looking at us and serving us when we journey forth; He relieves us of worry and of the fear of falling or sinking to the ground." And all Christendom is there, the entire church, both the church militant and the church triumphant. Those who have gone before joyously await the dying member. "And if you remain steadfast in faith, they all uphold you with their hands. When your soul departs, they are there to receive it. You cannot perish." And the Christians still living surround and support the dying person with their intercessions with which they remember the departing souls every day and every Sunday.

Thus man is alone with his God in death, yet he is not dependent on himself but on Him into whose arms he falls. The entire art of dying consists simply in firmly taking hold of this faith and, thus equipped, joyfully venturing forth. Luther's instruction on dying, as well as his own death, place the seal on the immovable center of his message: We are justified before God by grace alone. In the hour of death's inexorable trial, of what avail are the merits that man supposes he has amassed during life? Woe unto him if he thinks he can derive even a fraction of cheerfulness in

13. Wilhelm Dilthey, *Gesammelte Schriften* (Leipzig: Teubner, 1921), 2:213.

14. For the following, cf. "Sermon on the Preparation for Dying (1519)," WA 2:690.16, 695.16ff.; WABr 5:240.42, 71.

death from deeds and accomplishments during his life! For "we are beggars; this is true."

The radical resoluteness with which Luther adopted the biblical "without the works of the law, alone by faith" is based, in the final analysis, on his view of death. Only that which passes the test of death can also stand the test of life. The aloneness of dying severs us from everything with which we could count for anything before God or man. Therefore even in life we should train ourselves to discard before God our so-called attainments and merits, all those things with which we think we might count for anything before Him. Only a man able to cast aside the most monumental accomplishments and the most soul-shaking conflicts as rubbish, who counts for nothing except the mercy of God, can make his way to the indescribable joyousness in death and the certainty of victory reflected in Luther's last words on dying. In his memorial sermon in Eisleben, Justus Jonas quotes Luther: "I would not want my soul to be in my own hands. For if it were, the devil would long since have possession of it; yes, he would snatch it away in a moment as a vulture snatches a chick. But neither the devil nor anyone else will tear it from the hand of Christ, to whom I have commended it." Years before this, Luther had declared in a sermon: "Nothing in this world—not life, property, joys, or pleasures—can produce such happiness as dying with a good conscience, in a positive and comforting belief in life eternal."[15]

That is the way Luther died. Jonas relates that Luther prepared for death an entire year. In his psalter and prayer booklet, which he always carried on his person, he had inscribed more than twenty comforting verses, as if he wanted to say: "Someday in my hour of death I want, with God's help, to select one of these verses and be armed with it against Satan and all the gates of hell." Despite much work, his last days abound in conversations about death and eternity. However, in the hours immediately preceding his death, he spoke little, but he prayed much. His friends report that he stood in front of the window every day for several weeks before his death and engaged in such fervent prayer that they were often astounded by his words (he often prayed aloud). Then he turned toward them, "happy as though he had again cast off a burden." Thus he also deported himself in death itself. The reports, which have transmitted every word, almost every sigh, do not contain a single word addressed to his wife and

---

15. "Sommerpostille (1536)," WA 22:101.14.

children, no greetings for his friends, no stipulations for the future of his church and his work, though he had worried often enough about what would happen to these after his death. He had settled all this with God; now it lay behind him. Communion with God was the only thing that still engrossed him. His soul had already begun its flight into another world.

Luther entered his heavenly home in accord with the prophetic annotation (alluding to John 8:51: "If a man keep My saying, he shall never see death") made in his Bible ten days before his death:

> "Never see death." How incredible these words are and how contradictory to public and daily experience! And yet they are true. If a man earnestly ponders God's Word in his heart, believes it, and falls asleep or dies over it, he sinks away and journeys forth before he is aware of death; he has surely departed blissfully in the Word thus believed and considered.[16]

This is Luther's legacy to Christendom: his final words against worry and death, his last childlike prayer, and his own dying, detached from all earthly cares. It is just as powerful as his legacies to the political world and to the world of the mind, and it reveals the same force of intellect. For it is not made up of mere ideas; it is steeped in reality. This triple legacy, which once more focuses the riches of this great mind as in a lens and then radiates them abroad, has, therefore, not become invalid today. It will ever remain operative because it concerns itself not with the questions of a day but with the eternal problems of humankind and because it has been gained from experience with the nearness of the eternal God. Therefore we should not attribute Luther's work, as Goethe did,[17] only to the might of his creative genius but to his timeless message, spoken by the real God to real man, the message in which we see the fulfillment of the prophecy of Psalm 118:17, words especially beloved by Luther, set to music by him, and written on the wall during his banishment at the Coburg: "Non moriar, sed vivam et narrabo opera Domini. Ich werde nicht sterben, sondern leben und des Herrn Werke verkündigen." "I shall not die, but live and declare the works of the Lord."

---

16. WA 48:162.

17. To Eckermann, 11 March 1828.